Non-book materials in libraries

Non-book materials in libraries

in libraries

a practical guide

Second edition

RICHARD FOTHERGILL

and

IAN BUTCHART

CLIVE BINGLEY **ᗷ** LONDON

12474

First published 1978
This second, revised edition published 1984
Reprinted 1985

British Library Cataloguing in Publication Data

Fothergill, Richard
   Non-book materials in libraries.—2nd ed.
   1. Libraries—Special collections—Non-book materials
   I. Title   II. Butchart, Ian
   025.17   Z688.N6

   ISBN 0 85157 345 2

Typeset by Allset in 10 on 12 point Press Roman
123458786858483

CONTENTS

v

vi

Part 1

THE BACKGROUND

CONSIDERATION OF TERMINOLOGY

'I have no great opinion of a definition, the celebrated remedy for the cure of this disorder (uncertainty and confusion)'.[1] *Edmund Burke*

Uncertainty and confusion both become apparent in any discussion of the terminology of non-book materials. The subject is invested with an excess of jargon and technical language; general and specific terms abound. The advent of microcomputers, viewdata and teletext systems into libraries and the ubiquitous term 'information technology' has further complicated the discussion.

A consideration of the literature on the subject is an obvious starting place for establishing a consensus view. What terminology is used in the general literature of non-book materials? Have these terms been standardized at a national or international level? Are there approved glossaries? If the specialists within the subject agree on standardized terms, do the non-specialists use them?

On checking the titles of books in this area, it is apparent that there is as yet no general agreement on a single term to describe the subject. *The multimedia library* (1982),[2] *Cataloguing audiovisual materials* (1980),[3] *Non-book materials* (1981),[4] *A guide to media resources in psychopathology* (1982),[5] *Video: information technology of the 80's* (1980)[6] are all relatively recent publications. Attempts to combine terms include *Audiovisual and microcomputer handbook* (1982)[7] and a particularly ingenious title *Non-book materials: their bibliographic control: a proposed computer system for the cataloguing of audiovisual materials in the United Kingdom* (1971).[8] A review of the written usages of individuals and organizations in the UK, published by the British Standards Institution (1976),[9] produced a similar range of general terms:

medium
non-book material and its synonyms audiovisual materials and metabook
non-book media and its synonym non-print media
multimedia and its synonym non-print materials.

Thus it seems that despite many efforts and much individual endeavour, no consensus about the one general term to describe this subject has yet emerged. Consequently, the terms used in this book need to be defined.

Media
The channels used for the transmission of a message, as in the distinction
between print, sound and vision. The channels are: *printed message*,
usually on paper or on a screen which can be writing, graphics or
photographs; *still pictures*, which are transparent for projection or
viewing; *sounds*, as in a live radio broadcast, or recorded as on a sound
disc; *moving pictures*, as in a live television broadcast or recorded on a
cinefilm.

Materials
This term is used to describe the complete range of physical forms for
the recording of information carried by the media, for example books,
wallcharts, pamphlets, videorecordings, sound recordings.

Non-book materials (NBM)
Strictly speaking this should mean all those materials which are not
bound into a book. However, it is used here to exclude any printed
message presented in the form of a pamphlet, leaflet, manuscript, map,
serial or music score. The range is therefore wide, and also includes
those which have been excluded above when they are re-presented in a
different form such as a map on a slide, serials on microfiche.
    Four materials may be used:
    1 Paper, which can be arranged in a variety of ways; cards, charts,
       art reproductions, portfolios, photographic prints.
    2 Film, which includes:
       (a) filmstrip
       (b) slide
       (c) cinefilm: 35mm, 16mm, standard 8mm, super 8mm
       (d) microform: 35mm roll, 16 mm roll, aperture cards, micro-
            fiche, microfiche jackets.
    3 Magnetic tape which includes:
       (a) sound tape: open reel, cassette
       (b) video tape: open reel, cassette, cartridge
       (c) magnetic disks
    4 Plastic, either flat and transparent or opaque and grooved:
       (a) transparent plastic: overhead projector transparencies
       (b) discs: gramophone records, videodiscs.
    Other materials are of course used in models and artefacts. Specimens,
which are actual objects themselves, are also referred to as NBM.
    There are also mixtures of these materials, commonly called kits.

Finally there are collections of NBM materials which can be electronically accessed at a distance, for example teletext and viewdata systems.

Document
A unit of material containing information. The emphasis is on the information content rather than the physical form of the material.

Form
A general designator for a particular material, for example, cine film, sound recording, microform, videorecording.

Format
A specific designator for a form of material; for example, cine cartridge, sound cassette, microfiche, videodisc.

Each form and format will be described in chapter three, together with technical terms concerning the components of equipment. Other than that and the foregoing list, this book contains no glossary of terms, and the reader is advised to turn to other works for such information.[10] *The Anglo-American Cataloguing Rules* 2nd edition (1978) has produced a measure of agreement between British, American and Canadian librarians. However, much work still remains to be done, particularly in the area of microcomputer terminology.

However, these are the works of specialists trying to establish a common language, and it remains to be seen how far non-specialists will use their terms and definitions. A phrase such as 'machine-readable data file' may have a clear meaning to the specialist who knows it is a generic term for computer software but it is unlikely to find much favour with the library client who is searching for a computer cassette or floppy disk. The librarian needs to be aware of this 'natural language' if he is to succeed in remedying 'this disorder'.

HISTORICAL DEVELOPMENT

It is generally agreed that the function of a library is the collection, preservation, organization and use of documents. However, it is the documents concerning one medium, print, that has dominated the operations of most libraries to date. This is hardly surprising considering the long tradition of writing beginning with the earliest cuneiform system in Mesopotamia circa 3000 BC. Similarly, the development of the codex with pages like those of a modern book by the first century AD points the way towards the long tradition in which one physical form predominated in the preservation and dissemination of knowledge in every literate society. The development of printing in the second half of the fifteenth century made possible a revolution in thought and scholarship through the spread of multiple copies. With its mechanization in the nineteenth century the increased demands from an increasingly literate society could be met. It is hardly surprising that the mainstay of most library collections is the printed word, particularly in book form.

The physical materials used for the other forms have been the result of inventions of the late nineteenth and twentieth centuries. The more important dates for the various forms are presented below.

1 *Still pictures*
   (a) Film
       1841 William Henry Fox Talbot. Paper negative using the Callotype process. The true beginning of photography.
       1884 George Eastman. Roll film system patented and the development of the film slide. Prior to this date only lantern slides used, which were glass with an image printed on them.
       1888 First Kodak mass-produced camera.
       1912 Rudolph Fischer patented basic principles of the Kodachrome process for colour photography.
       1924 First crude picture containing all colours on a three-layer type of film.
       1935 Kodachrome first marketed. Development of 35mm (2 inch X 2 inch) colour slide.
       1951 Polaroid camera.
       1952 Theory of holography patented by Dennis Gabor.
       1960s Development of lasers made production of holographic pictures possible.

1976 Microprocessor controls exposure in a camera.

1982 Kodak disc camera.

(b) Microforms

1839 John Benjamin Dancer. First microphotography.

1870 Microforms sent by pigeon during Franco-Prussian War.

1901 Victorian age — commercial microphotographic views sold mounted on pen-holders, manicure sets, etc.

1906 Idea of microfiche proposed.

1928 Eastman Kodak Co. Use of microfilming to prevent bank frauds.

1970 *Books in English* produced on microfiche.

1978 Whitakers *British books in print* available on microfiche.

2 *Moving pictures*

(a) Cinefilm

1870-93 Eadweard Muybridge. Experimented with photographs and eventually made films of animal and human locomotion. Simple cameras and projectors used.

1889 First cinecamera in which the successive pictures were taken on a strip of film with a single camera.

1893 Thomas Alva Edison invented the nickel-in-the-slot cinematograph machine.

1895 First cinefilm made by L Lumière.

1914 First animated cartoon *The dachsund*.

1922 Technicolour process used for *Toll of the sea*.

1922 First sound recording on film.

1923 First practical 16mm camera projector and compatible non-flammable film. Prior to this date all films were made on 35mm.

1927 Sound on film with Fox-Movietone News.

1932 First practical sound on 16mm film.

1932 Introduction of standard 8mm film cartridges.

1950 Magnetic striping of 16mm film enables amateur makers to add a sound track.

1952 Cinerama.

1965 Kodak introduce the 'super 8' film.

(b) Videotape and television.

1908 First successful electronic transmission of a picture between London and Paris.

1926 John Logie Baird demonstrates first mechanical television transmission.

1932   Radio Corporation of America demonstrated all electronic television.

1936   British Broadcasting Corporation launched the first 405-line public television service.

1940   Colour television system developed.

1958   Videotape marketed.

1965   PAL scanning system patented.

1965   Demonstration of MVR videodisc recorder.

1967   Colour television broadcasting introduced in the United Kingdom.

1971   Some twenty different 'videocassette' systems under development.

1972   BBC introduce digital TV.

1977   Philips 1700 videocassette recorder.

1979   Philips Laservision digital videodisc system.

1981   'Kiddidisk' videodisc which allows viewer participation.

3 Sound recordings
(a) Discs

1877   Thomas Alva Edison. Patented the phonograph using a sheet of tinfoil wrapped around a cylinder.

1889   Emile Berliner. First recording on a flat disc.

1889   First use of sound recording in academic research.

1920s   Use of electrical recordings.

1933   Stereophonic gramophone patented.

1948   Columbia Company introduced long-playing record using vinylite.

1980   Philips and Sony introduce compact digital discs.

(b) Sound tape

1899   Valdemar Poulsen. First practical system using a wire magnetic recorder.

1927-28   Introduction of steel tape and coated paper tape.

1930   Cellulose acetate tape used.

1940   PVC tape used.

1960s   Philips compact cassette developed.

1968   Dolby 'A' system for reducing tape hiss.

1980   Sony Walkman miniature cassette recorder.

4 Microcomputers and viewdata

1945   ENIAC (Electronic Numerical Integrator and Calculator). First fully electronic computer.

1956	Burroughs E-101. First desk-sized computer.
1969	Silicon chip designed as the central processing unit of a computer.
1971	Intel introduce microprocessor.
1973	Computer coded labels introduced into supermarkets.
1974	Hewlett-Packard programmable pocket calculator.
1974	BBC CEEFAX service.
1975	Altair home computer in kit form.
1975	Videogames.
1976	APPLE microcomputer.
1979	Prestel service launched.
1981	Sinclair ZX81 microcomputer.
1983	Telesoftware service via Prestel and BBC CEEFAX.

How were these inventions and developments reflected in library collections? There is a parallel with the early history of libraries in that there is a general progression from service to select groups to service to the general public. Such a picture may be seen with collections of NBM, particularly those of sound recordings.

Private collectors were early into the field recording folk songs, and making anthropological recordings. The first instance of sound recording being used in academic research was by J Walter Fewkes who recorded the prayers, tales, and songs of the Pasamquoddy Indians in 1889. The first officially recognized collection of sound recordings[11] was established in Vienna in 1899 for the language and dialects of Europe. Later collections such as the British Institute of Recorded Sound (1948) relied heavily on the donations of individual collectors. Other national institutions were also keen to establish an interest. The Library of Congress had copyright concerning paper prints or contact prints of motion pictures by 1894, but sound recordings were not covered by federal copyright law until 1972. The BBC established its sound library in 1935 to satisfy its own growing demands. But there is little other evidence concerning the beginnings of many NBM collections. However, there is some indication of involvement by public libraries, particularly in the United States, from an early date.

Illustrations collections
These included prints, photographs, materials cut from periodicals, and lantern slides. The first known picture collection was begun in 1889 at Denver Public Library, Colorado. In the UK the emphasis

seems to have been on the collection of local illustrations, in particular photographs. Local photographic societies sponsored surveys, and in 1908 some twenty systematic collections had been preserved in local libraries or museums. Lantern slides were in use in a number of libraries and in 1923 Kent County Library had a collection of six thousand. Hereford County Library in 1926 had sets of lantern slides for forty-four lectures on subjects agreed with the rural community council. Illustration collections were available in half the municipal libraries in London and the Home Counties by 1939. However, Campbell,[12] writing in 1964, suggests that these were still peripheral in most UK public libraries and that there was nothing to compare to the developments in the USA where at least three public libraries held over one million illustrations. The closest British comparison was Birmingham Public Library, with some 200,000.

Sound recordings
In the USA public libraries were early in the field. That at St Paul, Minnesota, established a collection in 1913 and by 1919 had a stock of six hundred records and an annual issue of 3500. In the UK the first gramophone record service to schools was organized by Middlesex County Library in 1936, although it was soon transferred to the education department. Hereford County Library was the first public library to make discs available on loan to the general public in 1945, and Walthamstow was the first municipal library, in 1947. By 1950, there were fifty public library authorities lending gramophone records.

Cinefilm
Collections were slow to emerge in the USA but by 1922 eleven school systems had established them and by 1945 approximately a dozen large urban public libraries had organized film services. As early as 1929 the Cleveland Public Library had cooperated with a local movie house to publicize the film *Scaramouche*. In the UK little has been discovered to indicate any services to the public, but the children's librarian of Rochdale in 1930[13] has been reported as using film primarily to encourage reading! Even now, there are few loan collections for the general public.

Yet it should not be thought that librarians were slow to realize the potential of film. A writer in 1912 stated that 'a few years ago there were people who prophetically said that the cinematograph would not live long: it was just a craze, the popularity of which would soon

9

diminish, but we are compelled to acknowledge that the moving picture is a force to be reckoned with'. He cited its use to train medical students and in this way 'a large number of unnecessary operations are obviated'.[14]

Video, viewdata and computers
Librarians have not been slow to introduce videorecordings into their libraries. The resource centre growth of the 1970s saw a steady increase in educational establishments of collections of videorecordings. Similarly the domestic videorecording boom in the UK in the early 1980s was matched by lean services in many public libraries.[15]

Librarians have also been at the forefront of pilot work on viewdata services to the public, and while it is too early to comment on the developments concerning the use of microcomputers, the British Library has already sponsored work in this area.[16]

This short history of the development of collections of photographs, slides, sound and video recordings, and cinefilms in libraries is slanted towards developments in the public libraries of America and Britain. There were some developments in other types of libraries but there is still a lack of research into the early history of NBM collections. One writer has suggested that the lack of written evidence concerning the early collections of sound recordings may have been because they were 'considered ephemera and as such were likely to be disposed of; therefore, the librarians was reluctant to make their presence official by accessioning or cataloguing them'.[17]

The interest of librarians
Why were librarians so slow and in some cases hostile to the inclusion of NBM in their collections? Four reasons may be considered:

1 The long history of the book and the printed word as the main medium for recorded information.

2 The librarian was a collector and preserver of books and not of all forms of information carrier.

3 The strong belief that the book was an educational force and the other forms were mere novelties.

4 The cost and fragility of non-book materials.

In spite of the absence of detailed research, some general points may be made. Media other than books have been readily accepted by the general public. The spread of cinemas, the large sales of sound discs, the number of home movie makers and photographers indicate a

10

favourable use of all these forms. Yet librarians have often been in opposition to these other forms and linked this closely to a defence of books. In 1917 Doubleday questioned 'what may be the educational value of the picture palaces after sixty years or more of existence, is and must be a matter of speculation. In the writer's opinion they can only hope to serve as auxiliaries to libraries much as libraries are now an auxiliary to education; and they may never even attain to that utility'.[18] An anonymous writer some twenty years later believed that 'films are substitutes for reading. At the present time they are, at their very best, poor substitutes; at their very worst, they are pernicious'.[19]

Film was considered necessary in order to encourage reading rather than appreciated or valued in its own right. McColvin (1927) commenting on extension activities said 'the chief objections are that suitable films are difficult and expensive to obtain, and that they are not sufficiently related to books. Without a doubt they would attract a different public.'[20]

The librarian has also worried about the expense, safety and fragility of NBM. The cost would be prohibitive 'for a rate-supported institution to bear the expense of such a scheme . . . It is surely carrying our ideal of public service to such an extreme as to make it sentimental and American . . . To keep on adding to our extraneous undertakings will mean that we shall have soon departed so far from the fundamental idea of the public library that we shall regard the issue of a good book as a mere side-track'.[21] Savage was particularly concerned with the damage to discs by borrowers 'scraping the life out of them with steel needles or . . . blasting them with a blunt needle'.[22] Cinefilm was not being used in 1931, Sayers suggested, because of the 'obstacles of inflammable films and local regulations have made its use difficult'.[23]

During the early period of libraries, their champions defended books on the grounds that they were of educational value to the general public. Paradoxically, after 1945 NBM were excluded from libraries on the grounds that they were only of value to educational institutions, and not to the public. The only form that did develop outside the educational setting was the sound disc, and even here it was seen as an adjunct to music. One writer in 1964 commented: 'Since librarians first began to discuss gramophone records, those in favour of them have on various occasions stressed the value of non-musical recordings — such as sound effects, local council proceedings, play readings, and, in particular, language-teaching records . . . It seems doubtful whether they will ever be of great significance in public libraries'.[24]

11

Thus the major impetus for the development of collections of NBM after 1945 came from the educational system. Even when the public library was supplying a service to schools, the librarians were chiefly interested in books and ignored other materials. It has been a long road away from this position.

The value of film in education was stressed in 1948 by the National Committee for Visual Aids in Education which sought to establish 'what types of material should be purchased, and how best to establish local visual aids libraries.[25] As a result, local education committees were advised to set up lending libraries for 16 mm film and to support the establishment of a national film library by the Educational Foundation for Visual Aids. These recommendations were eventually implemented.

Attention during the 1950s and 60s was also focused on resource-based learning and in 1970 both the National Council for Educational Technology and the Schools Council established projects on resource centres,[26] the former for higher education and the latter for schools. These considered that the key area was the organization of recorded knowledge to meet the individual learner's needs. Both stressed the importance of libraries collecting all forms of materials. The Library Association recognized this in a number of policy statements culminating in 1973 with *Library resource centres in schools, colleges and institutions of higher education: a general policy statement*. This document stressed that 'books, duplicated and audiovisual materials complement each other in their contribution to teaching and research, and should be regarded as part of a unified collection'. It remains to be seen whether this view is reflected in the activities of all librarians, not only in the strictly educational sector, but also in other types of library as well.[27]

It is interesting to compare the hesitancy shown by librarians to the earlier NBM and that shown to the more recent formats. The great interest in videorecordings was perhaps fuelled by the belief that this was a service that could be financially profitable. Similarly the great public interest in the 'new information technology' and the monies provided by national government has resulted in the Library Association establishing an Information Technology Group and producing a policy statement in this area.

The financial rigours of the 1980s have resulted in threats to NBM in libraries. Sound recording collections, in particular, have been closed and even a famous slide collection, that of the Victoria and Albert

12

Museum, was threatened. However, these problems have not arisen because of the dislike of NBM by librarians but because the public representatives such as local government councillors and Government Ministers have seen them as of lower priority compared to other computerized forms of information provision.

VARIETY OF APPLICATIONS

Communication between human beings is through the senses, the most powerful of which is sight. In competition with other senses, sight dominates in the reception of information, a factor which has to be taken into account in the production of audiovisual materials. NBM carrying messages to users may be designed to stimulate any of these senses, taste, smell, touch, hearing and sight. In practice few make use of taste, partly because materials would be consumed in the process of communication, but mainly because storing information in this way is ineffective as the quality changes over time. There is a teaching kit produced by the sugar manufacturers which contains little canisters of different types of sugar for sampling. These naturally do not survive for very long.

Nor is smell a commonly used sense with stored NBM. In the broadest interpretation of this word, chemicals and cooking materials may be included, but even in the most comprehensive library of the present or future these are unlikely to form a significant proportion of the documents that are stored and used. Nevertheless, a few books have been produced for young children in which scratching the page produces an odour which may also be tasted. There have also been attempts at films in the commercial cinema in which appropriate aromas have been released into the auditorium at particular moments. The difficulty has been the removal of one odour from the atmosphere before the next one is released. Because smell is a relatively unimportant human sense, the advantages in atmospheric conditioning expected by the producers have not been achieved. Indeed, taste and smell are both more likely to be long-lasting irrational associative senses which may result in responses contrary to that of the communicator. A user may link a smell of onions with a personal nightmare, so that its appearance in the cinema may not act as an associative stimulant towards the food being served up on the screen. Curiously, such personal and individual associations are retained much longer through taste and smell than through hearing and sight.

Touch is a very significant sense which has been relatively unexplored in NBM. Too many objects have been locked away behind a sign 'Do Not Touch' in the past, although a relatively free atmosphere is now being encouraged in many museums. However, this is often ignored through the inhibitions introduced by previous attitudes. Yet from birth, exploration of objects by hand-contact has formed an important part of information gathering. Caressing and feeling also stimulate

14

strongly sensual senses which are an important adjunct to artistic, cultural and emotional experiences for both learning and leisure purposes. It is therefore an important part of the appreciation of art to be able to touch sculpture and cloth materials, in order to explore the surface and the texture, just as it is helpful in the learning of geology to feel the relative roughness of rocks. The manipulation of apparatus in technology or science museums is a valuable adjunct to the information gathering offered by the exhibits. While excessive physical handling of such materials may cause deterioration, nevertheless the opportunity for users to do this should not be entirely excluded. It is particularly encouraging that some museums are now lending their exhibits to users for such experiences, just as some libraries are offering art reproductions, models and other artefacts. Another sector in which touch is important is in the use of equipment by the handicapped. Controls for devices for the blind depend on buttons and keys which can be identified by fingertips, frequently producing voice outputs. In many cases, microprocessors are used between the blind user and the apparatus. For those with other physical handicaps, a large variety of switches are available which work through microprocessors to help such users control different equipment including NBM devices.

The values of sound and sight need no elaboration. It is often overlooked that sight dominates sound, and many people find it much more valuable to listen to dialogue and music with their eyes shut in order to eliminate visual distraction. The more visually realistic the message, however, the less it encourages imaginative participation. Someone reading a novel has imaginatively to construct both the appearance and the sound of the characters involved. Hearing a dramatization of this work leaves only the visual experience of the characters and the setting to be imagined. The film of the book provides the user with all the information except the touch, smell and taste of the atmosphere. Perhaps because of this, it can be argued that books are re-read more often than dramatic recordings are re-played, and re-viewing is generally less frequent still. A natural identification with characters varies little in each situation, although the physical appearance of a particular actor may inhibit such a participation in a visually realised recreation.

These responses are important factors in the borrowing rates of materials, and are the basis of one of the problems behind the selection of programmes for mass distribution. Naturally there are exceptions; and there are constantly changing records for the re-seeing of films such

15

as *E.T.* However, the principle is sufficiently strong to be of concern to producers and distributors of the different media.

On the other hand, audio and visual experiences are close to the manner in which individuals learn about their environments and interpersonal relationships. They are therefore sensory channels through which information and understanding are expected for efficient mental processing. The need for such stimulants sometimes leads to a state which may even be called an addiction. The printed word is often less readily processed than the information provided by sound and picture by people brought up in an audiovisual environment. Indeed they may need to turn words into audiovisual images before absorption.

Frequently, these media can carry information more concisely and directly than the printed word in a book. Because there are generally fewer imaginative requirements in mental translation, the nuances, inflections and relative emphases are less ambiguous, the comprehension quicker and more complete. However, good presentation of information demands simplicity and careful explanation, because paradoxically the user finds it more difficult to consider the meaning of a single word or phrase in an audiovisual programme than is the case with a printed book. Information in a book can be more complex and more completely cross-referenced than that in an audiovisual presentation. Videodiscs and computer programs offer many opportunities for revision, reviewing and recapitulation which approximate most closely to similar options with a book.

The applications of the various forms of NBM have to be considered in terms of the sensory stimulation they produce, together with the balance between such responses. It is also necessary to be aware of the different characteristics of the formats, most of which are implicit in the descriptions which follow in this book. Such characteristics result not just from the format itself but also from the environment in which it is used. For example, a film, *The whisperers*,[28] may be viewed in a commercial cinema in which the surrounding darkness isolates the senses to complete concentration on the audiovisual experience being transmitted. Participatory involvement is strongly encouraged. The same film may be shown in a classroom in only partial blackout, the senses alerted and distracted by the other activities within the room and the interpersonal relationships with the other students and the teacher. Or the film may be viewed on television, the impact effectively changed by the environment, the objects in the room, the ease of movement around it, the facility for disappearing to the kitchen for refreshment.

16

There is also a total absence of group response which is an important additive in the cinema, and a differing relationship to the medium, based on the relative sizes of the image and the expected perception. These facets need consideration in any understanding of the value and organization of NBM, but a detailed examination will not be given here. The example above does, however, indicate three completely different settings for the same item, each with a different overtone of emphasis. A viewing in the cinema is usually approached with a desire for entertainment; the school setting is more naturally didactic and the viewers in this case will be expecting educational or learning value. If such a film is selected from the range of television channels, the choice may have been made mainly for enjoyment, but there is also a perception that it may enrich one's understanding of society and the environment.

None of these terms – entertainment, learning, enrichment – can be considered mutually exclusive. Indeed, their overlap is apparent in each setting, for some cinema-goers will be enriched and the students in the classroom will certainly expect to be entertained. However, it is equally clear that the same document can be enjoyed in each setting. Users look to NBM for all three types of experience, but to segregate materials into each one is difficult. Visual material, in particular, is hard to categorize because the user brings to it such differing backgrounds of experience, expectation and perception.

As explained earlier, NBM consist of a wide variety of different materials, some of which may be used together as kits. The simplest forms are combinations of two items, sound tape and slides, filmstrip and booklet, but some kits are considerable collections of different formats. Thus one prepared on child abuse[29] by Newcastle Polytechnic in conjunction with the Open University contains twenty items, including two books, small instruction cards, small booklets, two plays, a pack of special playing cards, three sound tapes, and a set of slides.

While the majority of these kits have been prepared for educational purposes, the definition of learning must not be confined to the school environment. A few years ago, the *Observer* newspaper produced kits in support of a series of articles on the history of Britain in its colour supplement. *A making of the British* kit[30] could be purchased which included information cards, supplementary articles, slides, and a sound disc or tape. These were available to and purchased by the general public, not just teachers, and while some were undoubtedly used in schools, others were purchased for their general interest value. Certainly not every purchaser was an academic historian. For many, the materials provided added interest to the information contained in the articles, giving a different perspective and providing an extension of general knowledge. Certainly kits tend to be instructive rather than purely entertaining, but it would be wrong to conclude that they are not frequently of value to a general user.

In the broadest context therefore NBM are used for entertainment, learning and enrichment. In the commercial world, microforms are used for administrative purposes. Commerce also makes widespread use of NBM for advertising, promotion and sales. Slides, sound tapes, discs, cinefilms and videotapes all find a place in the travelling bag of the contemporary salesman, providing him with opportunities for expressing more directly and explicitly the applications and values of his products. For larger concerns, supporting general entertainment films is a means of advertising, and petroleum firms and tourist boards are considerable producers. International companies also use NBM for communication between the various subsidiaries. Videotape recordings of company plans or board decisions can be transmitted rapidly between branches and replayed to provide the receiver with clear presentations of procedures and future developments, together with a feeling of personal interest and concern from a remote headquarters.

NBM are also frequently used as a means of recording events. Sound recordings, still and cinefilm and videorecordings are the commonest forms used. The finish of a race may require a photographic record to differentiate the places, or the climber may use a camera to freeze that unique moment at the summit of the mountain. They may be for personal satisfaction or as a means of proving that the achievement has been completed. News and events of all kinds are captured in a different perspective by NBM, making a wide use of media. Whereas books and other traditional means of keeping records tend towards interpretations of happenings and people, NBM tend to closer representations of reality although inevitably the producer of sound and pictorial records does have some selection criteria. A verbal description of the Cod War and fishing in the North Sea requires imaginative interpretation from the reader, probably from a base of total inexperience, whereas a film, however selective the pictures, brings closer the sense of the battle for survival among steep waves in the small boats. Seeing Bertrand Russell talk about his philosophy adds further perspectives and understanding through the force of his personality as compared with reading the theories.

Nor should valuable records be restricted to just important events or notable people. The development of oral history on sound tape perpetuates the feelings of common people as they react to their environments and the daily intercourse of their activities. The programmes on BBC television in early 1978 *Caught in time* resurrected many old cinefilms taken by amateurs around their localities. Interest was not just confined to the settings and clothes of the periods in which the films were made, but also the social mores of the people, their behaviour and attitudes. In the same way that Phiz's drawings in the novels of Dickens give a sense of the nineteenth century, the dresses and clothes add a further dimension which provides a deeper understanding of life at the time. When examined with an appropriate program, recording census and similar details on computer stores offers extensive sorting and research opportunities which would be impossible from the printed records. In this case, the NBM provides a facility for examination and exploration which cannot be experienced in any other way.

NBM are also a source of study in their own right. Knowledge, understanding and theory are developing rapidly. In the late 1950s, the theory of film was discussed in very few books, by Rotha, Grierson, Manvell, Seton, Montagu, Jacobs and of course Eisenstein. Most writing about the cinema was about its stars and their love lives, not its history and theory. Now thirty years later, there are lecturers in film studies at universities, and degrees in media and communication studies in which the movies play a central part. The theory of semiology has developed to introduce a new approach to the interpretation of film and television. Studies of radio are developing insights into the cultural values of this medium. Other NBM like music on disc and still photographs already have their own theoretical structure and analysis.

In summary, the argument developed here is that NBM extend the range of the senses in exploring documents for information. In doing this, the user is employing the methods he used in the earliest days of his development, exploring his environment through aural, visual and tactile stimuli.

NBM are used to carry messages for entertainment, enrichment and learning, and are also increasingly used for administration and storage in business and commerce; communication between parts of businesses; sales promotion; records of events; and studies of the media in their own right.

Part 2

THE USER

INTRODUCTION

The term 'user' has been defined in a number of different ways in connection with libraries. Here it is being used to indicate a person using non-book materials, whether or not in a library context. The term 'non-user' therefore indicates somebody who does not use NBM rather than somebody who does not make use of libraries. In contrast the term 'client' describes somebody who actually makes some use of NBM within a library context whereas a 'non-client' describes anybody who uses NBM but has no knowledge of or desire to use them in a library context. An example may make this clearer. A safety officer who collects a film from his office and shows it in a factory is a *user* of NBM, while one who *lectures* on safety in the factory may be described as a *non-user* of NBM. If, however, he was to go to the company library and borrow a film on safety he would be a *client*, whereas if he did not know that the company library had any NBM or refused to use the library he would be called a *non-client*. The relationship is shown in the following diagram.

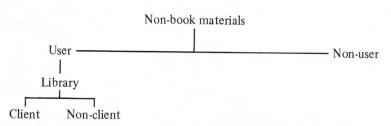

This is not merely playing with words, for it is important to consider the user of NBM outside the library context, which will reveal the potential market for the services of the library. For if librarians believe that the purpose of the library is to assist the economic, educational and social progress of the community, then their first duty is to analyse the use made of NBM by that community and to determine if, how, and perhaps most important *to what extent* the library can help.

This use cannot be defined too narrowly, for the full range of possible demands mustbe considered even if at the end the lirbarian concludes that help cannot be offered. The view which sees NBM within the public library context as being limited to sound recordings of music or entertainment confronts the belief that these are not just 'vehicles for artistic experience' but also a means of conveying ideas, information,

22

learning and instruction. As Unesco (1968) has stated for one subject: 'The emergence of exciting and creative new forms for the presentation of scientific knowledge contributes to the progress of education and enriches the cultural heritage of mankind'.[1]

It is not the aim of this book to describe and analyse the impact that NBM have had on society. However, it is important to realize that the individual user has an immense range of information sources available. Within individual homes there are radios, televisions, gramophone records, sound tapes, art reproductions, models, kits, photographs and viewdata services. In 1982 one million microcomputers were sold. Indeed some would claim that the information sources not found within the home are books, newspapers, and periodicals. In our day it is difficult to be a non-user of non-book materials.

A wide range of subjects and experiences are available: scientific exploration on television series; rock music concerts in stereo on the radio; posters as free gifts in magazines on subjects as diverse as 'Child safety in the home' or 'Uses of glue'; sound cassette guides around a stately home; videogames. Within a factory, school or office an individual is similarly exposed to numerous NBM: the training film on safety; the factory radio station with its own DJ; listening to the sound of recorded heartbeats in medical school; preparing a CSE project on the mass media; desk diaries on microcomputers; computer software on the genetics of the fruit fly.

THE VARIETY AND RANGE OF USERS

Users of NBM may be divided into two groups which, although not completely distinct, point to differing needs.

The producer
This type of user is one who, in creating a document in book or non-book format, has to extract previously recorded information from one or more forms of NBM. For example, for a television programme on Gary Cooper, the production team would incorporate material from his films, newsfilm, radio interviews and still photographs.

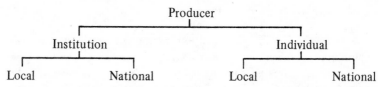

The diagram demonstrates that there are both individual and institutional producers. These may be differentiated into national and local, national in this context meaning that the document produced will be sold or distributed beyond the reaches of the institution or individual producer. This is analogous to the process of books being published. In contrast, a local production is one that is primarily designed for use within the institution or by the individual. For example, an individual producing at a local level could be a student creating a tape-slide presentation for a seminar about Beatrix Potter, drawing upon her writings, contemporary still photographs, and slides of her cottage. An example of an institution producing at a local level would be an educational technology unit creating a tape-slide for a law lecturer incorporating maps, pages from law books, photographs and drawings. School children produced a variety of microcomputer software including games such as 'Froggy'. Realizing that there was a market for their products they formed a company JSD Software and distribute nationwide.

In summary, the producer is a user who finds information in a variety of formats (be it book or NBM) and uses it to create something new.

The private user
This type of user takes a finished product in order to extract information from it. He may accept or reject that information but he makes

24

no attempt to create his own document. Thus a student who plays a sound cassette on 'Birds of the sea shore' has as a result gained knowledge of that subject but does not take parts of that recording and create his own document. Similarly, the parent who buys a copy of a sound cassette telling the story of Black Beauty in order to keep his children quiet on a long car journey is not intending to reorganize that recording. The private user may well be choosing the item not for himself but for a known audience. For example, the training officer in a library may select a videotape presentation on enquiry techniques to show to a group of reference librarians.

The producer and private user described above appear in all aspects of society, and the following sections may help to show how wide-ranging is the demand that these users can make on NBM.

In education

There is a danger in saying that education is the province of the school or college librarian and that other libraries do not need to bother about it. This is rather akin to the argument that some public librarians used to put forward concerning services for children – 'Up to the time they go to school they cannot read so they do not need the library. Once they are at school they have the school library so they do not need the public library. Once they leave school they are adults and can use the public library'. Such a parody could result in the newly fledged adult ignoring the public library for which he finds no use at all.

However, the librarian should be aware of trends within education which may alter the pattern of demands made on the library for information. There can be little argument about the attitude of the future clientele: their work within school is showing young people that non-books are powerful tools. This has already had a direct result on school libraries with the development of the resource centre. It cannot be stressed too highly that NBM has permeated into all aspects of education, although it may not have reached as far as some claim. Major stimulants to this spread have been the growth of the idea of the student as an individual learner, the concept of resource-based learning, and the project method, all of which suggest that if the student is searching for information then he must have adequate resources in all formats. For example, the student interested in local history may well study via books, filmstrips, still photographs, specimens, maps. This should not be thought of as a recent development, although the use of electronic

25

aids has developed during the latter part of this century. At the Beamish Open Air Museum, County Durham there is an example of a late Victorian classroom which includes maps, wallcharts, a magic lantern, specimens, even a teaching kit. What may be new is the belief that these are more than teaching aids, but the very basis of individual student learning.

The rapid introduction of microcomputers at all levels of our educational system is producing a computer literate generation who see computing software as a natural part of their information requirements. They organize and search for information using simple data management systems, such as 'Micro Query'; they learn about the stock market through simulations on the computer; and they relax playing 'Space Invaders'.

Even if one is not sure how far these developments may affect libraries outside education it is salutary to see the figures concerning the number of students and teachers. In the United Kingdom in 1980 from a total population of 56.3 million some 10.5 million children attended school (nursery, primary, secondary and special), 1,700,000 students were undertaking full or part-time further and higher education, about 1,600,000 people were attending Adult Education Centres, and there was a total of 700,000 teachers in schools, further and higher education. The US National Center for Education Statistics estimated the attendance at all of the country's regular educational institutions at 57,565,000; this was 25.7% of the total population of the USA as of 1st September 1980.

It can be seen that these represent sizeable percentages of the population of each country. If all these people are being involved with NBM in the educational sector, it is likely that many of them will be making similar demands in future outside it.

Private users within education
Within primary education this experience illustrates how far NBM and its equipment has become a normal part of the lives of some children.

A project on China − 'It is the policy of the school to have a School Project each term . . . Visits to places or institutions that might be useful are booked, transport arranged and outside sources of information sought, eg parents with a special knowledge or skills, local people who can help in some way. Films also have to be booked well in advance . . . Next the problem of reference materials − how do you get any practical experience of something like China? Were we going to rely on books?.

26

We discussed the way they felt would be the best to tackle the project. They wanted to make lots of models, they wanted visits, they wanted films, slides and tapes and "can we do a play?". Luckily I had spent six years in Hong Kong and had a fair amount of interesting materials which I felt would stimulate them right at the beginning. I was able to show them slides, play records of Chinese music and tell them stories from China'.[2]

In secondary education the Bullock Report (*A language for life*, 1975) mentioned a school using the facilities of an outside body: 'We have seen the work of some teachers who make excellent use of film as a focal point for talking and writing, as an aid to thematic work, where it is associated with related literature and as a medium for study in its own right. In devising a course for fourth and fifth year pupils one English department had tried over a hundred films in the space of a few years, most of them hired from the British Film Institute. These were rarely full-length feature films. As one teacher put it: "There are many excellent short films which are shown in film festivals and then are seen no more. Like short stories they fit well into double lessons".'[3]

Chapter 22 of *A language for life* offers many such examples. In a report whose main aim was to consider 'in relation to schools all aspects of teaching the use of English, including reading, writing and speech',[4] the committee clearly saw NBM as valuable. The producers of NBM have not been slow in recognizing needs in this field. Publishers such as Pinnacle have produced a wide variety of children's stories on cassette, and there is also a monthly sound cassette periodical retelling children's stories. A glance through the publications of the Schools Council[5] will demonstrate how widely the various NBM have been used to produce bright, attractive teaching packages. Even the computer developments in schools are providing a variety of NBM. For example *Mary Rose* Ginn, 1983 looks at the archaeological work on the ship through a kit which includes one computer cassette, ten survey charts, 21 drawings of artefacts and other finds, one colour booklet, one cut-out model, and a book of notes (ISBN 0602 25078 1). This pattern continues into higher education.

Pat Noble in her work *Resource-based learning in higher education* notes: 'Picture the learner in a resource-based system: busy with set tasks from a course workbook; submerged in a world of sound with headset and cassette player; trying to solve the decision-making problems with other students before rejoining a patient computer terminal; tuning into radio or television transmission; scanning a set of slides to

27

find essential information; seeking out a teacher for help or guidance to other sources. All these activities belong to a resource-based learning system whether within institutions or at a distance from them. Learning in all such systems invites transaction with stored knowledge'.[6] Examples of the above may be drawn from all aspects of higher education.

There has also been considerable interest in NBM as of value in Distance Learning.

The Open University is the first full-scale multimedia system of higher education. A student is involved with television and radio programmes, sound cassettes, still photographs, specimens, videotapes. As a producer of NBM the Open University makes heavy demands upon its library.[6] The library, however, provides the usual services of a university library for academic staff. In addition, the multimedia university university courses require multimedia services to the staff in the preparation of course materials: appropriate illustrative material has to be sought and made available — this includes the clearance of copyright for publication. Material is acquired and documented to these ends' (Helen Harrison, 1973).[7] The Open University also provides study centres throughout the country which are well equipped with NBM and the relevant hardware. Detailed proposals for the use of NBM in the 'Open Tech Programme' are contained in Twining.[8]

Outside the educational sector there are a number of academic associations and professional institutions producing NBM. These include the Historical Association, the Royal Institute of British Architects, the Law Society, the Institute of Chartered Accountants.

Producers within education
In the previous section the use of NBM has been considered in relation to the teacher and student as private users, in other words their individual use of the available documents for study and teaching. However, teachers and students in all sectors of education must also be considered as potential creators.

The primary school child involved in a project on the local park may take still photographs of the trees, interview the park-keeper making use of the school cassette tape recorder, obtain photocopies of early maps of the area, and borrow from the school library a filmstrip on the animals that may be found in a park. He will write of his experiences in compiling the project and package the complete work in a portfolio. At secondary school level there are numerous examples of children and staff being involved in film making, discussing a plot, writing the script

28

and then shooting the film. Teachers are also involved in educational broadcasts by local radio stations. The pupils and teachers at Selwyne School, Essex use a computer simulation kit based on the Voyage of Discovery in the fifteenth and sixteenth centuries. A pupil has written a computer program which clarifies the process of trading and makes possible many of the authentic variations in commodities and prices.[9]

Lecturers in higher education are also producers. A glance through the catalogue of the Higher Education Learning Programmes Information Service (1981)[10] reveals many examples. Educational technology units have helped the individual lecturer to produce very professional and sophisticated learning packages. However, these units have often confined their role to offering help to academic staff, limiting assistance to students to a training in the use of equipment, there are though exceptions. For example, one polytechnic has regularly run courses for librarianship students which involve them in creating tape-slide presentations for use in their own studies. A useful description and perhaps more importantly an analysis of some of the problems of other student productions may be seen in an article by Ravilious.[11]

At work
The Kodak survey (1976)[12] suggests that within firms two departments emerge as the major users of NBM: training, aimed at middle management and salesmen, and marketing, aimed at advertising, public relations and sales.

From the point of view of the employer the main purpose of training must be to achieve maximum efficiency. The armed services are major users of NBM for training purposes, particularly in the field of programmed learning. Other users include industrial employers such as British Leyland, Dunlop, ICI; in the commercial sector such firms as Marks and Spencer, Boots; and the nationalized industries such as the National Coal Board, British Steel Corporation, the Post Office. The Midland Bank in 1983 purchased VHS video players for installation in 1800 branches and offices for staff training and customer information.[13] Mothercare introduced in 1982 videodisc players for a nationwide campaign of its new products.[13] Abbey National in 1982 purchased 100 tape-slide machines for its regular employees communication network.

Viewdata systems have gained most success in the business world. In particular the travel industry has installed sets in the majority of their branches. Banks and financial firms have introduced private user systems for quick access to such information as commodity prices. Vast numbers of training films and specialist films are made for firms such as Unilever, Kelloggs, Scottish and Newcastle Breweries to motivate the work force, increase profits and to introduce new legislation such as the Health and Safety Act. There are some 20,000 training departments in the UK and 91% of them are using NBM to a greater or lesser extent. NBM gives an extra punch, adding effectiveness to presentation.

Publishers have also used NBM. For example, in order to launch the book *The mists of Avalon* by Marion Bradley, Michael Joseph is distributing a two and a half minute videofilm to selected bookshops. This gives a dramatic synopsis of the novel, plus a brief selling line. They have also provided posters, streamers, and sample copies. Penguin have provided on Prestel a catalogue of their non-specialist works.

As producers of NBM, industry was also considered in the Kodak survey and the results suggested that production needs were met both internally and externally. Most organizations produce their own flip charts whilst forty per cent produce their own films and videotapes. Overhead projection slides and 35 mm slides fall between these two limits. These organizations also produce material for use outside the firm. British Gas has educational aids for sale or gratis distribution to schools, and also produces films for internal use.

There is also a demand for NBM to assist in the planning and implementation aspects of work. Fairfax (1976) reports that 'a recent Aslib slide librarian conference brought together librarians providing slides, not only in education and training, but also for architects, planning departments of local authorities, meteorologists and scientists in industry and research organizations. Materials for this audience will be usually purchased from specialist producers or made within the organization'.[14] An example of this type of use is seen in a service provided by the local government unit, East Sussex County Library, which provides sound cassettes for councillors and local government officers. These give supplementary and background material on local government issues, and are particularly 'valuable in supplying an introduction to completely new topics . . . . for instance, new legislation like the Community Land Act and the Employment Protection Act'.[15]

NBM are not restricted, though, only to the training and marketing aspects of business organizations. The development of the small business microcomputer has increased the use of the computer to control finance, mail letters, and plan and model business projections. The British Government has recognized this by funding the provision of microcomputers for doctors and a large-scale electronic office at British Leyland. And microforms, in all their different formats, are used widely for information storage in the administration of commercial enterprises. Specific uses include microforms of patents and technical drawings, staff records and business transactions.

In leisure activities

All libraries, consciously or not, cater for leisure activities. However, within this context the public library plays perhaps the leading role concerning activities which take place outside the work place or educational establishment. These will include hobbies, club membership, sports, classical music, slide-shows. The merit, intellectual or otherwise of these activities need not concern the librarian. What is important is the fact that they involve a large number of individuals. Thus individuals in their homes listen to Beethoven on the radio, learn French from a sound cassette, or watch soap-operas on television. Probably the major leisure source is television.

In February 1981 the average time spent watching television by those aged five and over was about 20 hours, with children and the elderly watching the most (Social Trends 1982). The desire for home entertainment resulted in some 3.5 million sales of videorecorders in the UK by 1982. This was 15% of the world total with the USA having some 5.3 million sales. Video magazines have been produced on a wide variety of topics and leisure videorecordings are a feature in many High Street shops. The *Observer*[16] reported in 1983 that 'for the first time British sales of personal computers have hit the magic million mark in a twelve month period 1982 . . . also reveals a total installed base of 1.35 million machines a tripling of sales last year'. The BBC television series *The computer programme* was watched by seven million people and some 38,000 BBC microcomputers were purchased. A further 65,000 people bought the National Extension College book on *30 hour BASIC*'.

Other leisure activities besides television viewing are undertaken! Scouts and Guides had over 1.3 million members in 1982; youth clubs some 771,000 members; and clubs based on outdoor pursuits 152,000 members.[17] The organizations involved are generally both users and producers of NBM, perhaps as a way of keeping members interested in summer pursuits on cold winter nights! In the same way, national art galleries (attendance 1982: 5,764,000) and museums (attendance 1982: 17,111,000) also offer replicas of exhibits. One

31

enterprising firm is now offering 'artzak'; it hires out art works to firms for their board rooms. This has been a common practice for some time in a number of local education authorities, for schools, and several public libraries also offer the same kind of picture-loan service.

A church society considering a visit to the Holy Land may want to borrow a film or slides on the subject. The local council that is twinning its town with one in Germany may find the need for a few German phrases learnt from a language record. A local pressure group anxious to avoid the siting of an oil refinery in its area could usefully borrow a study kit such as *Distribution: siting of an oil terminal*, aimed primarily at sixth-formers but of obvious general interest, by Shell Mex BP Ltd, and Bath University School of Education.[18] A person trying to understand the construction of his car may gain more help from an overlay transparency than a series of diagrams in a book. Many librarians, whilst recognizing this use, may feel unable to justify buying the material in this format, although many libraries have it already, but bound into book form — *Colliers encyclopedia.*[19]

Librarians are aware of many of these leisure demands and have certainly attempted to satisfy some of them. This is particularly true in the case of gramophone records. Westminster Public Libraries have loaned records since the 1930s but even here there have been constraints, in particular the emphasis on classical music. However, the issue of records and tapes has continued to increase from public libraries reaching over 13 million in 1980-81.[20] Pinion[21] in 1982 reported that some 59 public libraries were considering setting up video libraries. A number of authorities have also established computer clubs in their branch libraries.[22]

Yet the impression remains that there is little systematic enquiry into whether or not particular users require NBM from their local library. Despite the development of NBM usage for leisure, it is still difficult to find evidence for H C Campbell's remark (1973) that 'There can be no doubt that public library users are interested in obtaining materials in forms other than print'.[23] There is certainly evidence of a growing demand for sound and videorecordings but this is not an indication of a general demand. As Swank (1953)[24] has pointed out it is a mistake to think of NBM as a homogeneous category.

NEEDS AND REQUIREMENTS OF USERS OF NBM

To what extent does the demand from users involve the functions of the library? Ely (1970) has defined a library as follows: 'A *function* (not a place) *whose responsibility is systematically* (there must be a plan for acquisition related to the needs of the institution to which it is attached) *to collect information* (information is used to include realia and non-book materials), *classify it* (the system must recognize the requirements of the retrieval system), *store it* (storage for retrieval purposes may require conversion to appropriate form) *and upon demand* (the art of identifying existence of a unit of information must be efficient and systematic) *retrieve it and assist in adapting it to the use to be made of the information*'.[25]

It is difficult to offer evidence for the view that users think of libraries in this way with regard to their requirements for NBM. They may well not see themselves as wanting NBM at all. The rapid growth of the library resource centre has possibly resulted because NBM have been considered by librarians to be on the fringe of library activities. Perhaps this is most apparent during times of economic constraint when what are seen as non-essentials are the first to be cut to protect the book fund. The other factor is that users may well see the library as a place for print material, and feel that other information sources belong elsewhere. The chief librarian of the Toronto Metropolitan Library Board (1972) has pointed out that 'whereas the library has remained the undisputed source for the organization of printed material in the past it does not hold this position in the area of non-print'.[26] The organizers of Information Technology Year 1982 took this view and it took considerable efforts to persuade them that libraries were information providers and could make use of the new technology.

As has been stated, one of the library's main functions is to collect documents, whatever their form, and throughout this book it will be argued that lessons already learnt about user needs and requirements for books may be used with modification for NBM.

The needs of the private user and those of the producer are similar in many ways, and there is one fundamental principle that is common to both, although its interpretation is perhaps different according to the community served. This is the paramount requirement to satisfy the user's need, and the user's right of access to all information sources in all forms. Unfortunately, at the present time NBM are not as readily available as books. The user has only limited access to those items

33

which are being offered. There is little opportunity to select retrospectively from the mass of recorded information. On the other hand, readers know that within the library system any particular book, no matter what its origin or level, can usually be obtained. The user of NBM does not have this choice because he is tied to the whims of the publisher. He has to buy a particular record for himself, for if it does not have mass appeal it will be deleted. A television episode can only be enjoyed once. Access to it is controlled by the policy of the TV service, unless it is illegally videorecorded.

The following may better help to illustrate the difference between the treatment accorded to books and NBM. The lecturer who wishes to comment on the work of Jane Austen needs to make little effort in purchasing or borrowing her novels. However, one who wants to comment on the films of Robert Altman has to attend public showings of the films or purchase or hire videorecordings. There is little opportunity to obtain access via the free public library system. To purchase or hire the films would prove exorbitantly expensive, even if they were available. Indeed, the right of access is further limited, because not only does it depend on the cinema's ability to show the film, but also on the distributor's willingness to make it available.

The freedom of access so precious in the world of books has been achieved because libraries have collected and stored information as represented in books, and have provided the facilities for its dissemination for both purposive and recreational needs. The words that spring to mind are that libraries enable clients 'privately and voluntarily to choose their own readings' (Enright, 1972).[27] Without this facility the information recorded within NBM becomes the property of the institutions that own the copyright or those who can afford it. The charging for these newer services is restricting their use to those who are already 'information rich'. Access to services such as viewdata are beyond the scope of the majority of the population. Children can only gain access if their parents or the institutions they attend can afford the costs and believe the services have a higher priority than other information services. One computer advertisement reads 'so the money you would normally have spent on a good set of encyclopaedias for your children would now be more effectively spent on one of the new breed of personal computers'. The library further offers the client the opportunity to use information sources privately, without a mediator. Perhaps an inherent danger in some student-centred learning schemes is that the teacher pre-digests the information for the learner, directing him along

34

certain routes. The student uses learning packages with no opportunity to compare and contrast the information in them, rather as if the Bible were only available in a filmed version with no access to the original. The library offers him other viewpoints and other routes.

Librarians must respond to the challenge of organizing NBM for they should be 'concerned with the products of the life of the imagination, the intellect, and the spirit of man; all formalized communication formats are of interest to librarians; audiovisual materials and services should have equal weight, equal concern, equal familiarity, and equal support of library administrations and staff to those of printed materials. Integration of planning and programmes regardless of subject, format, or age level served is required for the library to continue as a relevant agency'.[28] In order to achieve this the library must act for its clients, by providing information about what exists and how access can be gained. This implies the provision of bibliographical tools which are current, retrospective, offer evaluation, and state where the materials may be obtained. Individuals and institutions will require further information services geared to their specific enquiries. Furthermore, access to the materials in many cases will require collections organized in the way books have been. The private user and the producer will require all of these services although their approaches may well differ in purpose and degree. Equipment will be necessary for the full implementation of much of this material and will require similar services.

Thus the needs of NBM users may be focused on three areas which have direct relevance to libraries: What documents and equipment exist? How does the user gain access to documents and equipment? And how does he or she use the documents and equipment provided?

The national producer does not have to face these problems to the same extent as the local producer and the private user. There will often exist an institutional collection administered to meet specific demands, such as the BBC's film library. Where pressure of time is less, the national producer is likely to use external sources such as commercial picture libraries.

However, Hancock's comments (1973) should be noted: ' . . . for the producers of the media, the principal requirements are convenience and speed. A television company needs rapid access to film and tape footage; the ease with which a sequence can be located, retrieved and displayed is often the crucial factor behind whether it is used at all. The same is partly true of less professional users. Even for the private individual, a main interest is the ease with which he can find and secure what he wants'.[29]

35

DOCUMENTS AND EQUIPMENT

What documents and equipment exist?
A client may request a set of slides on blacksmiths suitable for showing to a group of ten year olds. A similar request could be made for equipment, an organization requiring, say, an overhead projector that could be used as a slide projector, costing no more than £300. Both these enquiries may well lead to a need to see the items themselves, but at this stage a collection is not necessary. Requests can also be retrospective (for example 'what videotapes exist on interaction analysis since Rackham wrote on the subject?') or current ('have any sound cassettes been produced on the changes in the tax system as a result of the recent budget?').

Such demands must be answered with the same range of information as to subject, authorship, format and full bibliographical details as would be given for printed material in the *British national bibliography*. The demand may be for access by purchase, borrowing, or for reference, but the important fact is that the existence of the document or equipment has been recorded. If librarians searching for an index or catalogue reference to printed material cannot establish the existence of the work, it is assumed that either they have failed to use the tools correctly, or that the enquiry was incorrect, or misleading to begin with. It is very rare indeed for a book not to have been recorded in any bibliographical source. Yet this can well prove to be the case with NBM, because of the imperfections of the bibliographical organization involved.

Many clients' demands in this area could be satisfied by the creation of a British National Media Record with many of the attributes of BNB. However, there also seems to be needs and requirements that may be better met through information services for NBM. These will use the tools described above but they will also need to create their own tools to satisfy requests.

Information services may be divided into two types.
1 Those supplying information only for a particular type of client The British University Film and Video Council Information Service is concerned with the production, availability and use of audiovisual materials in higher education. The needs of its clients may be seen in a sample of typical queries received by the information service:
— 'Please send me a list of British organizations, governmental and non-governmental which make films on engineering, medical and scientific subjects.'

– 'Do you know of any audiovisual materials on the history of industrial relations?'
– 'I am preparing a series of lectures on Greek drama. Can you suggest any films or videotapes I might use?'
– 'Could you send me a list of slide suppliers in the field of physics?'[30]
These enquiries are answered without direct access to a collection of NBM, but through books, pamphlets, appraisals, bibliographies, catalogues and an information file.

2 *Those supplying information on both print and NBM for a subject*
The Commonwealth Institute's purpose is to foster among the people of the Commonwealth a greater knowledge of one another and a better understanding of the importance and worth of the Commonwealth. Its library and resource centre satisfy an ever-increasing demand for information on all aspects of the Commonwealth. Bibliographies on Commonwealth countries, graded reading lists on specific topics of study, and books are available from the library. The resource centre provides filmstrips, slides, records, cassettes, tapes, overhead projector transparencies, illustrations, wall charts and products from Commonwealth countries.

How to gain access to documents and equipment

Demand for NBM may be satisfied by a reference collection, or the client may require a loan service. The user may be happy to travel a considerable distance to a national collection, or might require a local service for immediate use.

At the national level there may be the equivalent of the British Library Reference Division, that is, a central collection containing a wide range of NBM, linked to a programme designed to acquire all items as they are published and to make them available for reference. Some users may feel the need for a similar national reference collection for equipment. There is a National Microprocessor and Electronics Centre which displays leading makes of microcomputers. Also at a national level the example of the British Library Lending Division could be followed in supplying clients with NBM in the same way that books and periodicals can now be obtained.

There are no institutions which fully satisfy these demands for national reference and loan facilities. There are, however, a number of collections which partially satisfy the reference demand, for example, for particular formats, the National Sound Archive and the British Film Institute/National Film Archive. Other formats like still photographs are not covered at a national level.

37

The picture is further complicated at a national level by the number of organizations that keep subject reference collections of NBM. For example, the Victoria and Albert Museum has a slide collection, as does the Design Centre, and the Imperial War Museum has a sound records archive.

Clients require quick access to loan and reference facilities, and these may be met at an area and local level. At the area level there has been the development of reference collections such as the ILEA Central Library Resources Service to teachers, librarians and media resource officers. This has a reference collection of various types of commercially available materials which can be used to complement books in schools. A client can visit this service or contact the telephone information centre. It is likely that at national and area levels provision will be for reference and copying facilities only and this by itself is unlikely to satisfy clients' demands for a fast service. There are exceptions, of course, in that many film users rely on external hiring agencies and they are prepared to accept this delay.

However, the local service would assume importance for most clients as a loan service, helping, for example, the student teacher wishing to use NBM on a teaching practice the next day, the works manager who wants a film on safety for showing in a week's time, or the child requiring a slide set about the area he or she is visiting on holiday. At a local level there is also the need for access to equipment. The public library has not to date supplied equipment, but this practice is fairly common in educational and industrial institutions. (Gateshead Public Library has enabled its local community to access viewdata equipment in its branch libraries.) Even here, however, it tends to be for use within the library area, and the librarian will have to consider whether or not the client requires to take it elsewhere. Linked to this, and an aspect often neglected, the question is whether or not the client has access to the correct environment for using NBM. This may be as straightforward as a room with blackout facilities, or rather more fundamental, such as the example from Norman Beswick of the African from one of the developing countries who said that *their* problem with NBM was the lack of electricity!

How to use documents and equipment

Many librarians take a neutral position with regards to information. They certainly regard it as their duty to help clients *find* the information they require but there has been only limited attention paid to the question of helping clients *use* information documents and tools. This is partly dependent on adequate guiding, but unlike the case of printed material (librarians do not find it necessary to teach their clients to read) they may find it vital to teach clients the correct method of handling slides and operating the slide projector. Of course many music librarians do find it necessary to warn users about stylus care, but this is usually in the form of verbal or printed warnings. Few find it important to hold sessions on stylus care or on the maintenance of the record player.

There is also the question of information concerning use of NBM and its equipment. Should the industrial trainer be tutored by the library in the correct way of using the slide with a small group, or when not to use the videotape recorder? This may not take the form of straightforward teaching but may involve the library in providing instruction sheets with each machine, pointing out not just how to operate it but also the best way to use it to achieve a particular learning goal. It will also be important for the library staff to understand the possible uses of the material and equipment. Does the librarian know how to use the filmstrip projector in story-telling sessions in the children's library? Or how to introduce a tape-slide sequence into a presentation on aspects of the library to clients?

It is at the local level and in particular with the individual producer that the library can assist in adapting information to new uses. This assistance may involve the library in two ways:

1 The establishment of a production unit as part of the library A client who lectures on popular art may choose some long-playing record covers from the record collection in the library and ask the librarian to reproduce them as slides. The library will clear copyright, arrange with the library photographer to have them shot and mounted, and then deliver them to the lecturer. Indeed this is the equivalent to a lecturer asking the subject specialist in a library to prepare a bibliography on popular art.

2 Staff involvement The librarian may work with the client to adapt the information as part of a course (as at the Open University) or work together with a lecturer to create a teaching package (for example on children's literature). Packages have been made in this way including sound tapes of poetry reading, slides illustrating picture books, and extracts from books of the winners of the Carnegie Medal. Students have consulted this package in the library and then found further information relevant to their own needs using retrieval techniques taught by the librarian; the student's final work being marked by the lecturer and the librarian together.

ANALYSIS OF CONSTRAINTS

It is important to consider the constraints which can prevent the development of an effective NBM library. From some of these librarians have little chance of escape, but others have been created by librarians and could be overcome by them with some thought, careful planning and perhaps some luck, to the benefit of the library's whole clientele.

The traditional view of the library
Throughout their education and in their professional life librarians have used the printed word and are well aware of its value. Their contacts with NBM may have been limited and they might see no reason why libraries should consider supplying these materials. Such a belief often carries a moral undertone implying that in some ways books are superior and richer in spiritual and intellectual values: it is considered acceptable to sit outside on a glorious summer's day and read a book, but a sign of moral turpitude to sit on the same lawn under the same sun and to watch a programme on a portable TV set.

There is no doubt that books have some technical advantages — for example, a page can be referred to over and over again, or the index can quickly help to pinpoint information. In comparison, anyone who has tried to trace a particular piece of information on a sound cassette will know how difficult this can be. On the other hand . . . the song of a thrush can be described in print but a sound recording describes it much better. Photographs of the foetus increase our understanding of the miracle of birth in a way that mere words cannot.

Unesco (1968) states: ' . . . that film ranks as intellectual work, in the same way as books, newspapers and periodicals, and that all such intellectual works should benefit from all measures conducive to the development of culture, to technical progress and to the intellectual and moral advancement of mankind, without any discrimination based on the material form on which works or on the vehicle through which they are transmitted . . .'.[31]

This first constraint against the use of NBM must be seen then as a simple misunderstanding of the role of the library — which is, to supply information in whatever form it is required.

Clients' demands
A library necessarily reflects the demands of its clients, and it would be pointless to offer a service that is not required. However, this alleged

constraint may hide a value judgement, suggesting that there is no demand because users do not think of the library as a supplier of NBM. Indeed they may like to see NBM in the library but have not been asked. The record of librarians' assessment of user needs is weak, as the music librarian of Bromley Central Library, D J Munro, commented in a survey (1975) which found that audio users were a minority. 'This minority is growing. It would be most useful if the more detailed tastes and borrowing patterns and trends of this minority could be assessed by means of a survey on a metropolitan or even national scale'.[32] The limited research on sound cassette loans in public libraries, both in the UK and the USA indicates that many of the services users do not otherwise use the library facilities.[33]

Users are often not aware of the value of having NBM available. In a school where there are individual departmental collections of teaching aids, the teaching staff can often see no necessity in having this material centralized into one place. This may well lead to a waste of resources, the geography department having a model of Hadrian's Wall to show its underlying geographical features, the history department holding the same model for its historical value. Such a model could also offer a stimulus to other departments that may not have considered it as a teaching aid – the English Department reading Auden's poem on the Roman Wall for instance, or a school group organizing a climbing trip to the area. The librarian can have a role in the development of users' awareness of the potential of all forms of recorded information.

Even when NBM are available in the library, users may not be aware of it. As it is two-thirds of the population do not make use of the public library service. In a market research survey in Burnage for Manchester Public Libraries (1975), 99% of the sample were aware that they could borrow books from the library. Awareness of the availability of records, cassette tapes, slides and framed prints was very low, at 25% or less.[34] The need for the library to publicize its services is obvious, yet financial limits often prevent this. Pinion's research into public library video lending services concluded by stating[35] 'Public libraries have, generally speaking been slow to publicize their services, having had little outside competition where books and sound recordings are concerned. Video libraries demand a much more aggressive approach, particularly by those authorities establishing a service on a self-financing basis'. This need to publicize NBM services further is also true in academic libraries; 'surprisingly many academics had little idea of what

42

the library could offer in computerized information, despite advertising our service, as we thought, widely'.

The 'book fund first' syndrome

Library budgets are often under pressure, and sometimes cannot cope with the demand for books and periodicals. Before offering NBM many librarians consider it necessary to improve the basic book fund. Yet the UK Public Libraries and Museums Act (1964) places a duty on library authorities 'to provide a comprehensive and efficient service'[36] and states that 'in fulfilling it duty . . . a library authority shall in particular have regard to the possibility of . . . securing that facilities are available for the borrowing of, or reference to, books and other printed matter, and pictures, gramophone records, films and other materials sufficient in number range and quality to meet the general requirements both of adults and children'.[37] It is interesting that the emphasis here is on form, rather than why public libraries exist. Contrast that statement with one which states that public libraries today '. . . are fundamentally involved in the transfer of ideas, the stimulation of imagination and the development of adult learning through the use of all forms of communication media'.[38] Such a belief yields little to the finance argument, which it places in the same category as the belief that education is all about learning to read so that you can fill in your income tax forms.

However, it cannot be denied that the constraint of finance is an important one, nor that printed material is the major source of transfer of information at the present moment. Yet it is dangerous to consider NBM as something which can be dropped at a time of financial restraint: at a future stage when money does become available the library may find that the material is completely unobtainable. As has been pointed out 'these "new" services must be seen as an integral part of the library's role, and adequate and continuing finance must be provided. Otherwise, if the futurologists are right the world in general will bypass the library'.[39] It is perhaps better to adopt the policy of providing in estimates a material fund in place of the former practice of separate provision for books, gramophone records, etc.

Equipment

This argument usually takes one of two forms. Either it runs that clients may be unable to use sophisticated equipment and that therefore it is better not to supply such materials; or, the home equipment is necessarily expensive, and it is therefore better not to supply any

43

materials for it rather than risk disappointing those people who cannot afford it. This argument is perhaps most convincing outside the educational sector, and in particular within the public library. It is certainly true that many adults are unable to handle equipment competently, but it seems likely that the educational system will produce more and more people well able to use such equipment, and that they will expect to find forms of entertainment, education and training other than books.

The relative cost of equipment is steadily reducing, and more people *will* soon be able to afford it; the real danger is that they will be disappointed with the library provision and seek advice and help elsewhere. This is not a plea for the sanctity of libraries, but rather that recorded information be kept together for the benefit of clients. Adequate guiding in using equipment and perhaps supplying it for reference use are the first steps.

Subject v form
The message transmitted by a film of an athlete running is not the same as a slide set of the same subject. The librarian must consider not only the subject his clients are interested in, but also the appropriate forms for it. Yet in some libraries the subject is subjugated to the form. The public library's disc collection has always been concerned with music, so the music librarian was often made responsible for all record purchases. However a large number of fields are covered by recorded sound, including drama, poetry, social interviews, political debates, commentaries on important issues, and these could be of interest to all subject librarians.

Forms of communication can also change the way we look at our own experiences. Seymour Papert has clearly stated how he believes computers will affect our society. 'Computers can be carriers of powerful ideas and of the seeds of cultural change, and they can help people form new relationships with knowledge that cuts across the traditional lines separating humanities from sciences and knowledge of the self from both of these. It is about using computers to challenge current beliefs about who can understand what and at what age'.[40]

The DES working party (1976) felt that it was still necessary to emphasize that new media materials are far too frequently linked 'in peoples' minds with entertainment, whereas they can be as effective purveyors of information and of education as books, in some cases even more effective — and certainly can be as beneficial when used in conjunction with printed sources. Well organized in a library situation the new materials could have the instructional value of television without some of its disadvantages and faults.[41] This report further questions the need for storing NBM according to its form, rather than integrating all books and NBM in subject divisions. The problems raised by this are further discussed in chapter four under the heading of Storage.

Traditional client divisions

It has been observed in public libraries where the adult and children's sections have been merged that the move often benefits the adult looking for a simple introduction to a subject. No longer constrained by the librarian's artificial decision that a book will be of use only to one particular group of clients, he or she is now able to find a simple introduction in a children's book.

Yet the readability of a book is still a constraint. A child with a reading age of ten interested in ships might be induced to take out a book more suitable for a marine engineer. NBM to some extent overcome this barrier of client division, as they are more comprehensible across the age range. A slide of an oil tanker can be used by both the child and the engineer. The information received may differ, but there is not the same initial barrier to understanding the language of the message.

Traditional subject divisions

Melvil Dewey desribed how during a long sermon 'while my mind was absorbed in the vital problem, the solution flasht over me so that I jumpt in my seat and came very near shouting "Eureka"'. He had conceived, in 1873, 'a solution to the problem of orderly and efficient arrangement of books in a library'.[42] In his resultant scheme, the whole of human knowledge was divided into ten main classes, and many libraries since then have arranged themselves according to the Dewey Decimal Classification. But the artificial subject divisions pose problems, and particularly in the case of NBM. For example, a slide of a diamond may be of use to the chemist studying crystallography, the student learning to cut glass, the mathematician concerned with volume, the art lecturer concerned with shape, or the economist interested in forms of wealth. The librarian must consider each of these needs and decide to what extent the library retrieval system can meet them. This problem will be discussed in more detail in chapter four under the heading Cataloguing and classification.

Browsing

Librarians have usually been aware of their clients' need to browse, but worry over the fragility, durability, security and cost of NBM has introduced the notion that this material must be stored separately or even locked away. Some may feel that closed access policies are still necessary for some forms of NBM, but most forms can be safely integrated with the book stock. If this latter policy is adopted, someone looking for the novel *The hobbit* will through the 'serendipity of browsing' find also the sound cassette of this work.

Future shock

Librarians may be unable to assist clients properly because of their own lack of knowledge or even fears concerning NBM and its equipment. Alvin Toffler (1970) has aptly summed-up this inherent conservatism and lack of self-confidence as 'future shock', a 'concrete force that reaches deep into our personal lives, compels us to act out new roles, and confronts us with the danger of a new and powerfully upsetting psychological disease.[43] However he cannot hide from the truth of the statement that 'the use of the ubiquitous TV set as an information display and interactive personal electronic communication device will bring dramatic changes to the way in which we conduct our day-to-day affairs'.[44] Yet any change should build to some extent on the past. The library acquires, organizes, retrieves and issues units of information in book form, and these processes have been established after long practical experience. This book will demonstrate that NBM does not destroy these processes, and that what is changing is the nature of the demand — clients require now that the library should acquire, organize, retrieve and issue units of information *whatever their form.*

NBM AS ARCHIVE MATERIAL

Archives are not established to serve any particular group. Their sole aim is preservation, and they are the fundamental information sources upon which all other bibliographic organizations depend. Library services would be the poorer without them.

Some of the reasons for the necessity of our concern with the preservation of NBM are illustrated by the remarks of Mary Pickford, the silent screen actress of the 1920s. 'I never thought my films were important. I never did anything to save them. I just put them into storage and forgot them. I intended to destroy them because, frankly, I didn't want to be compared to the modern trend. If you look at the magazines of forty years ago, their writing is ridiculous. I mean it's so sentimental. I was afraid my films would be the same. When the Hollywood Museum started I tried to help, but found the tins of film were just full of red dust. Then we had two fires, one in our office building, another in the stores, and films were lost in both. Private collectors won't give up the pictures of mine − and they know they're bootlegged. But it's just as well − otherwise they'd be gone.'[45]

She mentions the establishment of an archival organization, the Hollywood Museum, to preserve material. The organization and preservation of Britain's heritage of books is firmly established in the work of the British Library, in particular its Reference Division. One of the objectives of the British Library is the 'preserving and making available for reference at least one copy of every book and periodical of domestic origin and of as many overseas publications as possible. The aim will be to provide as comprehensive a reference service of last resort as possible. If the reader cannot get what he wants nearer at hand he will know he can find it in the British Library'.[46] This is mainly possible because of the Copyright Act of 1911, which legally requires publishers to deposit one copy of each of their publications with the library. But the position with regard to the national heritage of visual and sound materials is not as well established. There is no national archive of NBM and indeed, 'it has already been decided if only by default that the British Library will not set out to collect audiovisual materials'.[47] There is no legal requirement for publishers of NBM to deposit material with any organization.

The National Film Archive is the only truly national and general collection of film, while for sound there is the British Institute of Recorded Sound. Neither of these collections has the benefit of legal deposit. They rely on donations and legacies for much of their material. The National Film Archive does receive gratis some material from the BBC, and the independent television companies pay the archive to preserve a representative sample of independent television programmes. A National Museum of Photography, Film and Television was founded in 1982 in Bradford.

There are other collections which have an archival function but this is secondary to their other roles. The BBC sound archive, where 'it is stressed that the most important object is to provide existing material for inclusion in new programmes',[48] is more concerned with its in-house responsibilities. The BBC Hulton Picture Library which has a collection of six million pictures, many of them unpublished and unique, 'is a commercial picture-lending library; it is neither a national archive nor a research institute, so it cannot help students or research workers unless it is a paying proposition'.[49]

A fuller listing may be found in Line, J 'Archival collections of non-book materials: a preliminary list indicating policies for preservation and access' British Library, 1977.

Yet NBM are valuable archive materials and there is an obvious need for the nation to:

1 Collect published NBM (such as the picture postcard, television programme, top twenty long playing records) and to preserve them.

2 Collect NBM of local interest, photographs of personalities, buildings, records of singers, sound recordings of noises (like the peal of cathedral bells, or the sound of the last tram). The local studies collections of public libraries have perhaps exploited most effectively this function of NBM.

3 Use NBM to preserve transient evidence, the growth of oral history being one manifestation of this. The historian who records on tape people's memories of the past offers the opportunity of access to the lives and outlooks of classes and groups who have left very little in the way of formal or written evidence. Gateshead Public Library have established a sound archive on the General Strike of 1926.

4 Use NBM to exploit more fully the material in the archives and give the public access to rare or fragile documents. The British Museum has published sets of slides of its rare coins. In Leicestershire, the use of microforms has provided children with a basic local history collection covering the whole of the county. Original materials from museums and public record offices have been indexed, photographed and supplied to some primary schools.

The major problem lies in deciding what should be preserved and what destroyed, and this decision should not be left to private collectors. As Mary Pickford points out they 'won't give up pictures of mine'. Because there is no national archive attempting to preserve all NBM, other collections have to worry about whether they are discarding the last copy of a document, and this function will probably not be central to its aims. There is no place of 'last resort', and this is further hampered by a lack of coordination between the existing archival collections, clients being unaware of the location of documents. For certain formats it is necessary to rely on the collections of individuals, and librarians may have to create location records for these collections. The National Photographic Record,[50] at Darlington, County Durham, has attempted to elicit by means of questionnaires the existence and composition of photographic collections held by libraries, museums, societies, individual collectors, and commercial collections.

Many of the collections have grown haphazardly with no systematic attempt to retain NBM. Lindgren (1951) states that the National Film Archive catalogue does not 'represent a comprehensive and carefully garnered selection of the period, but are the scraps of flotsam and jetsam, the wreckage of a vast output of film, which purely by chance have survived the destructive storms of time, and have drifted, if one may so express it, into the sheltered waters of the National Film Archive'.[51] The BBC sound archive only selects approxiately fourteen hours of radio time from a week's output of its national, overseas, and local broadcasting, and a corresponding amount for television. The Council for Educational Technology has funded the development of archives for local BBC Radio. Its Scottish counterpart has reported favourably[52] on the creation of an Orkney Sound Archive. The broadcasting of Parliament has stimulated the creation of a parliamentary sound archive at Westminster.[53] Pickford films survive because of illegal and non-copyright copies, and the same may well be true today about the output of radio and television.

While the priority must be to preserve this material, there is still a need to consider clients' demands. Paul Madden, the television officer of the National Film Archive, writes: 'There is no point in our just keeping material. We must be able to let people benefit from it.[54] The archive has available duplicate distribution copies of some of its film and will make stock available to the bona fide student on a reference basis. The Sound Records Department of the Imperial War Museum has collected more than 3500 hours of recordings on all aspects of war.

Listening equipment is available and small groups of eight to ten students can be accommodated. A further service is that teachers can record archival material such as the BBC recording of the Battle of Alamein, or an interview with a soldier who fought in the First World War trenches, and bring this experience into the classroom.

Finally, there must be concern for the physical preservation of NBM. Mary Pickford's 'red dust' clearly illustrates the problem for early films. The cellulose nitrate stock used was highly inflammable and moreover decomposes within fifty years. Unless the film is reprinted, the material can be entirely lost. It should be noted that film archives rarely project the preservation copy, a viewing copy always being printed. Glass plates of the early photographers too are easily damaged. Videotapes lose quality and eventually deteriorate until they are un-playable. A master copy of such material is invaluable if it is to be preserved. The advent of the laser videodisc may be a major advance in the preservation of material. For example, the International Museum of Photography has transferred some of its historic photographic negatives on to videodisc.

The nation's heritage of films, sound recordings, and still photo-graphs is in danger. Because so often only a few copies are published, the chances of survival are reduced. Imagine how our knowledge and understanding of Dickens would be restricted if copies of *Oliver Twist* had not survived. Yet more recent NBM have already disappeared. Brownlow[55] commenting on the silent film era suggests that later generations' views of that period have been distorted by the relatively small amount of material that has survived. Ballantyne has pointed out: 'Who is going to file electronic journals? Is anybody making an archive record of selection of pages from Prestel? Where will computer assisted learning packages be archived? . . . The National Computing Centre has estimated that between 6000 and 10,000 programs are commercially available in the UK at the moment. Think about it'.[56] Knowledge does not exist until it has been recorded, and that knowledge is lost if no copy of the document is preserved.

It is salutary to compare the national archival situation in the United States. The US National Archive had set up a division of Motion Pictures and Sound Recordings as early as 1935. The Library of Congress has the largest archival collection of NBM in existence. The motion pictures section has a collection of over 50,000 titles and adds between 2500 and 4000 reels each year. There is also an archive of some 300,000 sound recordings, although prior to receiving legal deposit in 1972, it had to rely on donations by record manufacturers. The library's Prints and Photographs Division has over three million photographs which unfortunately are not all catalogued. Perhaps an indication of the size of the Library of Congress collection is a report of the donation from *Look* magazine consisting of '17½ million black and white photograph negatives, 1½ million colour transparencies, 450 thousand contact shots and 25 thousand movie stills'.[57]

The determination of the United States to preserve its national heritage of NBM is hardly surprising, bearing in mind that it invented the majority of these new forms and formats. However it may also point to a greater awareness of the value of non-book materials as information carriers.

Part 3

THE MATERIALS

INTRODUCTION

Over the last few years, there has been an immense growth in the development of new technologies that affect the preparation, organization, storage and retrieval of information. For many people, the problems have become complex, for as soon as they feel they have mastered one new system, another one emerges with a whole new code of operating practice. There seems to be no possibility of this flood of new developments being stemmed, nor of the rate of change decelerating. Indeed the opposite seems to be the case. As new devices and systems appear on the market, so older ones are superseded and disappear, taking with them all too frequently the spare parts or materials that are needed to keep them in action. Decisions on what systems merit investment therefore become more difficult to take. There is little doubt that the 'life' of equipment is now shorter, not so much in its physical durability but particularly in its value to the user. Totally new concepts may appear which will further revolutionize the formats and equipment available, and the prediction of these or their value is not yet possible. For the user, however, it is the speed at which these new developments appear and are absorbed into the domestic environment that is particularly bewildering.

Recently, there has been much written about the office of the future and indeed the home of the future. In Milton Keynes, different buildings have been erected to demonstrate the reality of these forecasts, but they have only been using the latest manifestations of the technology as it is currently available. However, it is useful to try and see through these predictions to try and identify the trends that are taking place. For example, it is clear that there is a determined trend towards compressing information carriers so that they occupy less space and make storage and distribution easier. It is also apparent that direct access to information stores is a major target of the technology, although current attempts are often very confusing for the user. In all cases, the importance of the user's ability to interact with the information, control it and create his own stores is considered to be an important factor. Finally, another trend is to try and arrange that all types of information can be interpreted or carried by the one device.

Each of these trends can be illustrated in today's technology. Compression in size is shown in the growth of microforms, new film stock and the stores for the ubiquitous computer. The rapid development of satellites for broadcasting and telephone transmissions around the globe has brought many large databases of information into accessibility for the home, office and school user, and this is an area in which considerable investment is forecast for the future. Optical fibre lines and cable television networks will enhance the ability of people to be able to communicate directly with information stores, using their home computers as terminals, the major problems that face them being how to find out what is available, decide what they want and be able to discard the irrelevant. This process will revolutionize our approach to information storage and retrieval, and opens up opportunities for local access systems which have not yet been considered in any detail. For the user, it brings the information and excitements of distant lands closer, for it is not only databases that are at the end of the transmission lines, but also television programmes that can be broadcast via satellites into the domestic environment. The user's desire to interact and create his own materials is widely in evidence through the growth of programming with the microcomputer. Few are satisfied only with the games, and many are seeking to teach themselves how to develop their own, just as many people are now creating their own videotapes with camera and editing equipment. In developments with the microcomputer and with a system like the videodisc, it is apparent that the user is excited by the merging of media into a few formats. On the laserdisc, for example, it is possible to have still and moving pictures, at least two different sound tracks and a complete text system, and the storage space is very large indeed.

Laserdiscs are a format that is interesting to national producers for another reason, that of security. Too many of the modern systems can be readily copied or pirated by users, and this depletes the resources necessary for producing more materials. Non-magnetic discs of all types cannot be copied into reproductions of their own format by the general user, although they can be transferred to tape. ROM packs are computer program stores which are also difficult to copy and of considerable interest to producers as a format for distribution.

Many other developments are causing changes in information handling. Facsimile transmission may be the most economic means of obtaining back copies of material if they cannot be sent from a computer store direct to the user's own. Using computer interchanges in place of the post is becoming more common through a system known as electronic mail, and while it precludes the despatch of exotic greetings cards, it is very effective for instant communication on business issues. The success of these and the other examples of technology in the domestic and educational environment is the guideline on which their persistence and survival depends. One of the most exciting developments in recent years has been the laserdisc, as it offers such opportunities for data handling and information storage. However, there is considerable scepticism over its survival in competition with the videocassette recorder, which does not offer similar information handling capacity. If the laserdisc does not succeed in the domestic market, its availability for use in the other area is very much diminished, and of course the price will be discouragingly high. Thus, while perusal of the commercial uses of devices and good forecasting of likely developments can be helpful in determining the most useful equipment that will emerge, the successful exploitation of its use in the domestic market will finally decide on its viability. It is a regrettable fact that libraries and education on their own are an insufficient market to sustain the manufacture of devices at reasonable prices.

The effect of technological development has been to increase the variety of information-carrying formats that are available, frequently based upon the same medium. Partly this has been a direct result of technological advance, as for example in the developments of videocassette systems, but frequently different formats have emerged which make a system unique to a particular manufacturer, thereby shackling users to that company's equipment.

Such differences arise for a number of reasons, mostly relating to problems with patents and competition. For example, manufacturer X develops a cassette system for, say, slides. This is patented which means that other manufacturers can only use it under licence, which naturally requires payment to X. The public responds to the invention by welcoming it as a very successful method of storing and retrieving slides. Manufacturer Y sees that X has produced a market that Y can only enter in competition if he pays X for the privilege by paying his licence fee. To avoid this, Y develops his own system which, to avoid infringement of patents, must be different from X's, and the two compete. X's cassettes cannot be operated on Y's machines and vice-versa. For the poor user, the situation is full of difficult questions. Should he use such a cassette at all? If the answer is affirmative, then which system does he choose? If he favours X, has he any assurance that X will continue in business, or will he be forced out by the success of Y? Will X continue to have spare parts for his equipment? Will the lamps, for example, remain available? Will X be so successful that he will improve his cassette and make his new versions in such a way that they are impossible to use with his old equipment?

Pitfalls typified by these questions litter the pathway of development of non-book materials, and are part of the reason why some people shy away from them. It certainly has not always paid to be a pathfinder in the past, and yet in order to ensure that developments take place, it is essential that some users try to encourage manufacturers who are probing new territories, even though some will burn their fingers. To the prospective purchaser, the difficulties described in the questions above mean that very great care and often advice have to be taken in selection.

Some safeguard can come from choosing systems evolved by large international manufacturers. When the sound cassette produced by Philips, called the compact cassette, came on the market, there were in Britain two small companies offering cassette systems, the elements of which were totally different from each other and from the Philips system. Those libraries which purchased from the small manufacturers found themselves with equipment and materials possessed of a very short life. Others recognized that Philips, as a large international company, were likely to dominate all future manufacturing. And while there have been important technical improvements since that first cassette, all the Philips materials and equipment purchased at the beginning can be used satisfactorily now.

However, selecting the products of a large manufacturing organization is not *necessarily* safe. Technological developments may cause a company which has marketed one piece of equipment intensively to replace it with another, and the new equipment may not be compatible with the old. Such a situation occurred in the last decade with the arrival of videocassette recorders. The early European models sold well, but were not as successful in the domestic marketplace as the Japanese models that followed. The early machines disappeared and many users were left with recordings on tapes that were not compatible with later machines coming either from Japan or from the multinational European manufacturer who sold them the original equipment. Naturally there must be technical progress, and events like this will continue to occur, but it is to be hoped that wherever possible, materials developed for one piece of equipment will be usable on its improved successor, a feature often referred to as upward compatibility. In the field of computers, this is particularly important.

Such a situation results from the large number of international companies which are competing in the fields, none of them identifiable

57

as the market leader and therefore able to dictate design standards. Whereas in the photographic field the standards devised by Kodak are likely to become international ones, no similar individual company working in the area of videorecording has the same influence. For the user and the librarian, this situation is very disturbing. Money spent today might turn out to be a wasted investment tomorrow.

These problems could be overcome if there were accepted international standards to which equipment and materials were made. The purchaser could then be fairly certain that items would continue to be usable for a number of years. Because of the multinational standing of many of the major manufacturers, acceptance of a single national standard is not a sufficient guarantee. But unfortunately it is very rare for truly international standards to be produced until long after the pattern of production has been established. A number of agencies *do* try to sort out this very confusing problem. In Britain, the requirements of users are reflected in publications called USPECS (*User specifications*),[1] which are published by the Council for Educational Technology. These are written and amended by a large number of users and published after consultation with various manufacturing companies. They define the minimum standards for acceptable equipment and give guidance through codes of operating practice on the mechanical design of materials to be used with machines. While manufacturers are sympathetic to the requirements of users, these publications unfortunately carry little weight with larger international companies, or companies with a predominantly domestic market which is willing to buy whatever the drawbacks.

There are important links between the devisers of USPECS and the British Standards Institution (BSI). In some areas BSI regulations almost have the standing of law, and firms with equipment failing to meet some of them can be prevented from trading. In devising its regulations, the BSI makes considerable use of representatives from the responsible manufacturing companies. The devisers of USPECS and British Standards are represented in the International Electro-technical Commission (IEC) which attempts to promote international standards. The IEC includes representatives from European countries, America and Japan, largely delegated from the national organizations which parallel the BSI. The decisions of the IEC influence BSI and USPECS. Through these channels, then, some attempts are made to reach standard formats and procedures, but they are responsive channels and do not themselves dictate the trends.

As new formats and new equipment on which to use them arise, standards are initially those chosen by the manufacturer. If the system is successful or adopted by others, national or even international ones may be formulated, and these are increasingly being influenced by users. However, the increase in the variety of formats shows no sign of abating. Essentially users are looking for four groups of presentation, either independently or in combination with others. These are printed items, which can be writing, graphics, photographs on material or on a screen; still pictures which can be transparent for projection or viewing, or they can appear on a screen; recordings of sounds; moving pictures. With the exception of realia and artefacts, all information carriers can be sorted into these four groups. However, the technology has provided users with a wide range of different means of organizing and distributing these, and hence the confusion of formats and equipment that has followed. However, within all these developments and variations, manufacturers are only making use of basically four types of physical material: paper, which may carry photographic emulsion; film, a celluloid-type base with photographic emulsion or diazo dyes; magnetic material fixed to a base of either tape or a flat disc; plastic, either flat and transparent or opaque with grooves or pits. Different forms, sizes and configurations of these four materials are organized to provide the different formats in which the four basic media groups are presented. In addition, users can obtain materials from telephone and broadcast sources, but the local storage of these items is on a similar range of physical material.

From the user's viewpoint, there is too great a range and variety of formats, and it would be very much more convenient if these were limited to a few. However, selecting these raises a number of difficulties, the most important being the way in which the user's own equipment is selected. Constraints on manufacture prevent new developments, and inhibit research into new products which may be advantageous. Some products will disappear anyway as their particular advantages are superseded by new developments. Film loops are now rare, and videocassettes are now gradually replacing non-commercial cine films. It will take some time, but it is certainly possible that the compact laser audio disc will replace the vinyl long player. However, the disappearance of magnetic tape is less likely at present, as this is the format on which the user can make his own recordings. Thus technical and market forces have their own impact on limiting the formats that are available.

In general, information carriers should have the following characteristics: they should be capable of individual use; capable of broadcasting

59

to a large group; capable of storing information prepared by national producers; capable of storing information prepared and arranged by the private user and local producer with minimal processing; capable of securing the information to prevent accidental loss or replacement. Most of the formats that will survive have most of these characteristics, the main area of contention being whether or not the individual user can prepare and arrange his own material or whether it is only available on the particular format from a national producer. Pressure from users can be significant in the final appearance of a format. It was that pressure that encouraged the development of cassette-type packaging for microforms, film, sound and videotape because storage, retrieval and utilization are so much more convenient in this way. However, as a result of the individuality of manufacturers and their separate innovations there are many different and incompatible types of cassette available. While various attempts at standardizing materials and specifications continue, their effect on limiting the variety of formats marketed is not very decisive.

The remainder of part 3 is organized under the headings of the different physical materials utilized in NBM. The physical properties of each will be discussed, together with the appropriate care and maintenance. Then there is a section describing the various formats into which these materials are made. This is followed by a description of the equipment necessary for each format, with a final section giving simple guidance on operation, a manual of practice for the librarian.

THE MATERIALS

Paper

Care and maintenance of paper collections require the following points to be considered:

1 Poor quality paper such as newspaper deteriorates rapidly in sunlight. At all times they are not being used, extracts should be kept out of the light.

2 Paper surfaces and edges damage easily with handling. They can smudge from finger marks, and edges tear unless protected. Punchholes made through paper for storage purposes often tear further. Various protective devices like lamination, edge-binding, hole protectors can reduce these problems.

3 Printed sheets from spirit duplication fade with light. Copies that are stored should be kept out of direct light. If master stencils for duplication are preserved, they should be stored with separating sheets between them. Ink stencil masters should be hung or suspended.

4 Paper that is rolled retains the curvature. Reverse rolling cracks the surface veneer and encourages deterioration. It is preferable to hang such rolls with weights at the bottom to flatten them.

5 Dirt on paper can be cleaned with an ordinary eraser. Unless a special washable surface has been applied, washing is more likely to destroy paper than clean it.

6 Photographic paper has a layer of photographic emulsion on the surface. While this has been chemically fixed, it will deteriorate with misuse. Sunlight bleaches photographic colours, including black, and there is a tendency towards yellowing of the paper also. Scratching the surface will scrape away the emulsion. Dirt may be washed off the surface with a damp cloth, but drying should not take place in an oven or over a radiator. Unless great care is taken to weight the corners the paper will curl as it dries. Dust should be gently removed with a soft brush or with a puffer. Blowing is not recommended because of the effects of dampness.

Film

Photographic film has a layer of emulsion attached to a polyester base material. Careful observation will show that the backing is shiny whereas the surface with the emulsion is dull. Another way of identifying the surfaces is to hold the transparent film to the light. When the picture is the correct way round, the viewer is looking at the base surface, with the emulsion on the reverse towards the light.

The image is created in the emulsion by chemical response to light, and is fixed there by processing with other chemicals. Where there are holes along the edge of the film, they are used to pull the film through the projector. On 16mm cinefilms which have optical sound tracks, a white line of varying width or with cross-hatching can be seen on the side of the film opposite that carrying these holes, and this carries the sounds.

Some microfiche are produced on non-photographic film. This may be diazofilm, usually black, blue or sepia in colour, and evident because the writing is normally processed in white against a coloured background. The base is again a polyester plastic film with the diazo dyes attached to it. They are produced by a photographic original being contacted with the diazofilm, exposed to ultraviolet light and processed by exposure to ammonia and heat. Another film used for microfiche is called vesicular film, the writing appearing black with a white background. This is also a diazotype film with similar but not identical processing. In producing a microfiche, a negative of the original is used and the result from a single process is either a negative-type diazofilm or a positive-type vesicular film as described above. Some graphics on slides are also produced on diazofilm occasionally.

Good care and maintenance of film material should be concerned with the following points:

1 Storage out of sunlight is important as all chemicals bleach. Colours only fade with prolonged exposure, however, and short duration viewing will not lead to deterioration. Diazo and vesicular films are less stable and should not be used for archival purposes.

2 Abnormally high humidity encourages bacterial and fungal growth in photographic emulsions. This is difficult to remove when established and advice should be taken from photographic specialists. Diazo and vesicular films do not suffer from this problem.

3 All emulsions are very easily scratched. The polyester bases are more difficult to damage in this way, but the emulsion is comparatively soft. Once scratched, there is no method of repair.

4 Grease marks from fingers, often with accompanying dirt, readily adhere to both surfaces of the film. Careful rubbing with lint-free tissue or photographic cloth may assist in erasing such damage. Ensure that the film is dry before storing.

5 Both surfaces, but especially the polyester base, attract dust. This is an electrostatic reaction, and can be discouraged by using cleaning

cloths that are described as 'anti-static'. Dust can also be removed with a soft brush or puffer.

6 If paper is used to cover film material, for example sleeves around microfiche, it should be sulphur-free to prevent chemical reaction with the silver salts in the emulsion.

7 Glass covering over film may induce the formation of 'Newton's rings' if a trace of water is trapped between the two materials. The rings cause rainbowlike effects which change shape with the heat of projection. Anti-Newton glass which prevents this action is available.

Magnetic tape

The tape is made of a polyester base to which oxides of iron and chromium are attached. Examination of the tape shows that one surface is shiny, the polyester base, and the other dull, the layer of oxides. By magnetization and rearrangement of the magnetic fields borne by these oxides, a message is recorded on the tape which can be 'read' by a device in the playback machine. The quality of the tape depends on a number of factors: non-stretching of the polyester base; the adhesion of the oxide to the tape; the density of the oxide. The finer the 'grain' of oxide the better the quality of the recording.

The formulation of the oxide has developed and changed with technical advances. Some manufacturers claim improved recording quality with the use of chromium dioxide (CrO_2), and the latest development is the expensive metal tape, a combination of metals on the same polyester base, with even better recording characteristics. Both these two types of tape require an electronic change in the recorder used for playback, and this is either automatic or at the touch of a control on modern equipment. Most tapes make use of a mixture of ferric (iron) oxide and chromium dioxide, and others are only the ferric variety. To assist in identification and help standardize manufacture, the IEC have agreed to a numbering system which should be marked on all cassettes. These numbers reflect the magnetic properties of the tapes and not the quality of the product. IEC 1 is the ferric oxide tape, IEC 2 the chromium dioxide, IEC 3 ferrochrome and IEC 4 the metal tape. Unmarked tapes are available and are often used with microcomputers where the quality of the coating is not so significant.

In use, the oxide surface of the tape is pressed very closely against the playback head within the machine. The closeness of this proximity is an important factor in determining the quality of reproduction. Any dirt or grease (which collects dust) is transferred from the oxide layer

63

to the head and introduces a barrier between them, so it is important to keep this layer free of foreign matter. Any handling, marking or repairs should be on the polyester surface and not the oxide layer. When the tape is wrapped around an open reel or in a video cassette, the polyester layer is outermost and protection is relatively simple. However, in a sound cassette, the oxide layer is outermost and relatively easy to damage.

The care and maintenance of magnetic tape is concerned with the following points:

1 The tape must be reeled flat and smoothly. No part of the tape should be twisted, bent or creased.

2 All tapes should be played periodically to prevent the magnetic print-through of the message from one layer to the next.

3 Dust and dirt readily accumulate on and between the layers of tape, partly as a result of electrostatic attraction. Tapes should be kept in a dust-free atmosphere as far as possible.

4 High humidity causes dampness to form between the layers of tape. Fungal growth is encouraged and the tape layers tend to stick together.

5 Because the recording on the tape is the result of a magnetic process, it is important to store tapes away from the influence of magnetic fields. These can be caused by electric motors and dynamos, but to be really damaging, the fields must be very strong. Vacuum cleaners, for example, are harmless, but some metal-detection devices, as used for example at airports, produce strong fields which can be destructive.

Magnetic disks
These are used for recording computer programs, and the library will commonly deal with those disks which are not sealed in dustproof containers. The covering which records the program is similar to that on tapes, usually ferric oxide, and the disk itself is held within a card protective jacket, from which it should not be removed. Various slots are present which expose the recording surface, and these must not be touched (see figure 1).

Care and maintenance of these disks should be concerned with the following points:

1 The disks must not be bent or distorted.

2 Dust and grease seriously interfere with use and they should be protected from these hazards as far as possible.

3 High humidity causes dampness and encourages fungal growth.

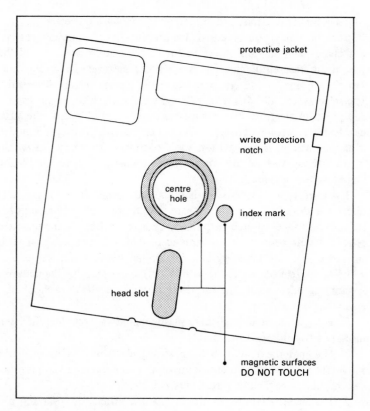

Figure 1. Floppy disk showing its parts

Excess temperature, including exposure to the sun, causes the disks to bend.

4 Because the recording on the disk is the result of a magnetic process, it is important to store them away from the influence of magnetic fields. One corrupted piece of recording can prevent a program being used.

Plastics

Plastic can be used in a transparent or opaque form. Flat transparent acetate or polyester sheets are used as the base for overhead projector transparencies, and opaque circular and grooved pieces are used as recorded discs. The polyester for overhead projector transparencies can be written on with special quick-drying inks, adhered to by self-adhesive film and letters, and printed on by standard processes.

Recorded discs are processed by pressing from a master negative. For audio reproduction, the curvature of the bottom and sides of the groove are responsible for representing the message. There are three varieties of videodisc, each approaching the recording issue differently. The selectavision disc has a very fine groove in which the stylus travels, and picks up electrical capacitance from the pits within it. In the VHD disc system, there is no groove, but as the pick-up on the player is guided over the surface, it too registers the capacitance from tiny pits within it. Both these types of disc are sensitive to dust and grease, and handling should be avoided.

The third type of disc is the laserdisc, also available as the compact disc for audio recordings. Underneath the surface layer is an aluminized reflective surface covered in pits. By focusing a laser beam on these pits, different reflections are produced, which form the signal. This surface is virtually undamageable in normal use, and may be handled without any fear of interfering with the signal or damaging the material. As nothing rubs or cuts the surface in normal use, the discs should last a very long time.

Care and maintenance of these plastic materials, excluding the laserdiscs, involves the following points:

1 The material readily bears a strong electrostatic charge which attracts dust. Wiping with anti-static cloth is helpful, and various other devices, like an anti-static pistol, are available.

2 The materials must be flat to operate efficiently. Warping and twisting under excessive heat or distorting pressure should be avoided, and this sort of damage is irreparable.

3 Surfaces are easily scratched, and the marks are permanent.

4 Dampness encourages fungal growth, and may arise in conditions of high humidity. Surfaces may adhere together through water tension. Specialist help should be sought if this occurs.

5 If dirt gets into grooves, various liquid cleansing agents may be used to loosen it. However, it is important that this liquefied dirt is removed by a powerful vacuum or else it will solidify again. The record must be thoroughly dried afterwards.

THE VARIETY OF FORMATS

Paper collections

Little need be said about collections of paper materials. Charts and folders of loose sheets are commonplace, and the sizes and quantities are variable. It can be expected that these formats will continue to be popular both for educational and domestic use.

A change in the structure of the textbook is beginning to emerge. Some are now published in a loose-leaf format, the pages held in a ring or lace binder. All the pages can be removed individually and extra pages added also. Diagrams and photographs which are referred to frequently need only be printed once, and extracted for repeated study. Some medical books are now published in this way, and other subjects are likely to follow.

Combinations of books and loose-leaf pages inside an attached folder is also a format which is beginning to be used. The standard book is not a static format, but one which will evolve in combination with other arrangements and media.

Film

Transparent film is used in a number of different formats.

The filmstrip

The filmstrip is a collection of images organized in two different forms, the single or half-frame and the double or full-frame. The differences between them are illustrated in figure 2, showing also the relevant dimensions. The single frame strip is usually passed through the viewer or projector vertically, the double frame strip horizontally. At the beginning and end of the strip are lengths of black film, the leader and trailer respectively, which are used for attaching the film to its carrier.

Filmstrips are usually supplied in small circular canisters and accompanied by notes explaining the content of the pictures.

Slides

The photographic slide, sometimes referred to as a transparency, is a single frame of transparent film, usually held within a mount made of cardboard or plastic. Glass is sometimes used to cover and protect the film with the mount. There are two common formats, the dimensions of which are shown in figure 3. The 35mm format has the same dimensions as an individual frame of a double frame film strip, and is

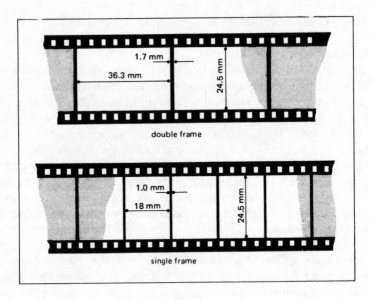

Figure 2. Filmstrips: double and single

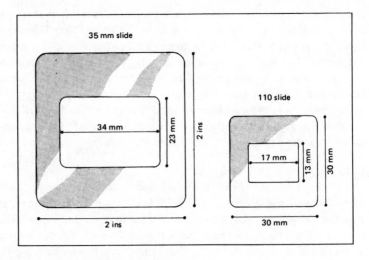

Figure 3. Slides: 110 and 35mm

68

the more widely available one commercially. The 110 format has only recently appeared on the market in Britain and is almost exclusively for home use.

The dimensions of a slide can be increased to 250mm square, suitable for an overhead projector. Some slides are made 60mm square, but these are now rare, and require a special projector which is not commonly available.

Cine film

The cine film is a sequence of images arranged vertically, which gives the appearance of movement when projected on to a screen at the correct speed. A variety of formats are available, their arrangements illustrated in figure 4. These are:

1 *35mm with sound track:* This format is almost exclusively used in public cinemas. A double sized frame, 70mm, is also sometimes used for Hollywood epics.

2 *16mm with optical sound track:* This is the common format for distributing films to small clubs, schools and business sources. The film should be projected at 24 frames per second, a reel of 400ft (120m), lasting about 11 minutes (36ft or 11m per minute). In some films, the optical sound track is replaced by a brown stripe which is the same as a thin piece of sound tape. This carries a magnetic sound track with all the properties of magnetic tape, and it can naturally be erased. Optical sound tracks cannot be altered in this way.

3 *16mm silent:* This is now comparatively rare. The film has sprocket holes on both sides, and should normally be projected at 16 frames per second, a reel of 400ft (120m) lasting about 16 minutes (24ft or 7m per minute).

4 *8mm standard (regular):* This may be silent or with a magnetic stripe for sound. The film can be projected at 16 frames per second (silent), 50ft (15m) lasting about 4 minutes (12ft or 3.6m per minute), or at 24 frames per second (sound), 50ft (15m) lasting about 3 minutes (18ft or 5.5m per minute).

5 *8mm super:* This may be silent or with a magnetic stripe for sound. The film can be projected at 18 frames per second (silent), 50ft (15m) lasting about 3 minutes (15ft or 4.5m per minute), or 24 frames per second (sound), 50ft (15m) lasting about 2½ minutes (20ft or 6m per minute).

To distinguish between the two 8mm film standards, look carefully at the different frame or picture sizes (standard 4.37 X 3.28mm,

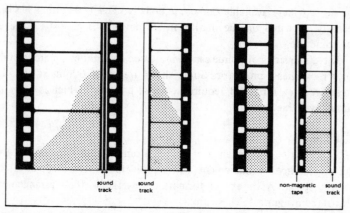

Figure 4. Cinefilm: from left to right – 35mm, 16mm sound, 8mm standard and 8mm super sound (Note: diagrams are not in proportion)

super 5.35mm × 4.01mm) and the shape and position of the sprocket holes.

All types of cine film are usually stored on open reels, each end having a long blank piece of film acting as leader or trailer for attachment through the projector. An attempt has been made to introduce 50ft and 100ft cartridges for 8mm film to protect the film from dust. In use, these cartridges require special projectors, each type of cartridge requiring its own model. However, to date, this system has not been very successful.

The continuous loop cassette has proved more successful as a means of storage. In this the 8mm film plays in a cyclic mode, the film continuing without end within the container. Silent film loops are contained in the cassette illustrated in figure 5, those for super 8 being coloured blue, those for standard 8 being clear plastic. The duration of each loop should not exceed three minutes if the film is to pass through the projector without difficulty. To ensure smoothness of operation, the film is usually specially 'oiled' by the manufacturer. If the film breaks or twists inside the cassette, it is possible to open it for repair, although the procedure is intricate and requires patience.

Both sound and silent films may also be held in other cassettes of varying shapes and arrangement. Each is usually unique to its own projector and not interchangeable. While some are used for information films, and the Open University distributed copies of its television transmissions by this means in its early days, the predominant use for

70

8mm sound cassettes is in the area of marketing in industry.

Cine films should be checked for breakages and tears. The latter are usually found around the sprocket holes, these being extended or the whole film ripped. Sometimes holes are also found in the sound track where a user has threaded it wrongly. Wherever this occurs, the torn film has to be cut out and the two ends stuck together. While thin self-adhesive tape is available for this purpose, it is better to splice the ends together with special cement. The repair is stronger by this means, though awkward to effect when dealing with 8mm film. It is important to realize that the continuity of the film will be broken through this and that the image will 'jump' on the screen. Because the sound track runs ahead of the image, the piece of sound excised in this process will refer in part or completely to frames of film that will be seen after the point of repair.

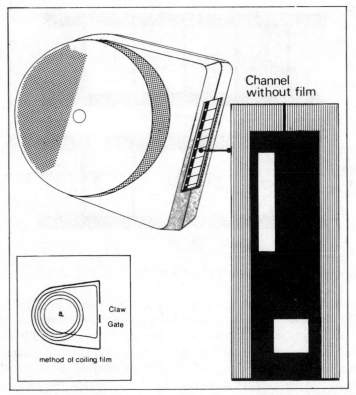

Figure 5. Loop cassette

71

Microforms

Various configurations of microform are available:

1 *35mm roll film:* The film has no sprocket holes, and may be in an open reel or, very rarely, a cartridge. The images in the frames are arranged horizontally, as in a double frame filmstrip with the same dimensions.

2 *16mm roll film:* The film has no sprocket holes, and is supplied in open reel, cartridge or cassette formats. The images may be arranged in comic-mode (often referred to in other formats as portrait shaped) or in cine-mode (often referred to in other formats as landscape shaped), as shown in figure 6. There may be a single strip of images, the simplex format, or a double cine-mode line of images, duplex in the same direction or duo in opposing ones.

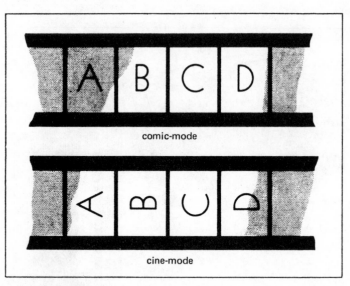

Figure 6. Microform: cine and comic modes

Roll film is used on open reels, in closed cassettes or in cartridges. While open reels are usually interchangeable between those machines which accept them, both cassettes and cartridges are made with different mechanical configurations and may only be used with equipment specifically designed to accept them. They are therefore not necessarily interchangeable between machines. A cassette contains two reels, the film passing from one to the other in either direction: a cartridge

72

contains one reel, the film being withdrawn from the cartridge and wound on to a receiving open reel. The important advantage of them both is the protection from handling and dust that is given to the film, and the cassette has the added value that it can be withdrawn from the equipment without rewinding back to the beginning. The open reel can only be cumbersomely used in this way and the cartridge requires the film to be totally rewound before it can be removed. While attempts are still in progress to produce a standard cassette which is universally applicable, this has not yet occurred.

3 *Aperture cards:* These are pieces of card with a window into which the microfilm is inserted. The card is usually approximately 187mm X 82mm (7¾in X 3¼in), can be written on for reference purposes and notched for mechanical sorting or computer information and retrieval. The latter can also be performed through machine-readable marking. The microfilm is usually directly affixed to the card, or it may be inserted into a thin jacket (see below) which is itself fixed to the card. Commonly one 35mm frame is inserted into the window, but a number of 16mm frames may be used instead.

4 *Micro-opaques:* The micro-images are printed on a card in a grid formation, either photographically or by an offset litho process. Because they are viewed by reflected and not transmitted light, they are relatively inefficient. Only one major publisher, Readex Microprint Corporation, uses them, for British and American government material. They should be avoided as an obsolete format.

5 *Microfiche:* The micro-images are arranged in a grid formation on a transparent film, 148mm X 105mm (the A6 dimensions, approximately 6in X 4in). A strip of eye-readable writing is placed along the top edge for identification. The number of frames may be varied with the reduction ratios used, but certain standards are emerging either through common practice or the British Standards Institute.[2] 60 and 98 frame formats are usual for microfiche of documents, the latter being more common, using a reduction ratio of 24X from the original.

The recommended arrangement of frames is in the portrait shape (comic mode) and should be read in this orientation. Where the original allows, the page may be spread over two adjacent frames. Regrettably some publishers intersperse images read this way with ones read horizontally although printed in the same fashion, so that the user has to turn his head sideways, reinsert the fiche sideways, turn the machine on its side or if available use an image-rotation control.

270 frame format is the commonest arrangement for COM fiche

(computer output on microfiche), using a reduction of 48X from the original. The images are printed in landscape shape with the long side horizontal, parallel to the top edge of the fiche. Through special processes reduction ratios up to 150X have been used (ultrafiche), and are utilized by particular businesses or for unique purposes.

Microfiche can also be presented in *jacketed formats*. A jacket is the same size as a standard microfiche, usually with a strip at the top for labelling, and a number of double layered plastic channels into which lengths of microfilm are inserted. The common form is a five channel jacket which accepts non-perforated 16mm film, but other versions exist for 35mm film. The do-it-yourself version, the jacketed fiche, is easily amended and rearranged, and of course can accumulate frames, the five channel variety achieving a maximum at 60. Copies in standard format can be made from the jacket acting as a master fiche. In filling the jacket, it is usually advisable to use a mechanical inserter as the two layers of plastic forming the channel are necessarily difficult to separate. Illustrations of microfiche are shown in figure 7.

Magnetic tape
This will be considered under the two main divisions, sound and video.

Sound tape
This is commonly available in three formats, open reel, cassette and cartridge. Tape may also be separately glued to 16mm and 8mm cine film to provide the base on which a sound track may be magnetically recorded, and this has been described in the previous section on cine film. It is important to note that stereo, quadrophony, two track, four track, etc, are functions of the tape recorder/player and *not* of the tape or its mechanical arrangement.

1 *Open reel:* This format is becoming increasingly uncommon for the dissemination of copies of recordings, but it is still widely used for the preparation and storage of masters or originals. While wider tapes are available for specialized purposes, for example studio recordings for the preparation of originals for discs, the usual width of tape is 6.3mm (¼in). The tape is supplied wound on a reel, the magnetic surface on the inner side, the reels usually of 8cm, 13cm or 18cm (3in, 5in or 7in) in diameter. 26.5cm (10½in) reels are also available. The amount of tape and the playing time available varies within two parameters, the thickness of the tape and the speed at which the recording is made. The thinner the tape the more there is on the

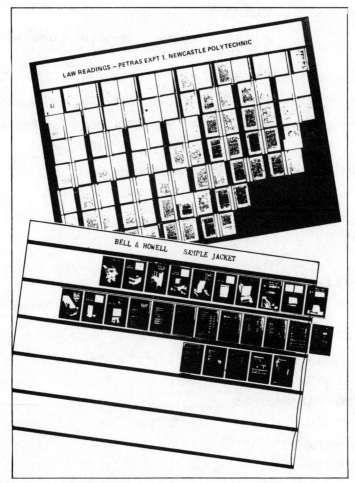

Figure 7. Microfiche: standard and microfilm jackets

reel, but also the more likely it is to stretch or break.

There are no standard codes to identify which tape is which, so the user has to identify this at purchase. Tables 1 and 2 give playing time for lengths of tape of different thicknesses recorded at different speeds. Speeds are measured in inches per second (ips).

Using both tables together it is possible to calculate how long a particular tape will play or record passing once through the recorder at a certain speed. For example, an 18cm (7in) reel of standard tape

SPOOL SIZE | **TAPE TYPE**

	standard		long play		double play		triple play	
	m	ft	m	ft	m	ft	m	ft
8cm reel (3in)	54	150	62	210	90	300	135	450
13cm reel (5in)	180	600	270	900	360	1200	540	1800
18cm reel (7in)	360	1200	540	1800	730	2400	1080	3600

Table 1. Spool size related to tape type and tape length

TAPE LENGTH | **TAPE SPEEDS**

		19cm/s ($7\frac{1}{2}$ips)	9.5cm/s ($3\frac{3}{4}$ips)	4.75cm/s ($1\frac{7}{8}$ips)	2.4cm/s ($^{15}/_{16}$ips)
m	ft				
45	150	3.9	7.8	15.6	31
65	210	5.5	11	22	45
90	300	7.5	15	30	60
135	450	11	22	45	90
180	600	15	30	60	120
270	900	22	45	90	180
360	1200	30	60	120	240
540	1800	45	90	180	360
730	2400	60	120	240	480
1080	3600	90	180	360	720

Table 2. Minutes of playing time for one pass through the tape recorder for different lengths of tape at different speeds

(360m) at 9.5cm/s (3¾ips) speed lasts 60 minutes. It is very important to store tape indicating the speed of the recording and its duration, usually as a function of time, but tape length may be given also.

Tapes are supplied with coloured leaders and trailers, which are lengths of coloured plastic tape at the beginning and end without the magnetic surface attached. On these may be written information concerning the recording, but their primary purpose is for attaching the tape to the plastic spool. This is usually done by slotting a short length of the leader (or trailer) through the notch on the spool (see figure 8). Sticky tape may be used with care, but is not necessary and not recommended.

Between the leader or trailer and the magnetic coated tape is sometimes found a short length of silvered tape. This affects the tape recorder as it passes through the record/playback channel and in those machines with the appropriate facility causes the machine to stop. This is useful in preventing the tape flapping round on its spool after it has finished recording or playing.

When stored, the loose end of the tape should be fixed into the reel, either using a special plastic clip or a piece of adhesive tape. In this

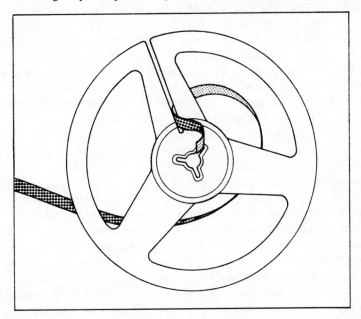

Figure 8. Attaching open reel tape to empty spool

77

position there is no danger of damage as the adhesive should be attached to a leader, or in its absence to the plastic backing of the tape and not its magnetic surface.

2 *The sound cassette:* First developed by Philips during the 1960s the cassette now meets international standards.[3] Indeed, Philips released the patents in order to encourage such a universality. At the time, other systems were being introduced, but these have now disappeared. It is possible that a larger cassette will emerge from Japan, but this has long been promised without anything actually materializing in commercial form. Small cassettes for dictating machines are also available but these are not discussed here.

The compact cassette has standard dimensions (10.2cm X 6.4cm; 4in X 2½in) and features. The tape is 3.8mm (0.15in) wide, and in the cassette the magnetic coated surface is on the outward or exposed surface. All cassette recorders and players run at a standard 4.75cm/s (1⅞ips), and this means that cassettes are sold with predetermined playing times. These are commonly C30 (15 minutes each side), C60 (30 minutes each side), C90 (45 minutes each side), C120 (60 minutes each side), so that the sum of the time produced by playing it completely through one way, turning it over and playing it through again is the number given to the tape. Tapes for computers are generally shorter and of lower quality material. The common lengths are C10, C12 and C15, and while longer tapes may be used, it takes such a long time to find the program that the shorter length is more suitable. The thickness of the tape decreases; C30 and C60 tapes are approximately that of triple play open reel tape, C90 and C120 becoming progressively thinner. The inside of a cassette is shown in figure 9.

The tape passes from one spool to the other actually remaining within the cassette, so it may be removed from the playing machine at any point without any necessity for rewinding. Within the cassette, the tape is kept in position by a series of guides, and is attached at each end to the respective spindles by strong adhesive tape. When fully wound to one side, the user will notice that a leader or trailer of transparent or coloured tape is visible. When stored fully rewound in this way, there is no chance of damage to the magnetic coating, as this is protected within the cassette. The leader or trailer takes between five and seven seconds to pass, so no recording can be made during this period. In early cassettes a silvered portion of tape was inserted between leader and coated tape to provide an automatic stop, but this facility is now handled by a sensor which determines the dif-

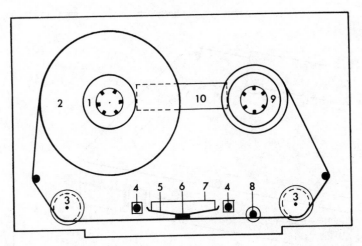

Figure 9. Diagrammatic view of the inside of a cassette: 1=gearing of the left-hand supply reel; 2=left-hand supply reel; 3=guide roller; 4= guide pin; 5=pressure spring; 6=felt pad; 7=baffle; 8=capstan; 9=gearing of the right-hand take-up hub; 10=inspection window

ferent thickness or density of the coated and leader sections.

The quantity of tape within the cassette may be seen through the window on its surface. Some cassettes are held together by screws, and this has the advantage of easy access for any necessary adjustments and repairs. Others are sealed and access is very difficult. At the rear of the cassette are at least two lugs, pieces of plastic covering a hole (see figure 10). When present, normal use of the cassette is possible, including the recording or erasure of sound. But they can be snapped off, in which case accidental erasure is precluded because recording is not possible. This means that if a cassette with the lugs removed is returned by the borrower and its programme discovered to be tampered with, it can be definitely established as deliberate interference. As the cassette has two playing sides, there are two lugs: with the cassette flat on the table with the exposed tape facing you, the lug referring to the upper side as per label is the one at the back on the left.

Other important features to note on a cassette are the pressure pad behind the tape, usually a small piece of sponge rubber which is supported by a spring, used to keep the tape in firm contact with the recording surface of the playing machine; the notched rings in the large holes which engage the spindles on the machine and help to keep the tape

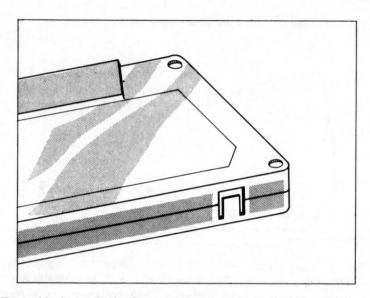

Figure 10. Lug at back of cassette to prevent accidental recording

properly wound in the cassette, the four holes at the front, the inner pair providing access for pins to hold the cassette rigid, the outer ones allowing access for a rotating pin which with the wheel in the playing machine actually propels the tape at constant speed from one half of the cassette to the other.

3 *Cartridge:* This form of container is becoming less popular. The tape is wound from the reel and back within the same containing box, the coated surface facing outwards. It is the same tape used for standard play open reel, 6.3mm (¼in) wide, and plays at 9.5cm/s (3¾ips). Because the tape is a continuous loop, it is not attached to the reel, and has no leader tape. However, there is an inserted strip of silvered tape which is used to create a signal to change the track being played. Cartridges can only be recorded on specialized and expensive equipment which is not normally available to the domestic user. It is also impossible to locate specific passages on the tape so selective replay is not possible. However, as they do not need rewinding, they are useful for continuous music.

Splicing sound-tape All sound-tape can be edited and repaired with very little noticeable effect on the sounds being recorded or replayed. Clicks or other sounds of interference are hardly distinguishable.

When a tape is recorded, the message is passed on to a segment of tape which varies in length according to the size of recording head and more especially the speed of the tape. The faster the recording speed the longer the space between the different elements of the message. For a tape to be edited, therefore, it is an advantage to have the original recording made at as fast a speed as possible.

When splicing the tape, it is helpful to use a commercially produced block which will help to hold it in exactly the right position (figure 11).

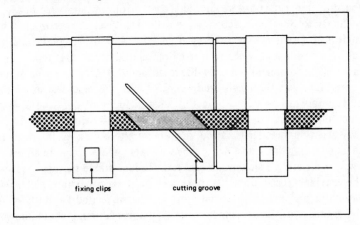

Figure 11. Tape on editing block

Before starting, check the exact points that you wish to join together; marking the shiny rear surface with a chinagraph pencil will help to keep the points identified. Place the two ends to be joined on the block so that they overlap, the two points to be joined on top of each other over the cutting groove, the shiny backing surface uppermost. With the tape fixed in this position, the tape is cut on a diagonal by passing a sharp blade through the groove. The two ends will now be accurately butted against each other. Adhesive splicing tape is then attached to the surfaces, and any overlapping edges trimmed either by a slicing mechanism on the block or by a sharp blade. The tape may now be removed from the block and re-used.

All widths of tape may be edited and spliced in this way, but it is easier to do with the wider ¼in tape than with the cassette tape. Not only are the possible recording speeds faster with the wider tape, it is also easier to handle and manipulate than the thinner cassette material. Appropriately sized blocks are available for each width of tape.

81

Videotape

Almost all videotape is now made with chromium oxide as a major constituent of the magnetic coating. Before discussing the arrangement of the tape in its various carriers, some description of the recording mechanism may be helpful.

The tape is passed across the heads in the recorder at a certain speed. The heads are revolving at a high speed as well. The product of the two gives a 'head-to-tape' speed, the general rule being that the higher the rate, the better the recording. Tape 'writing speeds' vary between 850cm/s to 3800cm/s depending on the quality of the recorder. With such high speeds between the head and the tape, the magnetic coating suffers considerable wear from friction, and it is rare that tape manufacturers recommend a longer life than about 1000 passes. These are passes in which the heads are in contact with the tape, not in rewind or fast forward modes. Any count must include not only those made when the programme is replayed but also when it is being recorded.

When videotape first started, manufacturers created machines to fit their own specifications. Thus the same tape, while usable in terms of size on different machines, could not produce stable pictures because the machines used different tape and head speeds. Other electronic variations also existed, but the most significant related to the tape. In the summary of the existing types of tape organization, it should not be thought that all differences between manufacturers have been ironed out. There has been considerable progress in eliminating incompatibilities, but there is still a long way to go before all video tapes are usable on all machines. Apart from differences in width and packaging, there is no apparent sign on the tape as to what machines the tape was recorded on or whether the programme is in colour or monochrome. Labelling should therefore include all this information, together with an indication of the timed length of the programme. The figures given here refer to machines playing in the PAL 625 line system used in the United Kingdom and will vary slightly from other systems. Note that the video image and sound occupies the whole tape and that it plays only in one direction.

1 *Open reel tape:* The commonest spool diameters are 12.7 (5in), 17.8cm (7in), 20.3cm (8in) and 24.7cm (9.7in). Because different manufacturers produce tape in a variety of thicknesses, these figures bear only a tenuous connection to tape length.

50mm (2in) tape is used almost exclusively with equipment developed for broadcasting. Two different tape speeds are usual, 39.7cm/s and 19.85cm/s, and the tape is commonly reeled in lengths of 702m, 1465m and 2196m.

25mm (1in) tape is used increasingly either for broadcast purposes or for making master recordings which are re-recorded for distribution on smaller tapes. Different equipment has different tape speeds. Thus IVC uses a tape speed of 17.2cm/s, Grundig 20cm/s. A reel of 655m (2150ft) will give one hour's playing time on IVC.

12.7mm (½in) tape is available for a number of machines, the majority now standardized to the EIAJ-1 format. (EIAJ stands for Electrical Industries Association of Japan.) The tape speed is 16.32cm/s, and is commonly available on spools with diameter 12.7cms (lasting about 30 minutes) and 17.8cms (lasting about 60 minutes).

6.25mm (¼in) is produced for one type of equipment by Akai. 330m of this tape on a 12.7cm spool gives about 30 minutes' playing time at a tape speed of 23.8cm/s.

Open reel tape is wound with the magnetic surface on the inside and the polyester base layer outwards. There are no leaders or trailers as used with sound tape, and the tape end is fixed to the other coils with a plastic clip.

Editing of open reel tape is not done by cutting and joining, but electronically. If the tape breaks, a temporary join may be made using adhesive tape, making sure it is *only* applied to the backing surface. However a copy should be made as soon after use as possible to prevent further damage from the splice.

2 *Cassettes and cartridges:* Increasingly, videotape is being stored in containers, cassettes and cartridges. Cartridges are basically an open reel within a box, the tape when played in the equipment being automatically extracted, threaded and played. It can only be extracted from the equipment after the tape has been rewound into the cartridge. The only extant form of cartridge is a container for the standard EIAJ system that uses tape at a speed of 16.32cm/s. Cartridges are available for 15, 30, and 60 minutes playing time.

Cassettes are enclosed systems in which the tape is wound from one reel to another, both within the container. Thus the cassette may be withdrawn from the playing equipment when the programme is not complete and without rewinding. Table 3 outlines the significant figures for the various systems presently available.

U-Matic cassettes use the widest tapes of the various cassettes described. They are available in 10, 15, 20, 30, 40, 50 and 60 minute sizes. A small plug on the underside of the cassette may be removed to prevent accidental erasure. This may be replaced if the tape is required for use again. Unrecorded tape is marketed with the letters CA in front of the number which usually indicates the time it lasts, CS for that to be used with the portable version of this recorder.

VHS is the format of cassettes which is manufactured by the largest number of companies. The cassette is the largest of the three systems principally used in the domestic market, although the tape width is the same. Tapes are available in the following sizes, E30, E60, E120, E180 and E240., where the numbers represent the playing time. The longest tape is also thinner than the others and may be less robust. Another size of cassette known as the VHS-C is produced to fit into portable recorders for use with a camera. The cassette is smaller although the tape is identical, and it may be replayed in the standard machines by inserting it into a dummy cassette of the correct size.

Name of system	U-Matic	VHS	Beta	Video 2000
Principal manufacturer	Sony	JVC	Sony	Philips
Maximum playing time (mins)	60	240	215	480
Tape speed (cm/s)	9.5	2.34	1.87	2.44
Tape width (mm)	19.05	12.7	12.7	12.7
Container dimensions (mm)	221 × 140 × 32	188 × 104 × 25	156 × 96 × 25	183 × 111 × 26

Table 3. Significant features of various cassette systems

The major rival to the VHS system is the Beta format. The cassette is smaller and there is no need for a different size for use with portable recorders. Tapes are available in the following sizes, the figures in brackets being the playing time in minutes of each, L124(35), L250(66), L370(95), L500(130), L750(195) and L830(215). The thinner tape is in the last two sizes of cassettes.

Two firms are currently involved in manufacturing the third domestic format, Philips and Grundig. Known as Video 2000, it is unique in that the tape can be used in both directions. The cassette is inserted into the machine, played through fully from left to right, withdrawn and turned over and played again. This is because the recordings are made on only half the tape at a time. Because of this system, the playing times are given in minutes in brackets for one side only in the list of available tapes, VCC120(60), VCC240(120), VCC360(180) and VCC480(240), the last size having the thinnest tape. As the cassette is small, portable recorders use the same ones.

Each of the cassettes of the three domestic systems have plastic lugs which can be broken off to prevent accidental erasure or over-recording. All cassettes can and should be stored in their own or specially purchased boxes. While the cassette itself provides some protection from dust and other hazards, and is a very convenient and simple method of handling videotape, they should nevertheless be treated with care.

Magnetic disks

These disks are used with computers as the backing store for information recording or more commonly in the library as the store for programs. The slower alternative is the cassette, referred to under that heading.

Large computers use disk packs but these will be stored within a computer service area and are not discussed here. Also available are 'hard' disks or Winchesters, which are kept in sealed and dustfree containers. Very large storage of computer information is possible with them, but they are unlikely to be kept in a library and so will not be referred to here. This section concentrates on 'mini' or 'floppy' disks which are separately filed for use with micro or stand-alone computers. At present, they are supplied in two sizes, 132mm (5¼in) and 203mm (8in), although there are proposals for smaller disks of 76mm (3in) diameter to work with microdrives. As these are not commercially available yet, no comment can be made.

There are two different types of disk, hard and soft sector. When information is stored on a disk, it is placed in a sector, the address of which is stored in the disk's catalogue and instantly identifiable to the computer. Information is stored on the disk in concentric circles called tracks, each track being divided into sectors. The numbers of these vary between computers and the system they use, but in one example there are 40 tracks on a disk, each divided into 10 sectors. Others may be more densely packed and therefore able to store more information, for generally each sector can hold 256 bytes of computer information. Because computers and disk systems vary, there is no compatability between the models of the machines, and it is necessary to be certain that an individual disk is used with an appropriate computer. When new

85

disks with no information on them are used, then it is necessary to prepare the disk before information is recorded by overwriting it with the appropriate formatting codes which divide it into the relevant sectors. Such a disk is known as a soft sector disk as the arrangement of these divisions can be altered. A hard sectored disk has the divisions permanently assigned, and the formatting activity is used to appoint the addresses for each one. Such formatting is done from a computer program supplied by the manufacturer. On examination, a disk that has been formatted has no visible change to it, and so it should be labelled as necessary.

Disks should be kept in their protective jackets and also in paper sleeves to preserve them from dust and grease. Like all disks, they are stored most conveniently and safely in an upright position and not subjected to undue pressure or extreme conditions. They do wear out from use, and even if only a part is worn, it is better to replace them as the worn area may affect the delicate mechanisms of the disk machinery.

Plastic
Under this heading, two formats are considered.

Transparent plastic
This material is for use with the overhead projector and is available in various thicknesses commonly ranging from 0.05mm to 0.25mm, either as single flat sheets or as rolls. The roll is 25.4cm (10in) wide and of varying length. Attached by self-adhesive tape to a central core of cardboard, to the ends of which are attached light metal hubs with key-slots to align with the winding arms of the projector, the material can be used repeatedly. However there is a tendency for the edges of the roll to tear or crack.

Flat sheets are usually supplied in two sizes 26.7cm X 26.7cm (10½ X 10½in) and 26.7cm X 21.6cm (10½in X 8in). Different manufacturers supply slight variations on these figures. While some are stored loose in folders, others may be attached to a frame, the common external measurements being 30cm X 30cm (11.8in X 11.8in). While A4 sizes (31.4cm X 31.4cm) are being developed, they are unlikely to be very common. If sheets are kept against each other, paper should be inserted between them to reduce the natural adhesion between plastic. Because of a natural tendency to bend and warp it is wise to store them sufficiently compressed to maintain some rigidity.

Discs

Discs are marketed in 17.8cm (7in), 25.4cm (10in), and 30.5cm (12in) diameter sizes, the central hole for the spindle being about 7.5mm in diameter. This spindle need not be a tight fit, acting as it does as a centring device and not an aid to the disc's revolution. This is done by the turntable itself.

Recordings on discs are made at 33⅓, 45, and 78 revolutions per minute. The fastest of these speeds is obsolete, and the speed of 45rpm is restricted now to 'singles' of popular music. The length of time the recording lasts is determined by the length of the groove, but it is unusual for a 12in disc to carry a recording in excess of 25 minutes per side.

While the plastic material from which the disc is pressed is fairly strong, the groove itself can be quite easily damaged. It is inadvisable to place one disc directly on another, for this sort of stack playing will increase wear. Because the pick-up stylus physically vibrates along the groove as the disc is played the plastic material becomes gradually worn away. However, no rule can be laid down for the life of a disc as it depends on the weight of this contact between stylus and groove, and this varies between record players.

To play accurately, discs should be as level as possible on the turntable. Bending and warping are common from exposure to heat and damp, or are the result of distorting pressure. Discs should therefore be stored vertically, not leaning in either direction. The disc's wrapping is also important to exclude dust. The disc should be placed in the paper sleeve, the opening of which should be against a sealed edge of the cardboard sleeve.

Videodiscs

There are three types being developed and manufactured, selectavision developed by RCA and marketed in the USA only although proposed for Europe, VHD (video high density) developed by JVC and Thorn/EMI and currently postponed although marketing is proposed for Japan, and the laserdisc developed by Philips, Grundig and Pioneer and marketed in the USA and Europe. The first two work on the principle of capacitance and the discs have to be made of electrically conductive material. The third operates on the principle of reflection and thus the material need only be a polished plastic. Naturally there is no compatibility between them.

Selectavision is a 25.4 (10in) disc with a spiral groove for the stylus.

It is inserted into the player inside its jacket as it is very sensitive to surface damage. Each rotation of the disc produces four pictures, so it is not possible, without considerable expense, to use this system for still pictures. Playing time is about one hour per side.

The VHD disc has the same dimensions as the selectavision but has no groove. Instead, there are spirals of pits from which the stylus detects the capacitance necessary to create the picture. Each rotation produces two pictures and a system developed to allow for still picture. As the discs have not yet been marketed, further details of this system are not available, although it is known that it is hoped that the playing time will be one hour per side also. Unlike selectavision, it is also expected that VHD will offer two independent sound tracks to accompany the pictures, which means that stereo or bilingual productions are possible.

In contrast to the other two systems, the laserdisc is totally inert, and therefore can be handled. During playback, no stylus or other wearing agent rubs against the disc, the signals being translated from the variations in the reflections of a laser beam from the pits in the material. Two types of disc are produced, a one hour each side long play disc with stereo sound which has no still picture facility as more than one picture is recorded on each rotation, and a 36 minute active play disc with full control available over each frame. Both discs are the same size, 30cm (12in) in diameter, 3.4mm thick and a centre hole of diameter 35mm, and the player can recognize the difference between them electronically. There are 54,000 still frame positions available on each side of a laserdisc, each of them independently addressable, so the storage capacity for information is very large. Discs have programmes written on them at the manufacturing stage, and normally the user cannot produce his own. However, there are developments to make it possible for the user to purchase blanks of laserdiscs and burn his own recording on to it.

Developed alongside the video version of the laserdisc by Philips and Sony is the compact disc for audio recordings. The dics are currently only recorded on one side, and are 12 cm (5in) in diameter. 1.2mm thick, the centre hole has a diameter of 15mm. Their characteristics are similar to those of the long play laserdisc and have a playing time of about an hour.

EQUIPMENT: PRINCIPLES OF OPERATION

In this section, the various pieces of equipment required to view and listen to the various forms of material described in the previous pages will be explained in terms of the principles by which they operate. No attempt has been made to apply these features to a particular model. Rather, the section has been written in very general terms, and includes as many of the features as possible that are likely to be present. Important electronic parameters are also included, together with a simplified explanation of some of the figures given in commercial descriptions of equipment. The divisions follow those of the previous sections, dealing with paper, film, magnetic tape, and plastic derivatives in turn. Lastly, there is a discussion of the issues involved in all aspects of maintenance.

Paper
Paper materials do not normally require equipment in order to be used. Magnifying glasses may occasionally be used to view small print, but this is not often necessary. For charts and large pictures, suspending devices may be used. It is preferable that these do not damage the material, so that if hooks or pins are used they should go through prepared and protected holes. Clips are available in a number of forms, from pegs to bulldogs. One of the most successful is the Klemmboy clip, which utilizes a plastic roller to trap the paper and hold it firmly.

Film
In the context of equipment film is transparent; it can only be viewed by means of light passing through it into the eyes. This light may be direct or pass through a magnifying system, or go through this system and then be projected on to a screen. Viewing directly, for example by holding a piece of film up to the light, requires no further explanation (figure 12a). It is, however, worth noting that some light distorts the colour quality of the picture being viewed, fluorescent tubes being particularly liable to do this.

Direct viewing through a magnifying lens is a simple system, usually only suitable for a single user at a time (figure 12b). Some arrangements require the interpolation of a translucent screen between the magnifying lens and the user, such a screen being called a rear projection as the image is thrown on the back and seen by looking at the front (figure 12c). In these systems, if the screen is made fairly large, it is possible

89

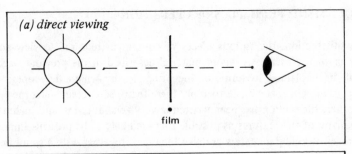

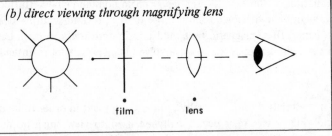

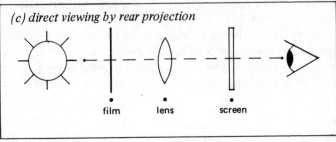

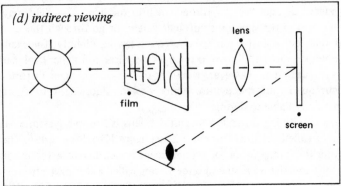

Figure 12. Various methods of viewing film

for several people to view simultaneously; but in practice the results are not very effective. This is further discussed later.

Indirect viewing via reflections from a screen is a more complex system, and is the one adopted for mass viewing. Because it is more restful for the eyes, it is also adopted in place of a rear projection system for individual viewing where long periods of study are involved (figure 12d). Unlike the other methods of viewing, this system has to have the film inserted laterally and vertically inverted before magnification rather than placed initially in the 'correct' alignment. In those rear projection systems in which light from the projector is reflected off a mirror, similar inversions have to take place.

In simple terms, all film viewing and projecting systems operate in the same way. The film is placed between a lamp and a lens, the latter magnifying the image. If the eyes of the user are close to the lens, that is within the focal length, the image is viewed as through a magnifying glass. If the eyes of the user are further away than the focal length, the image is inverted vertically and laterally by the lens and can only be viewed clearly by casting the image onto a screen.

The size of the image seen is determined by the power of the lens (expressed as the focal length) and the distance between the film and the lens. Adjusting this distance fixes the place at which the image is focused. That is why focusing is controlled almost invariably by moving the lens in and out of its carrier.

The image cast on a screen by a lens increases in size the further the screen is moved away from it. When this exceeds the size required, a lens with a longer focal length is introduced instead. Thus as a rule of thumb, the longer the distance between the lens and the screen (the 'throw'), the longer the focal length of the lens required. The appropriate lens can be selected using the charts (figure 13) provided the distance of the 'throw' and the size of the screen available are known.

While the lens in a simple magnifying situation (figure 12B) is usually constructed in a single piece, those in projecting arrangements are normally made of a number of separate parts carefully sealed at set distances apart in the lens holder. This is referred to as a complex lens, and is used to eliminate distortions of the light as it passes through the glass. As there is no opportunity for dust or condensation to occur between these pieces under normal conditions, there is no reason why they should be separated, and it is most inadvisable to attempt to do so. The complex lens in its holder may naturally be removed from the lens carrier to exchange it for another, for security reasons, or for simple maintenance.

91

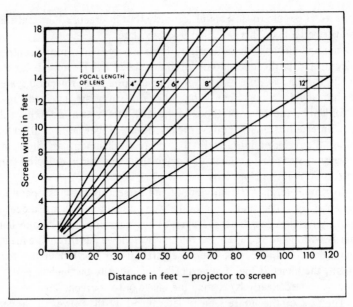

Figure 13(a). Lens selection: filmstrips and slides—single frame 24×18mm

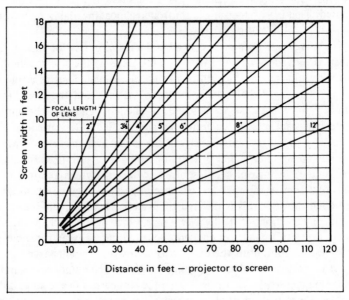

Figure 13(b). Lens selection: 2×2in slides—horizontal 36×24mm

92

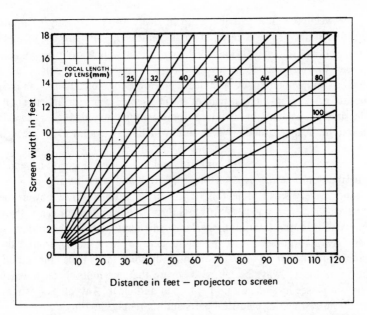

Figure 13(c). Lens selection: 16mm projector – millimetre range of lenses

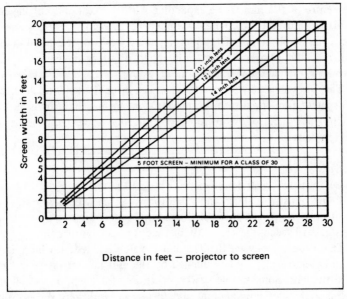

Figure 13(d). Lens selection: overhead projectors

93

Between the film and the lamp in many projectors may be found another series of lenses referred to as condensers. The purpose of these is to collect and marshal the light so that as much of it as possible passes through the whole area of the film and into the lens. This is further supplemented by a concave mirror either behind the lamp or occasionally as an integral part of it. The separate mirror and the condensing lenses may be removed for cleaning, provided great care is taken in noting exactly where and which way round each piece is placed.

Lamps in projectors get very hot, and unless some method of reducing the temperature is available, the film and even wiring may get burnt. In very small projectors or where the lamp is of low power, the case will have a number of air vents through which cold air can pass by convection currents around the lamp and cool it. In larger machines, fans are incorporated into the equipment to drive the air around the lamp. Such fans must operate continuously while the lamp is illuminated, and care must always be taken to ensure that the holes through which the air passes in and out are kept open and clear. Any blockages may result in overheating electrical parts and scorching the film.

Another result of the heat generated by the lamp is that the film may visually 'pop' — that is, go out of focus suddenly. This is caused by the centre of the film frame expanding with the heat and bulging forwards towards the lens. When this happens, it is no longer possible to focus the whole frame of the picture, and a weakness is created in that frame of the film so that it is likely to occur again on subsequent occasions, even at a lower temperature.

The foregoing points refer to all pieces of equipment which enable transparent film to be seen, no matter what format that film is in. The descriptions that follow therefore assume that these basic principles are appreciated.

Viewers
These are based on the system described in figure 12b, and are usually used for filmstrips, slides and microforms. Some will allow frames of cinefilm to be passed through them, but as these are not conveyed at the standard speed, they can only be used for casual inspection.

The distance between the lens and the film is fixed; any increase in magnification can only be obtained by the user moving his head back from the lens. Some simple viewers make use of daylight or room lights as the sources of illumination, and these can work very successfully,

94

particularly for casual inspection. For longer study, viewers with bulbs are preferable, powered either from the mains supply or by batteries. Because the light passes fairly directly into the eye, this is not a comfortable means of long-term study. It is also noteworthy that the edges of the picture are less clearly illuminated than the centre.

Viewers are usually made for one format of film only. Some models are available for both types of filmstrip or for two or three sizes of slide. With delivery and collecting chambers attached to the side, some slide viewers are made to allow the user to change slides through a stack of them fairly rapidly. A lever is pulled and pushed, the movement ejecting one slide into the collecting chamber and delivering another into the viewing position.

Filmstrip projectors
These are very simple projectors, their particular feature being the method of holding the filmstrip. While there are very specialized machines which use a cartridge from which the strip is wound, and others with chambers inside the body of the projector into which it is coiled, the majority work on the very simple principle of winding the strip from one holding spool to another through a fixed position between the lamp and the adjustable lens. It is important to keep the frames rigidly in the correct position for any movement causes the picture to blur out of focus. In one system, this is prevented by clamping the film between two pieces of glass, a method which also eliminates any possibility of 'popping'. However, it does introduce the danger of scratching if the strip is pulled sharply through its glass 'sandwich'.

The filmstrip is attached to the spools either by clips or adhesive tape, and by turning the spool, usually by hand, the film is wound from one to the other, each frame passing into the projecting position in turn. Variations on this introduce a further spool and make use of the sprocket holes on the edge of the strip to determine an exact movement from one picture to the next.

Not all projectors accept both formats of filmstrip. The key to deciding whether a particular machine does is to examine the size of the hole in the filmstrip carrier. If this is big enough for a double or full frame filmstrip, it is likely that the manufacturer also provides a masking mechanism which will cut down the size of the hole so that it is suitable for the other format as well.

Slide projectors

The complexity of slide projectors is dependent on the degree of automation involved. Hand operated projectors are usually based on a simple rotation or lateral movement of slides behind the lens, usually replacing each one in the carrier alternately. Controls are limited to mains power, lamp brightness and focusing.

Semi-automatic projectors provide a system for reducing the problem of changing slides. Instead of feeding them in singly, they are carried in a magazine. A hand-operated lever is employed to pull out a slide from the projecting position into the magazine, move it one place and push in the next slide. Normally they only operate in a forward direction, the magazine having to be pushed backwards by hand to allow a previous slide to be reshown.

The commonest magazine is a straight one carrying a maximum of 36 slides. Care should be taken in selecting them for not all are interchangeable between projectors. Circular magazines, taking about 80 slides, are also available for certain machines.

In automatic slide projectors, the changing of the slides is done mechanically. The changing mechanism can be similar to that on a semi-automatic projector, a lever carrying the slides in and out mechanically from a magazine held at the side of the machine, or through a partial gravity-feed mechanism. In this latter method a circular magazine is used, lying flat on the top of the projector, with a hole in the underneath immediately above the slot in which the slide fits to be in the projecting position. The slide drops into this position by gravity and is held there by light springs. When the signal is given to change the slide, an arm under it lifts it back into the magazine, which is then moved on to a new position by a lever. The arm then drops back into its bottom position and a new slide falls into place. During the movement which changes the slide in both automatic and most semi-automatic systems a shutter passes in between the lamp and the lens to prevent light shining on to the screen and showing the transfer action. A new development in some machines is the presence of a small hole in the shutter so that the black-out is only partial and therefore the contrast for the viewer is not so great.

The changing mechanism of an automatic projector may be operated in both forward and reverse directions depending on the signal given. Commonly the two signals are given by separate buttons, but in a few machines the difference between forward and reverse is governed by the length of time that the signal is given. Automatic projectors have control buttons on the projector and a socket for a plug (usually the DIN variety, see figure 14) which provides access for signals to be given remotely. The sources and results of these signals may be:

1 Slide changes by a remote control attached by a cable, carrying forward and reverse buttons, and usually a control for moving the lens for focus. Such a lens control only provides for fine adjustment.

2 Repetitive changes at set intervals, a simple adjustable automatic timing device which gives slide change signals at predetermined moments.

3 Changes caused by signals from a tape recorder.

3 Zeroing, that is, the projector automatically changing back to the beginning of the programme after the last slide in a sequence has been shown.

All the signals are conveyed electrically to the socket, and therefore the device providing the signals must be attached to the projector.

There have been increasing developments in the multi-slide projector show in which two or more machines are used. While one slide is changing, another machine provides the picture. The changes may be fading from one projector to another or snap changes, that is one going off suddenly at the same instant as the other lights up. The controls for this operate commonly through circuitry which not only affects the slide change mechanism but also the brightness of the lamp. At the present time, most of the systems operate on different signal arrangements and are therefore not interchangeable. A programme made with one system must be replayed using that and no other.

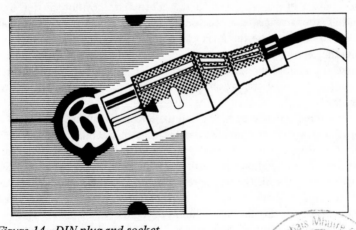

Figure 14. DIN plug and socket.

97

Microform readers

While the film may come in rolls, free, in a cassette or cartridge, or as a flat piece, the means of enlarging or projecting it are essentially similar. The film is placed very close to the lens to ensure the maximum area of light passes through the frame for magnification. Because the information is so small, the quality of the lens must also be good in order to achieve even magnification over the whole area of the image. The closeness of the film to the lens and the considerable magnification required also means that slight movements of the film cause abrupt changes of focus. It is therefore important that the film is kept rigidly in position, which may be done through a holding mechanism as with microfiche.

Paper copies of individual frames of microforms can be obtained using specially modified equipment called reader-printers. The copy is of the enlargement and of the parts selected by the user. Such equipment is available for both roll microfilm and microfiche.

Although there are viewers for microforms (see page 94) they are not very comfortable for extensive reading. The commoner arrangements of readers are front and rear projection. The latter is often considered less satisfactory because the optical and screen qualities tend to mean that the screen is unevenly illuminated, and the excessive brightness in the central area can cause discomfort to the eyes. With front projection, the light is bounced off a screen and this helps to reduce the bright spots. The front projection screen may be an integral part of the reader, but in a number of them it is separate and may even be a piece of paper placed in the appropriate position by the user. In this latter arrangement, because the lens-to-screen distance is variable, the user can increase the magnification by increasing it without changing the lens. However, it should be noted that as the magnification increases so does the size of the image, and therefore a larger screen is required to show the whole picture. Focus adjustment will also be necessary.

Various lines may be present on the screens. Some are introduced to provide a working outline around the edge of the image for particular magnifications. Where the reader is integrated with a printer, lines may be introduced to show the outline of the area which will be printed. More recently, with the widespread use of COM fiche many screens are made with a fixed or mobile horizontal line, a cursor which assists the reader in sorting through columns of figures.

While all front projection screens are white or slightly silvered, those used for rear projection are often tinted to reduce the problems of glare and visual discomfort. Blue, grey and occasionally green surfaces are available, and can be an assistance if reading passages of writing. However, users should be aware of the fact that coloured film will not be viewed in its original colours when these screens are involved.

Readers with both types of screen arrangement can frequently be altered for projection on to a room screen for mass viewing. While the equipment is usually designed for individual use, simple adjustments can often be made to remove the screen or tilt a reflecting mirror or swivel the lamp-film-lens assembly so that the light can be made to fall on to a big screen.

Microform readers are very simple projectors with few controls. Lamp brightness is usually fixed and remote control is not necessary. The exception to this is the recent development of a tape-microfiche system, discussed on page 118. A control to alter the oreintation of the image is present in some of the more expensive equipment. Operating by means of turning a prism placed between the lens and the reflecting mirror, this provides a method for turning the image 90° (sometimes 360° is available for roll film) in either direction, a portrait-shaped original thereby being turned so that it can be viewed as a landscape image.

Most readers now have the facility for changing lenses to give a variety of possible magnifications. Different methods have been adopted to do this. Some machines have to have the lens in position unlocked and then unscrewed before a different one can be inserted. Others incorporate a nosepiece to which the lenses are fixed, while others have them attached to a bar which is slid from one position to another. Selecting the most suitable lenses depends on the reduction ratios of the original material to be viewed. For 35mm film, it is likely that 10X and 20X are a suitable pair. 16mm film and microfiche will usually be viewed satisfactorily with 24X and 48X lenses, the latter being designed for COM fiche as well. Zoom lenses, having variable focusing within the same lens and often supplied for slide projectors, are not presently used with microforms. It should also be noted that the threading and physical dimensions of lenses usually mean that they cannot be interchanged between readers made by different manufacturers.

Focusing the image means moving the lens, usually by fractional amounts. Most frequently this is done by rotating the lens in its carrier by hand. However, this may also be accomplished by a remote mechanical connection to a control on the outside of the machine.

Readers for roll-film

Cassettes and cartridges are made to fit on particular machines, depending on the manufacturer of the container. When fitted to the reader, the film is either placed directly in the appropriate position between the lamp and lens or it is automatically threaded into the correct place.

Open reel film is attached and usually threaded by hand through the 'gate' between lamp and lens, the pathway marked on the reader. Winding the film from one reel to another can be done manually by turning the handles attached to the reel carriers. Because very long lengths of film can be fitted on roll-film readers, holding perhaps 2000 or more images, some machines have a motorized form of film transport. The speed of this differs between machines, and a manual override is essential to finally centre the image to be viewed. Incorporated also in many readers is a facility which enables the user to move the reflecting mirror up and down so that various parts of the image can be centred in the vertical plane.

With such a large number of images on a single roll of film, it is essential that the relevant ones can be located quickly and smoothly. There is no standard or universal system. Code-line indexes on the film between the images are sometimes used, but more commonly with motorized movement machines, a footage counter or odometer is used. Provided this is started from the beginning and the counter counts the same thing, in this case feet, the system is effective. Photo-mechanical methods which count blips or white spots on the edge of the film are also available.

Aperture cards

These can usually be read with equipment designed for microfiche, provided the carrier tray for the fiche is wide enough to accept the card. Some machines are made specifically for use with these cards, having a slot into which they are inserted. The readers have few controls, although a minimum of two lenses are essential.

Microfiche

Except in the case of the smallest readers, the fiche is always inserted into the machine inside a carrier. These may be transparent plastic or glass, keeping the fiche in exactly the correct position, and protecting it from damage as it is moved around. Usually the carrier opens automatically like an oyster shell as it is pulled towards the user, and the fiche is inserted into place. As the carrier is pushed back under the lens, the carrier closes. In some readers, the carrier is opened manually, but before doing so, it must be withdrawn from under the lens.

Locating the correct frame is done on an assumed grid system. On some microfiche, the identity of each frame based on this grid is marked, but frequently it is not. The system is based on every horizontal row being assigned a letter, A being that immediately under the title strip; and every vertical column being given a number, the one on the extreme left of the fiche being 1. Thus an X is placed in frame B3 on the grid illustrated (figure 15).

Because there is some variation still in the grids, position finding can be confusing. The common arrangements are: 18 frame fiche using 35mm frames — rows A to C, columns 1 to 6; 60 frame fiche rows A to E, columns 1 to 12 (this includes jackets although the vertical separation between rows is slightly greater); 98 frame fiche rows A to G, columns 1 to 14; 270 frame COM fiche rows A to P (omitting I), columns 1 to 18.

To locate the positions, one of three different methods is commonly adopted. Before describing them, however, it should be noted that each fiche grid demands the use of different scales. The machine scans the same distance from top to bottom whether the rows are from A to C or A to G, and therefore the scales have to be changed appropriately. The systems are:

1 Two independent markers move along the letters and the numbers. Thus to find B3, the letter marker is aligned with B, the number marker

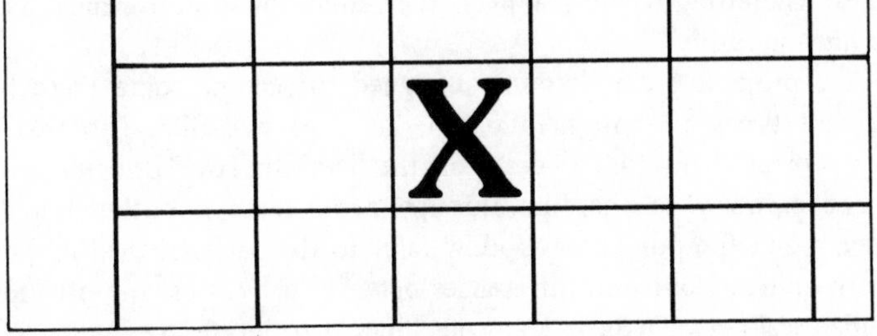

Figure 15. Microfiche: 'X' in frame B3

with 3. Usually this system requires the use of two independent controls operating horizontal (for numbers) and vertical (for letters) movements of the fiche carrier.

2 The carrier is moved until the selected letter and number are adjacent to or superimposed on each other.

3 A pointer attached to the carrier is pulled over a map of the grid which is attached to the reader. When it is placed over the selected square, the frame is ready to be viewed. Some machines provide facilities for interchange of maps for different fiche arrangements.

Cine projectors

The concept of movement produced by cine films is the result of a sensory phenomenon referred to as 'persistence of vision'. When an individual picture is seen, the details are registered in the brain and retained there for a short period of time. When another picture appears, that too is registered, and provided the frequency of the different pictures is above a certain level, they appear to represent a continuum, even though they are in fact rapidly changing. If there are slight changes between succeeding pictures, it appears that movement has taken place.

Cine film is just a series of still pictures, separated from each other by a thin black band, and the projector shows each one in turn. The black bands between each picture should not be seen. Thus the mechanism of a cine projector pulls a picture between the lamp and lens, projects it for a short time (one twenty-fourth of a second in the case of sound films), covers the lamp for a moment while it pulls the black line past and places the next picture in position, and then uncovers the lamp. Thus the movement of the film between lamp and lens is in practice a series of very rapid jerks and stops. In contrast, the film carries the sound record as a smooth continuous flow, and if it was replayed as a series of jerks, the ear would detect some distracting noises. Therefore, where it replays the sound, the projector must move the film smoothly.

Cine projectors are therefore designed to accommodate these two different types of movement on the same piece of film. Those which only project silent film operate on the 'jerk and stop' principle only.

The pathway of the film through a projector is outlined in the diagram and the points that follow refer to the parts labelled in figure 16. In spite of outward differences between projectors, the principles are identical between them. Many machines incorporate an extra sprocket drive wheel between the lower loop and the sound drum or pick-up head, and some free-running pulleys to change the direction of the film to the take-up reel.

1 The film on its reel should be attached so that the sprocket holes on it are on the right as seen from the projector lamp side.

2 Both sprocket drive wheels move at a continuous speed. The spikes on the edge of the wheels engage the sprocket holes, the first pulling the film into the projector, the second pulling it past the sound replaying area and out to the take-up reel. Because of the different size and spacing of the sprocket holes on the two different formats of 8mm film, these drive wheels have to be changed when the film type is changed (on projectors which allow this).

3 The loop here is essential to allow the film to be jerked through the gate below without breaking. By keeping the loop, the continuous feed from the wheel is changed into the jerk movement without mechanical tension in the film.

4 The film passes along a channel between the lamp and the lens. Ridges at the edge of the channel keep the line of the film exactly straight, and a spring-loaded pressure plate on the rear of the lens carrier keeps the film from coming out forwards. The film is pulled down by a claw which protrudes through a slot in the channel, engages a sprocket hole, pulls the film down and then releases it. Each pull down is the same distance as the height of a frame, so that an intermittent movement is caused by the slight interval between the claw releasing the film and another engaging the next sprocket hole up.

During the pause, the picture should be exactly in front of the hole in the channel through which the light from the lamp passes to the screen. If a black line appears at the top or bottom of the picture on the screen, the position of this hole has to be slightly altered. This is done by the frame control which may be a lever raising or lowering the hole position, or a screwing mechanism which does the same thing.

The movement of the claw and therefore of the film may be done manually with the drive motor off, although obviously not at the correct speed. This is done by turning a control called an inching knob or animator. If the film is placed in the channel by hand, rather than mechanically, it is advisable to move the film up and down slightly while turning the inching knob until the claw is heard and seen to engage the sprocket hole. This helps to reduce tearing of the film as it starts.

In dual format 8mm projectors, the channel with its slot for the claw and picture aperture has to be exchanged when changing between

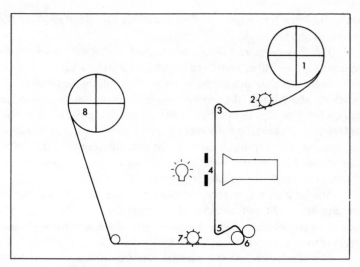

Figure 16. Stylized lacing diagram for 16mm projector (see text for interpretation of numbers)

standard and super 8. Film loops in cassettes work by the same principles, the pressure plate holding the film in the right position being built into the cassette itself.

5 The second loop plays a similar part to that of the first (no 3) in reverse. The film leaves the channel with intermittent motion, jerks and stops, and is pulled the rest of its journey by smooth continuous motion. In the absence of the loop, mechanical tension will break the film. Some projectors have an automatic loop former which senses the tension when it disappears and jerks sufficient out of the channel to remake it.

6 To replay sound, one of two methods is employed, depending on the manner of the recording. Magnetic recordings are 'read' by a head similar to that in audiotape recorders. Optical recordings are 'read' by light from a lamp passing through the transparent patterns on the sound track, the dimensions of the light being translated by a photo-electric cell into the noises recorded. For both to operate, it is essential that the film is kept very tightly against the head or drum or else the quality of the sound is defective.

7 The second drive wheel pulls the film continuously past the sound area at the set speed.

8 The take-up reel is driven by a belt at the same speed as the

drive wheel and wraps up the film constantly. This contrasts with the reel from which the film is started which runs freely.

Rewinding: Almost all projectors have a capacity for rewinding. Reverse wind through the projection path is slow, being at the standard speed of 24 frames per second on sound projectors. As the lamp can be turned on during the process, the amusing sight of backwards motion can be observed. All the sprocket drive wheels, including the claws, reverse their direction, the take-up reel free wheels and the starting wheel is driven to wind up the film.

When the rewind system is activated with the film outside the projection path, a gear has to be engaged if a high speed is required. When the film has been rewound, the gear must be disengaged.

Cassette loops cannot be rewound. They can only be moved in a forward direction.

Damaging the film: Poor projection is frequently the cause of film damage. The common points where this occurs are the following:

1 Sprocket drive wheels damage sprocket holes and film edges through faulty lacing and attachment.

2 The claws can cut the edges of the sprocket holes or across the film if it is not correctly placed in the channel.

3 The loss of the loops causes mechanical tension which will tear the film.

4 The failure to disengage the rewind gear will in some machines allow forward and reverse to operate simultaneously which will break the film.

Every instance of slight damage done to a film will be the site of a weakness during the future projections.

Automatic loading: A considerable number of projectors now incorporate a method of automatic loading. The leading edge of the film has to be trimmed, usually by a clip provided. When the film is inserted on to the sprocket wheel drive, with the motor on, it is automatically threaded, two curved levers forming the loops. If the film breaks or has to be removed during its projection, it is sometimes awkward to withdraw it.

Stop motion: Some projectors are supplied with a control which stops the film instantly. Unfortunately, this action does not always coincide with the film in the right position and the picture may not be seen because the shutter is covering the lamp. Turning the inching control will clear this. A heat filter is automatically introduced to prevent the frame burning, and this may mean that some refocusing is necessary.

Amplifier: The sound from the projector increases in volume to audible levels by means of an amplifier which is usually an integral part of the equipment. This is then connected to a loudspeaker which may also be within the projector or linked to it through a cable. Controls usually include an on/off switch, base and treble variables.

Lamps for all projectors

The power supply to projectors must be that for which the equipment has been designed, or adjustment has to be made. The lamp must be that listed in the operating manual. Some projectors have adaptations to increase the life of the lamp by operating at a lower voltage, which means that the equipment includes a transformer. If too high a voltage is passed through such a lamp it will break. Another possible adaptation is a control which allows the lamp to be used at two different levels of brightness. If the lower brightness is acceptable it should be used.

Changing the lamp is usually simple if the instructions in the manual are followed. Modern lamps should not be held by uncovered fingers as the grease causes a weakness in the glass cover.

Screens

The surface covering of the screen dictates the clarity of any pictures viewed. The brightness of the image is chiefly the result of the power of the lamp, but various factors concerned with the screen also have an effect. Principally these are the reflectivity of the surface, the amount of light which does not come from the projector that falls on it (called ambient light), and its position with relation to the viewers.

A matt white screen is a good reflector of light over a wide area. Other types, lenticular, beaded, high gain, have better reflective qualities, but these are only appreciated by viewers seated close to the centre line. Therefore, like rear projection screens, they are more suitable for small groups of viewers.

The reduction of ambient light is important. Where possible, hoods or covers are advisable to mask the screen if no other means of reducing it are available. Screens are like mirrors, and can distort if they are not correctly positioned. The surface of the screen should always be at right angles to the centre of the beam of light from the projector (or mirror if it is being reflected from one). If the projector is tilted upwards, then the top of the screen should be tilted forwards, or else the viewer will see a picture that is wider at the top than at the bottom. This distortion also causes some parts of the picture to be out of focus

106

because full focus of the whole image can only be produced if it is all in the same plane. Ideally, the edges of a screen should be slightly curved towards the projector so that the light rays on the outside of the beam also reach the screen at right angles. Correction of a picture that is wider on one side than the opposite is simply brought about by moving the wider side nearer the projector or the narrower side further away.

Magnetic tape players and recorders

Messages are recorded on tape by the magnetic realignment of particles on one surface. This action is brought about by changes in the magnetic flux on the head which rubs against the tape, the variations in that flux being caused by electronic translations of the signals entering the record circuits of the equipment electrically either from a microphone or from other electronic sources. As the flux alters, so does the alignment of the particles on the tape. Before the tape reaches the metal piece which conveys the message to the tape, it passes a similar piece which erases any sounds previously recorded on that part of the tape. This is done by transmitting a supersonic signal which realigns the particles.

During playback, the tape rubs against another or the same piece of metal, in this case inducing from the tape a direct replica of the flux that produced sound and/or video signals which a user can listen to and/or see. When the same piece of metal is used for both record and replay, there is an electronic switching which causes it to operate in the chosen manner, and this is selected by the controls operated by the user. The pieces of metal are referred to as 'heads', and thus there are present erase heads, record heads, and playback heads, the latter two sometimes being combined into one.

Equipment is designed to create the maximum fidelity between the recording made and the playback heard and/or seen. On the whole, the more expensive the equipment, the more faithful is the accuracy between the two. This is because of improved systems design to balance and correct possible distortions in the recording and playback systems. Generally it is the circuits involved in placing the message on the tape and reading it back afterwards which require these improvements and not the amplification of the message to an audible volume.

A number of international standards ensure compatibility between methods of recording and replay between machines. These apply universally to sound machines, but unfortunately there are a number of variations on video machines. Standards are more universally applicable within defined limits when the message moves from the video machine to the television set. One accepted standard throughout all sound and video equipment, however, is that the tape is recorded and replayed only when the tape is moving from left to right.

In the record or playback mode, magentic tape moves from the left reel to the right one at a fixed speed across the front of the heads, a series of spring pressure pads keeping the magnetized surface against them. The erase and record heads are activated in the record mode, the playback head in the playback mode. Only a certain area of tape is in contact with the heads, and great accuracy in levelling their plane is required to ensure that exactly the right portion is rubbing against them. If the wrong portion is in contact, the message is either absent or distorted. Because the ferrite material which makes up the heads is very delicate, great care must be taken not to break, scratch or knock them off their carrier. Friction between the head and the tape introduces wear which means that head replacement is sometimes necessary, and this should be carried out by a service engineer.

Although the spindle on which the collecting wheel rotates is driven round, this is mainly to keep the tension on the tape and ensure it is wound up. The delivery wheel usually runs freely. The movement of the tape is maintained at an even speed and pulled across the front of the heads by the rotation of the pinch wheel and the capstan which grip it. Variations in speed distort the signal; on sound equipment slow speeds deepen the noise, higher speeds cause higher pitch.

Amplifiers are attached to or are an integral part of tape players. They may have separate on/off switches, but the usual controls are volume and tone, the latter either combined or separate as base and treble. Slider controls tend to give a more sensitive response.

Soundtape equipment
Open reel tape recorders usually have a choice of speed, and the higher the speed the greater the area of tape on which the message is inscribed and hence the more faithful the reproduction quality. Thus a wide range of frequencies of sound are recorded and played back when the speed is increased. Because the various elements of the message have been spread over a wider area, editing between them can be done more easily. The three common speeds are 19cm/s (7½ips), 9.5cm/s (3¾ips), and 4.75cm/s (1⅞ips).

Cassette tape runs at one set speed, 4.75cm/s (1⅞ips) only, and there are therefore theoretical limits to reproductive quality. However, recent improvements to the quality of the tape and more especially to the electronics involved in recording and playback have meant that there is little practical difference in quality between the cassette and the fastest open reel.

The number of tracks recorded on a tape depends on the type of heads used. By looking at the head, the user can see if there are two pieces of metal attached with little separation between them or whether there is only one. Two pieces indicate that the machine is capable of four-track or stereo replay, one piece means that it is limited to two-track or mono only. The exception to this is the arrangement on the heads for tape-slide cassettes, the head arrangement being described later on page 116.

Figure 17 numbers the tracks and indicates their width on recordings made on open reel tape recorders. On the heads, the recording ferrites are placed for track 1 in mono or tracks 1 and 3 in stereo or four-track. Thus to play track 2 or tracks 2 and 4 respectively, the tape is wound straight through on to the take-up spool, lfited off and placed upside down on the delivery spindle and played through again. By doing this, on mono equipment, track 2 is now where track 1 was, on stereo equipment track 4 is where track 1 was and track 2 where track 3 was. The tape is now travelling the opposite way, hence the direction of the arrows.

If a four-track tape with messages on each track is played on a mono or two-track machine, examination of the area covered by the playback head will indicate that sound will be reproduced simultaneously from track 1 and track 2, the latter of course backwards. If the tape is wound through and turned over, then track 4 and track 3 backwards will be replayed. On the other hand, if a two-track tape is played on a four-track machine, examination of the heads will indicate that half track 1 will be reproduced, surprisingly producing little distortion from the original recording. Should this machine operate, however, as a fixed stereo recorder, then the lower head will reproduce part of the mono track 2 backwards at the same time.

Implicit in the comment in the last paragraph is that there is a difference between a stereo machine and a four-track one. In the former case both tracks 1 and 3, or tracks 4 and 2, play simultaneously, the first track number of each pair being reproduced through the left-hand speaker, the second through the right-hand speaker. Four-track machines on the other hand treat each track as a separate mono entity,

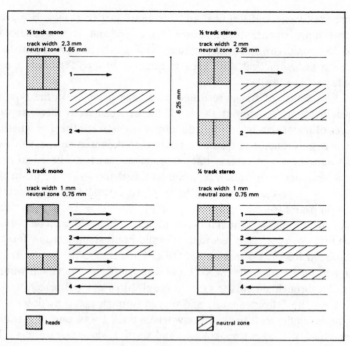

Figure 17. Open reel tape: track layout and dimensions

a switch providing the user with the ability to select track 1 and 4 *or* 3 and 2 depending on which way the tape is going. On some machines, the mode of the four separate tracks or stereo pairs, each track independently controlled for volume and tone, is selectable. This provides a facility whereby for example, a commentary can be recorded on track 1, background music independently on track 3, and then the pair played back simultaneously, their relative volumes separately modified.

In cassette tape recorders, the layout of the tracks is shown in figure 18. The very thin heads and even thinner separation between them are worth noting. In this arrangement the situation is much simpler. With the exception of cassette machines used for language laboratory work or in tape-slide presentations, the heads record and playback either stereo or mono only. There is no separate selection for the four tracks. Thus when side one is playing, track 1 (mono) or tracks 1 and 2 (stereo) are being used. When the cassette is turned over, the tape is

110

travelling in the opposite direction, track 2 (mono) or tracks 3 and 4 (stereo) being used. An examination of the arrangement of the heads will indicate that if a stereo recording is played on mono equipment, both the tracks, for example tracks 1 and 2 (stereo), will be covered by the mono head and the whole recording will be replayed. Similarly, if a mono cassette is replayed on a stereo machine, the two heads will cover almost all the recording and it will be reproduced virtually perfectly, although of course only in mono. Stereo reproduction means that the output from tracks 1 and 4 are transmitted through the left-hand speaker, tracks 2 and 3 through the right-hand one depending on the direction of the tape. Thus in contrast to open reel tapes, mono and stereo recorded cassettes are fully compatible with each other in terms of equipment on which they are played. It is worth noting that

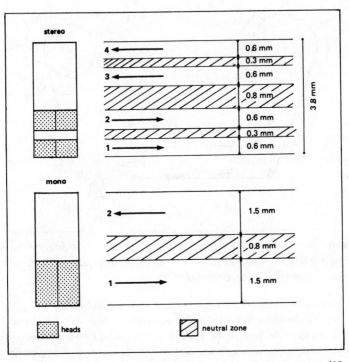

Figure 18. Compact cassette: track layout and dimensions (Note: numbering begins from the lower edge)

111

terms of equipment on which they are played. It is worth noting that the playing heads are on the bottom of their carrier, so that track 4 is at the top and track 1 at the bottom.

Outline figures (19 and 20) show the layout of open reel and cassette recording and playback arrangements. In open reel machines, the tape is laced so that it rests against the heads. When either record or playback modes are engaged, pressure pads and the pinch wheel are brought forward to maintain this firm contact. In contrast, when the cassette has been inserted, the heads are separated from the tape. Engaging record or playback modes causes the shift plate to carry the two heads and the pinch wheel to press against the tape, the pressure pad inside the cassette and the capstan spindle forming the other half of the sandwich. The pinch wheel can be moved in this way as it is a free wheel, the drive being provided by the capstan spindle.

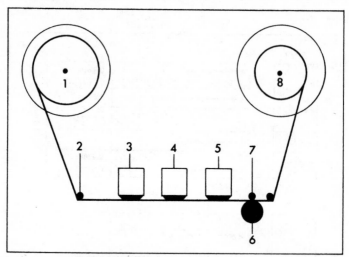

Figure 19. Open reel machine: pathway of tape — 1=delivery wheel; 2=tape guide; 3=erase head; 4=record head; 5=replay head; 6=pinch wheel; 7=capstan; 8=take-up reel

Erasure of previous messages on the tracks selected for recording is performed by the erase head quite adequately, although there may be some background hiss. Total erasure can be done more thoroughly by special equipment called bulk eraser, which produces a strong magnetic field when switched on. Erasure is complete over the whole tape within a few seconds.

112

Recording can be from a microphone or from electrical sources as the radio, other tape recorders, record player or electronic boxes. Microphones are not discussed in this book, nor is it practical to describe the channels of connection between other equipment and the tape recorder as these will vary between models. The point to note, however, is the impedance values (a term referring to resistance between interconnected devices, matching being achieved when the output impedance of one is within acceptable limits of the input impedance of the other) of the interconnecting machines. These must match to prevent distortion or in extreme cases potential damage. Consulting manuals will provide the relevant answers. Care should also be taken in matching impedance with external speakers and headphones. For user safety, the latter should be medium or high impedance.

The controls on the deck of a tape recorder which switch on the

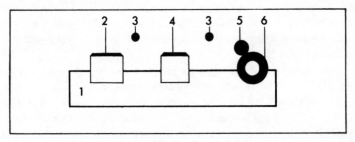

Figure 20. Cassette recorder/player: heads and pins – 1=shift plate; 2=erase head; 3=guide pin; 4=recording and playback head; 5=capstan; 6=rubber pinch wheel

record mode should be noted, so that accidental operation is avoided. A common system involves the simultaneous operation of two controls, that marked for record and also that for normal play. If there are dials to indicate the record level, these will usually light up. In their absence, small indicator lamps may be illuminated. The level of recording is shown by the dials or a magic eye (two bars of green which move towards each other as a sound is made), the optimum level being when the needle just fails to cross into the red area, or in the case of the magic eye the two green bars just fail to touch. Recorders with manual control can have this level continuously adjusted as the sound varies in volume, but in most there is an alternative system known as AGC (automatic gain control), which adjusts the recording level automatically to an even balance, based on the total volume of signals from all

113

sources being received. Where the recorder has separate heads for record and replay, it is usually possible to listen to the quality of the recording being made just afterwards by monitoring the sound from the replay head. The same principles apply to both open reel and cassette equipment, although in the latter it will be recalled that a recording cannot be made in the absence of the appropriate plastic lug on the rear of the cassette.

Some cassettes are recorded with the Dolby system, and the sign $\square\mathbb{C}$ will be noted on the cassette or its container. The Dolby system is an electronic device to reduce the background hiss that is endemic with tape recorders, particularly when the tape speed is low as it is with cassettes. It operates through a particular compression of the recorded frequencies. Many cassette recorders have the Dolby sign marked on them to indicate that the circuit is present to correct automatically the distortion to provide nearly perfect reproduction. If a Dolby recorded tape is replayed on a machine without this circuit, the quality of sound is still adequate and some slight improvement is possible by increasing the treble control.

While theoretically any cassette recorder can be used with a microcomputer, it is wiser to use one which is recommended. The important factors are the volume control which is frequently critical for effective transfer of information between the recorder and the computer, and the capability of the computer to interface with the motor control of the machine. Signals from the computer can then start the recorder and stop it after the program has been loaded. Some recorders are made with a switch that can be used to change its bias from audio to computer, and this can be helpful as it provides an evenness of response. If a transfer is taking place without an automatic disabling of the internal loudspeaker of the recorder, the user will hear a very unpleasant and loud noise. This can be eliminated by inserting a jack plug into the earphone socket on the recorder as this does disable the speaker.

Finally, in this section, a few words about a number of controls and special phrases which help in understanding the mechanism of soundtape recorders/players.

An *odometer* or revolution counter is often present. This consists of a series of three or four digits which revolve like a milometer in a car, but unlike that can be set to zero by an adjacent button. Unfortunately, they are not standardized between machines, although it would be comparatively easy to do this for cassettes where the size of the spool on which the tape winds is fixed. The digits indicate the number of

114

revolutions of the spool, usually the right hand or take-up one, which of course is not directly proportional to either length of the tape or time, for as more tape is wound on, the spool turns slower and each revolution collects more tape. If they were standardized and accurate both at play and fast speeds, the odometer reading could be used to identify points on the tape just like the numbered pages of a book. Where similar models are used throughout a library, rough accuracy is possible. A recent development in both sound and video recorders is the appearance of an odometer which counts in minutes/seconds/ tenths of seconds. These may be printed numbers or use an illuminated display, and naturally there will be compatibility between these.

Fast rewind and *fast forward* operations permit a tape to be delivered or rewound at high speed. In open reel machines, there is some wear on the heads when this happens, as the tape brushes against them, but in cassette machines this does not occur as the heads are withdrawn. The drive is by the centre spindle through the collecting spool and not by the capstan spindle and pinch wheel.

The *pause control* causes an application of the brakes on the tape drive mechanism and during its use the tape should not travel forward at all. This should only be applied during normal play or record, not when the tape is being driven at speed.

The next three items refer to specifications on the performance of equipment. *Frequency response* is a measure of the range of sound that can be replayed. The ear of a normal young child can hear sounds between 15 and 20,000 Hertz, but in the adult the band becomes progressively narrower. Equipment for listening to music should offer 40 to 15,000 Hertz and anything with a narrower band than 50 to 10,000 is not really acceptable even for dialogue alone. Variations from this should be less than ± 2 db (decibels).

Signal to noise ratio is a measure of the balance of recorded signal and the background hiss and machine induced noise. Measured in decibels, it should be −50 db or more (ie minus more db). Inexpensive tape recorders may be specified at −45 db which is tolerable but irritating.

Wow and flutter are terms referring to the distortions of sound caused by slow or fast running of the tape. Acceptable measures are less than 0.2%, the better quality machines giving 0.05%.

Tape-slide equipment
Increasingly popular is the system known as tape-slide (or slide-tape) which involves signals from a tape recorder causing the automatic

changing of slides. Thus it is possible to synchronize sound recordings with still pictures, and reproduce this audiovisual programme on demand. The system requires a fully automatic slide projector, the cable from the tape system being inserted into the socket into which the remote control lead is otherwise placed. While there are systems for use with open reel equipment, the common ones involve special cassette recorders. As the system only depends on the introduction of a special signal on the recording, the format of the tape is the same as that used in other recordings.

The system requires the addition of circuits and a record/playback head. The same head is used both to put the signal or pulse on the tape and also to recognize it and thus instigate the passage of an electric signal to the slide projector. A control is necessary to switch the head between the record and replay modes.

In open reel systems a pulsing box is placed against the side of the tape recorder, the position not being critical but roughly as shown in figure 21. The tape is wound round the special head on the box between the recorder's heads and the take-up spool. When switched into the record mode, a pulse may be recorded on the tape on the bottom track. Because the tape recorder is independent of the pulsing box, the programme may be listened to as the pulses are recorded. When playback is required, the box should be placed as nearly as possible in the same place so that the signal is sent to the projector at the same point in the programme as it was recorded. While the system shown in the diagram is one provided by a particular supplier, the principle is the same with equipment made by other manufacturers.

The system differs in cassette systems insofar as the head used for pulses is on the same carrier as the sound record/playback head. In order that pulses can be recorded while the programme is being heard, the head can be activated for record while the rest of the head and the recorder is in the playback mode. The protection against accidental recording does not operate for pulse recording. The box may be part of the recorder or separate, but the operations are independent of the rest of the machine. From the recorder to the slide projector, the signals from the pulses go through the box, the final cable going from this part of the system.

Inspection of the heads of cassette recorders will indicate whether it is capable of being used for a tape-slide system. The heads must cover both tracks 1 and 2 (stereo) or 1 (mono) and at least track 4. Tracks 3 and 4 are sometimes covered by a continuous head. The allocation of

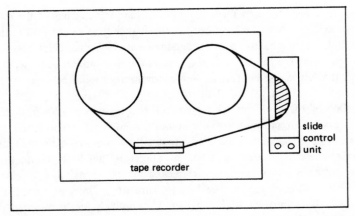

Figure 21. Arrangement of synchronization box for tape-slide using an open-reel tape recorder

tracks is now covered by an international standard:[4] tracks 1 and 2 for narrative, sound effects etc; tracks 3 and 4 for cue tones (pulses for synchronizing).

The frequency and duration of pulses or cue tones follow an international standard and have the following characteristics:

— For slide change: a frequency of 1000 Hertz (1 kiloHertz), the duration being 450 milliseconds.

— For automatic switch off: a frequency of 1000 Hertz, the duration being two seconds.

— For tape pause (see below): a frequency of 150 Hertz, the duration being 450 milliseconds.

Tape pause is a control which stops the tape automatically while the slide may continue to be viewed. Very useful in education, it gives the producer of the programme the opportunity to set the user a problem to be resolved, with the tape stopped for as long as it takes to complete. Usually a small red light glows on the recorder to indicate that the pause is operating, a restart button near to it ready to be pressed when the user is prepared to continue.

Another common system initiated by Philips provides for a slide change of 1000 Hertz of unlimited duration (this is governed by the length of time the finger is on the buttom) but no cue tone for tape pause.

Another international standard specifies the manner in which a tape-slide programme commences. This states that the first slide is

117

shown on the screen by manual control of the projector before the tape is started, the first cue tone causing the first slide to be changed to the second. Unfortunately, some programmes are available which adopt a system in which the first cue tone causes the first slide to be projected, and this can cause confusion. New programmes should be designed in line with the international standard.

One of the problems with tape-slide programmes results from the fact that at present most systems do not rewind synchronically. When a cassette tape is rewound the heads are usually withdrawn from the tape, so that cue tones cannot be picked up. Therefore they have no effect on the projector. Even if they were picked up, the signal they produce induces a slide change in the forward direction. The speed normally involved in rewinding is such that it would be unlikely for the projector to complete a change before the next cue tone passed its signal. Currently no attempts are being made to resolve this problem at an economic price.

Tape-filmstrip systems are also available, but there are few common standards of operation between the various pieces of equipment. Librarians will therefore have difficulties of compatibility if they purchase documents in this format.

Tape-microfiche
With the recent development of colour microfiche, there are discussions under way which suggest that colour slides might be reproduced in this format, particularly where they are used for private or small group viewing. This had led to the development of a tape-microfiche system, similar in programme construction to a tape-slide. The development is not widely marketed, but it offers some advantages. Because the cue tone is individual to each frame on the fiche, the order of the pictures can be altered without any change of the fiche itself. The speed of frame change is so fast that there is virtually no visible gap in viewing, eliminating the short blackout during change with slide projectors. A further advantage is that the present system is linked to a standard stereo cassette tape recorder, special heads not being required. This development is an exciting one for librarians as the storage/retrieval problem for a colour microfiche and cassette tape is so much less than for a set of slides and a tape.

Videotape equipment
Videotape stores signals which require a television set to replay. The domestic TV set receives its picture via an aerial plugged into an aerial

socket. This signal is commonly referred to as RF (radio frequency), and a set like this is known as a 'receiver'. However, the signal from a videotape recorder may be transmitted into the television set through a circuit which bypasses that used by the message through the aerial. This alternative access is referrred to as a video-input, and a set having one is usually referred to as a 'monitor'. Two types are common, one which receives a mixed signal called composite video which is the common source from cameras and videorecorders and the other called RGB (red, green, blue) which can be obtained from computers.

Because video cassette recorders of whatever system (see page 84), were designed for the domestic market, they connect normally through the aerial socket of the receiver. Alternative video connections are available. Some of these recorders have the added facility of a built-in tuner, that is they have the capacity to record a transmission on any selected channel directly from the signal received by the aerial. The receiver does not have to be switched on for this, and of course the user can record one channel whilst viewing another.

After a TV set receives its signal, electronic circuitry translates it into sound and pictures. In Britain, all television signals are trans-mitted in colour, and monochrome receivers show a black and white version of this. In colour receivers, the information received activates three different electronic 'guns' at the rear of the tube, one responsible for exciting red phosphors, another for blue and the other for green. The phosphors are fixed to the inside of the screen of the tube. To illuminate them the 'guns' scan in horizontal lines across the screen starting from the top left hand corner, and in Britain completing 625 lines before reaching the bottom. This is UHF transmission, the older VHF system having 405 lines to complete. The whole scan is completed 25 times every second, the controls over this scanning being delicate and achieved magnetically. Certain adjustments can be made to govern the size of the picture, the brightness of the illumination and the character of the colouring of the phosphors. Most other variations in the picture are the result of the transmission and interference between the masts which radiate it and the aerial attached to the set receiving it.

The system of the signal transmitted in Britain is called PAL. This is one of three such systems, the others being NTSC and SECAM. Dif-ferent nations have chosen different systems, the most significant supporters being shown here.

NTSC USA, Canada, West Indies, Japan, Peru, Taiwan
PAL Argentina, Australia, Austria, Belgium, Chile, Denmark,

Finland, West Germany, Italy, Hong Kong, Jordan, Nether-
lands, New Zealand, Nigeria, Norway, Singapore, South
Africa, Spain, Sweden, Switzerland, UK, Yugoslavia
SECAM   Bulgaria, Czechoslovakia, Egypt, France, East Germany,
Hungary, Iran, Poland, USSR.

With few exceptions, the field frequency for SECAM and PAL is
50 Hertz and uses 625 lines. In contrast, NTSC has a field frequency of
60 Hertz and uses 525 lines. These differences increase the problems of
compatibility, and the simple rules of thumb are: without the intervention of converters, NTSC programmes cannot be played with PAL
and SECAM equipment, and vice versa: PAL and SECAM can be interchanged but with the loss of colour. This means that tapes made in
America and Canada cannot be played in Europe and Australasia unless
conversion takes place. Some videotape recorders and monitors have
switches for conversion standards, but these are not very common.

The discussion so far has been limited to the receiver and monitor.
To project the message on the tube, the signals transmitted to the aerial
are complex. They include not only the audio signal but also visual
information, scanning for 625 lines and colour instructions. These same
instructions are recorded on the videotape, together with a number
more to ensure synchronization of the picture, so the system is a great
deal more complex than for sound recording.

The pathway of the tape is similar to that on sound recorders, from
the left-hand reel past the heads to the right-hand reel. However, there
are important variations. The method of contact with the heads differs
between models but generally involves a tight winding against them
rather than the use of pressure pads. While there is a capstan spindle/
pinch wheel driving system, it is placed between the delivery spool and
the heads, not after them, and is used to draw the tape from the spool.
The drive of the take-up spool pulls the tape past the heads. Thus the
tension over the heads and the speed and position of the tape is dependent on the relative speed between the two drives.

Apart from those using the quadruplex system with 2in tape for
broadcasting purposes, all videotape recorders work on the so-called
helical scan system. This means that the recording is made across a
slope, higher at the front, lower at the rear. By this method, as large a
surface area as possible is involved in holding the recorded signals. It
has a further implication, the tape having to move upwards over the
heads. Thus the take-up reel is normally on a higher horizontal plane
than the delivery one.

Not only does the tape move past the heads, the carrier which usually carries two heads also revolves at high speed. The same heads are responsible for recording and replaying the programme, depending on the mode being selected. The heads themselves are more delicate than those used in sound tape recorders and are readily destroyed through contact with rough surfaces and mishandling. Before the heads is a stationary erase head which is activated when the record mode is in operation. The input for recording may come from cameras, another videotape recorder, a receiver or monitor or direct from the aerial. Those from cameras, videotape recorders and monitors are direct video inputs which produce a more faithful recording of the original message than RF inputs.

On open reel recorders, once the tape is laced, turning on the machine produces instant replay. With cartridges and cassette recorders, there is a pause while the tape is automatically partially extracted from the container and laced around the heads before replay commences. In cassette recorders, there is frequently an additional adjustment before the tape is laced while the cassette itself is mechanically moved into position. The reverse occurs when the user wishes to stop the tape. Open reel tapes can be lifted off or rewound; cartridges are rewound back into the container before they can be released from the equipment; cassettes remain in the recorder while the tape is mechanically removed from the heads and they can then be removed, the position of the tape being in exactly the same position as it was when the machine was stopped.

Because of the complexity of the signals, most of them are automatically balanced by the equipment. Sound and colour signals are modulated internally, and any changes that the user requires should be done at the receiver or monitor. However, the range of external controls on videocassette recorders have increased considerably in the last few years, although they seem to have reached their peak now. Some of these are available on remote control pads which may be wired to the recorder or interact with it via pulses of infrared light. If both the television receiver and the videotape recorder operate on this latter system, then it is possible to get interference between the two signals and the wrong machine responding.

Many of the controls are similar to those found on the audiocassette recorder, but there are frequently additional ones to increase the versatility of the equipment and also deal with the visual elements. There is always an on/off switch for mains power into the machine, a forward or

121

play control, a stop control, fast rewind and fast forward, a control for recording interlocked with forward for simultaneous activation and an odometer (see page 114) to measure the revolutions of the take-up reel. There is also a control to eject the cassette which cannot be activated if the tape has not been released from the heads. Additional controls that are found on some machines include a pause or still picture feature, the former causing the tape to stop with no picture on the screen while the latter does the same with the picture in sight; picture search, which may have variable speeds, may be independent from the fast forward/fast rewind but on the other hand may be locked to them so that it only operates in play mode; slow motion. If a connection to an aerial is made, most videocassette recorders can record in the absence of the user and therefore have programme selection and timer controls, usually being able to start and stop the recording at the beginning and end of the transmission. Linked to this can be found indicators showing what place on the tape a particular recording was started and a 'go to' command which will wind the tape there automatically. On some, there is even an indicator which will show how much tape is left before the end.

Further controls may include colour lock, skew and tracking. Colour lock is usually automatic and is probably better left alone. Skew is adjusted to correct distortion in the upper part of the picture. Tracking may be adjusted if the picture appears with band distortions in the middle or at the top and bottom edges. The accuracy of picture reproduction is dependent on the relative speeds of the heads and the tape passage. By a number of sensors this is usually maintained accurately but automatic corrections may introduce visual defects, and the tracking control affects the head and tape speeds to modify these corrections.

All domestic videocassette recorders have tuners built in so that they can be arranged to select the various broadcast channels. U-Matic systems are made without this facility. In addition certain machines have electronic editing facilities and the appropriate controls. It is important to note that videotape should never be cut and taped, either for repair or for editing purposes, as this will damage the delicate heads. Instead, this is done by electronically adding to the end (assembly edit) or placing in the middle of a sequence (insert edit), and the more sophisticated machines offer these facilities. Many also provide controls for recording the user's own soundtrack alongside the pictures.

Sound from television productions is notoriously poor, and this is also true of videorecordings. However, there is a growing interest in improving this. Stereo facilities are being provided on certain television

122

sets and also from some recorders, and for some time the user has had the option of bypassing the sound channels from the recorder to adjacent hi-fi audio equipment. Now some videocassette recorders have introduced noise reduction systems like Dolby (see page 114) which the user may switch in for his recording. However, the level of improvement can never be very great until the electronics are generally improved for the space on the tape for audiorecording is 0.35mm at best compared with 0.6mm on an audiocassette, and the tape speeds which govern the frequency are so slow. Compare those in table 3 (page 84) with that of the audiocassette of 47.5mm/sec.

Finally, implicit in this discussion has been the principle of interchangeability between colour and black and white (monochrome) recordings. No difference is evident on the tape itself, nor can visual inspection determine whether there is a recording at all. If the videotape recorder is designed to record colour signals, then it will do so if the source of those signals is in colour. This is also the case if the recording is made from a broadcast transmission obtained through an aerial, even if the receiver is monochrome. The replay is naturally of the same colour signals but to see pictures in colour it is necessary for the receiver or monitor to be a colour set. All videocassette recorders currently marketed record and play back in colour.

Microcomputer
The appearance of this equipment in large numbers in domestic and educational settings in recent years makes it necessary for the library to consider storage of magnetic disks and cassettes which carry computer programs. Only microcomputers will be discussed here, as it is unlikely that general library work will involve the storage and retrieval of programs for more powerful machines.

Information is stored on disks and cassettes magnetically, and has to be loaded into the computer before use. As each computer model has its own system, there are difficulties in interchanging materials and any storage system has to be used with the appropriate equipment. Cassettes as stores are common because they are inexpensive and the equipment needed is a relatively cheap cassette player. However, as the programs are held serially, that is one item or bit of information after another along the length of the tape, it is a slow method of storage, and it also takes some time to find any individual program if several are stored on one tape. In contrast, the disk storage system is much quicker to access, indeed almost instantaneous, and eight items or bits of information are loaded at the same time, a system described as parallel. However, the disks are more expensive and the equipment necessary, disk drives, cost considerably more than the cassette players. After a disk has been inserted into the drive, label side upwards, the door flap is closed and the read/write head comes into close proximity to the head slot. Under the control of instructions from the computer, the disk is revolved inside its protective cover, the head moving along its slot until the program that is to be read or the place where it is to be stored is located.

The backing store equipment, either cassette player or disk drive, (see figure 22) is attached to the appropriate sockets of the computer which are usually marked for this purpose. Also attached to the computer will be a keyboard, usually part of it, and a television set referred to as a VDU (visual display unit). While a television receiver is acceptable, greater clarity of viewing is obtainable from a monitor. Other devices or peripherals may form part of the system as for example a printer, but these will not be discussed here. Parts or all of this equipment may be permanently fixed together in one container.

When a computer is switched on, it comes under the control of its operating system which monitors and organizes all the various functions of the circuits. The operating system is held in a ROM (read only memory), one of the integrated circuits attached to the board. One or more of these may be involved in carrying this information. As particular models of computers develop, one of the features that are improved is the operating system, and usually programs that were usable with an early system are acceptable to an improved one. Occasionally this upward compatibility does not happen.

Controlling the loading of the information from the backing store are either a cassette operating system (COS) or a disk operating system (DOS). These too are stored in ROMs and subject to improvement and change. Upward compatibility in these cases is less common, and especially with disks, the identity number of the disk operating system for a particular program can be essential information.

As the information is loaded from the backing store into the computer, it is transferred to the RAM (random access memory). Unlike the ROMs referred to above, the RAM is automatically emptied and the program lost when the power to the computer is switched off. Of course it is still present in the backing store and can be reloaded at any time. The size of the RAM is critical to its ability to accept the program that is being loaded. The measurement of the size is given in K (Kilobytes), one K being 1024 bytes of information, a byte being eight bits

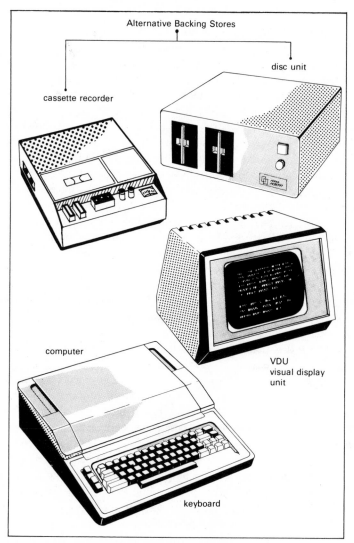

Figure 22. Parts of microcomputer system

or individual items. Knowing that the memory size of the computer is, for example, 16K does not necessarily mean that all the memory is available for the program. Other parts of the computer's operation may also be stored in the RAM in its working state, and this reduces the space that the program can occupy. Depending on the model, part of the disk operating system, the screen mapping instructions, language interpreter, networking system are examples of other information that may be temporarily transferred to the RAM. Sometimes it is possible to relocate sections of this memory but this will depend on the computer. However, it is important to know whether a program being loaded will fit into the memory, and this should be part of the information on the label.

Once the program is in the RAM, the computer can be instructed by the user to cause it to work or run. If the program was written in one of the many high-level languages like BASIC or PASCAL, the computer system has to translate the information into a form that it recognizes by having present the appropriate compiler or interpreter of that language. Unfortunately, languages too have been the subject of development and improvement and for some like BASIC there are now several different dialects. If the computer does not have the appropriate translation system for the language in which the program was written, it will not run. Even relying on the manufacturer is not always secure as upward compatibility has not necessarily been maintained.

If the program is acceptable to the computer, there is usually little difficulty in loading it from the backing store and using it effectively. However, general guidelines on the way in which a user controls a computer are difficult as each model has its own idiosyncrasies and particular instructions. Facilities too vary and have to be elicited from handbooks. This is a field that is rich in new developments, the processing circuits themselves subject to radical improvements in the near future as they increase in power from eight bit to sixteen and thirty-two bit operation. It is to be hoped that the problems of compatibility are tackled as the developments take place. One of the more pertinent changes will be the appearance of a new form of backing store known as a ROM pack. In this system, the programs will be 'written' directly into a read only memory which will be plugged into the computer. More robust than disks, faster in operation than cassettes, and used in some videogame players, they may well replace many of the current systems of distribution when they appear.

Plastic
Two types of equipment are involved in dealing with the formats described under this heading, the overhead projector and the disc or record player.

The overhead projector
This is similar in principle to a film projector, lamp light passing through a lens, the transparent plastic film, and a mirror system to reach the

screen. The mirror system which is positioned vertically above the centre of the film has the sole function of turning the beam of light towards the screen behind the speaker. At the same time it ensures that the picture has the correct orientation on the screen. The lens between the lamp and the transparent film is made to the Fresnel design. This is a system by which the curved convex lens is produced on as flat a plane as possible, and is made as a series of circles of the correct curvature set one inside the other. The lens so produced is not as high a quality as the full convex lens and is liable to produce distorted colouration at the edges.

The user works at the side of the machine facing away from the screen, placing the film on the glass platform or stage in the correct orientation for reading. When the lamp is switched on, the light travels through the film into the mirror system and on to the screen, focusing being done by raising or lowering the mirror system with respect to the stage. The heat generated by the lamp is dispersed by a fan, which must be in operation during viewing. Almost all projectors now use low-voltage lamps and a transformer must be present within the machine to adjust for this. A further control is responsible for varying the brightness of the lamp, and to reduce costs it is advisable to use the reduced setting if that provides adequate lighting.

The record player

The recording on a disc is in the form of waves and troughs on the side of the groove. In a mono recording, the waves are usually on one side only, but in stereo the left-hand wall holds the curves for the left-hand channel and the right-hand wall for the right-hand channel. The movements required by the needle or stylus in the stereo system are at right angles to each other and the distortion so produced in two directions is differentiated in the cartridge which carries the stylus. Because the movements require some flexibility in the stylus, it is essential that the correct type is fitted. A mono stylus and cartridge will not respond to both movements and will tend to damage the right-hand channel. Thus if a stereo record is to be played on a mono recorder, a special cartridge should be used.

The stylus is triangular in shape with a rounded tip, usually made of a chip of sapphire or diamond. The latter is preferred as it lasts much longer. The radius of the tip is about .0007in. A more expensive stylus can be obtained with the tip in the shape of an ellipse; this fits the curves of the groove more exactly.

127

The vibrations of the stylus are turned into electrical signals by the cartridge. Two systems are commonly available for this, ceramic and magnetic. In the former, two piezo crystals are distorted by the vibrations of the stylus, producing small electrical pulses. This is a cheap and strong cartridge but compared to the magnetic one it does not follow the groove so well and tends to introduce cross-talk between the two channels. If these probems are reduced, the cost exceeds that of the magnetic cartridge. This is more delicate, working by the vibrations of the needle introducing fluctuating magnetic fields which produce a current. It is more expensive and frequently is so manufactured that a worn stylus means the change of the complete cartridge.

As the stylus follows the groove, the cartridge and the pick-up arm are pulled across the record. There is no drive across, and various forces act on the arm to prevent a satisfactory flow through the channel. Thus the stylus has to be kept in the groove by sufficient weight but not too much to damage the walls; a ceramic cartridge needs a larger weight than the magnetic one. There is also a distortion effect due to friction which pulls the arm towards the centre and is compensated for by a bias. In good quality record-players these forces are balanced out in the construction of the pick-up arm and the recommended adjustments.

The sounds produced by means of the pick-up arm and the cartridge are then transferred electrically to an amplifier and thence to loudspeakers or headphones. The quality of sound depends on the shape of the stylus, which deteriorates through use, the accuracy of the shape of the groove, which is gradually worn away, the weight of the stylus so that it rides in the groove at an optimum pressure, and the speed at which it travels. Wear of the stylus or the groove can only be improved by replacement, the average life of a diamond stylus being the replay of 1000 sides. Some record players have weight adjustment controls on the counterbalance end of the arm, but corrections should only be undertaken with reference to scales. Any variations of speed of the turntable are the result of mechanical faults and require adjustment by an engineer.

For improved care of discs and use of the equipment, additional facilities are useful. A lever to lift and lower the stylus on to the disc obviates potential damage caused by the stylus hitting the disc too hard or at an angle, the latter causing scratching which destroys the edges of the groove. A reject control causes immediate raising of the arm, the turntable stopping as it returns to its resting position. When the stylus reaches a certain point, about 54mm (2¾in) from the centre of the disc, automatic raising of the arm and return to rest, the turntable stopping afterwards, is a common facility.

On some equipment, it is possible to play a stack of discs one after the other. This can introduce two potential defects and thus should be discouraged. When the groove on one disc lies against that of another, the friction between them induces wear and damage to their edges. There is also a drag effect which will introduce variations in speed and consequent distortion.

Laserdiscs
As laserdiscs are the only form of videodisc player currently available commercially in Britain, it is the only one that can be discussed here. Some description will also be given of the new compact disc for audio replay as this works on the same principle.

The recording on these discs is in the form of a series of pits in the surface of a reflective layer of material which is covered by a further layer of transparent plastic. Such recordings can be made on both sides of the disc, although compact discs are initially being produced with them on one side only. A short focus helium neon laser beam is focused on the surface of the disc and the shape and depth of the pits cause its reflection to be distorted. After being reflected back through a series of lenses, the distortions in the beam are registered by a photodiode which changes them into electrical pulses. These are interpreted by the electronics, amplified as appropriate and transmitted as signals to speakers or screen. The presence of other items on the disc surface like grease or scratch marks is ignored because they are out of focus of the beam. While the word laser can be construed as dangerous, there are many different powers of this instrument, and the one in this device is not powerful enough to produce any damage at all.

The disc is enclosed inside the player when it is being used and cannot be watched or touched at this time. This is because the videodisc revolves at a very high speed, 1500 revolutions per minute at its maximum, while the compact disc has a revolution speed between 200 and 500 per minute. Some noise comes from this speed of movement but this is masked in use. From the coded information analysed from the videodisc, the player can interpret where it is on the recording, produce sound in two separate channels, written information like teletext, which can be superimposed on the pictures, and the visual information itself. There are currently no record facilities, and if they are developed

129

commercially, they will allow for one recording per disc. It will not be possible to erase the pits and start again.

To produce television playback from the disc, the player is connected either to a receiver through the aerial socket or to a monitor through the video input. If full stereo sound is required, it is possible to connect the player's audio signals to the auxiliary input of a hi-fi system, although stereo television sets are also now being produced. Speakers and amplifier are not supplied with the compact disc players, but it is simple to attach them to existing equipment.

Playback of long play videodiscs offers the user few facilities. It is possible to do a fast search through the disc to find a particular sequence, and there is an index system. This assigns a number to each frame of the picture and the user is able to superimpose these to aid identification.

In the active play mode, the extra facilities of this system emerge. Speed of movement can be varied over a wide range and in both directions, and there is an almost perfect still picture. Each sound channel can be independently selected, and therefore each can be used for different purposes. Full teletext facilities are also provided. A further feature is the chapter and frame identification system. Each sequence may be described as a chapter and each frame has an individual identity. At the beginning of each chapter, a short description of what follows can appear on the screen together with a listing of numbers of the more significant frames. It is then possible to key in the number of the passage or frame that is required, and this will be located at high speed and with complete accuracy. On some machines there is also a port through which communication with a microcomputer can be made, so that full interaction between a computer program and the videodisc can be introduced.

The compact audiodisc is a standard laser format. The players offer the user a number of extra facilities which make access and use more convenient. One control gives the user instant movement from one track to another across the recording, but at times of uncertainty it also offers the facility of fast forward or reverse through a particular track. Pause and memory controls are further facilities. There is also a visual display panel on the player which can give the user information on the track number that is being played, how long it has been playing and how much longer it will last. As this is the beginning of this technology, it is likely that further developments to give the user further control over the content will emerge. It is important to note that interchange between laser videodiscs and compact discs is not possible.

Videotex
As a result of the development of the new technologies, the ease with which individuals can link up their home or work-base with large banks of information has increased dramatically. Whether this is done by broadcast, telephone or direct cable, the user has access to a considerable database provided he learns how to explore and find the appropriate pathway through the system. This is Information at a Distance by Electronic Systems (IDES), and is probably the most significant development for the user and the librarian that will affect them over the next decade. For some years, BLAISE and DIALOG, for example, have been accessible through the telephone system to approved users, but the mushrooming of available systems for both specialist and general users has occurred only recently. Later in this section, the two main public systems, broadcast teletext and viewdata (known collectively as videotex), are examined in more detail, but first a short discussion of the technology involved.

The user has to connect his reception device to the telephone system or to a direct cable to the computer holding the datastore that he wishes to access. In practice, the latter approach is not economic unless the distance is short, or unless it is part of a much more extensive cabling operation, as for example may occur with cable television. The connection to the telephone requires a device called a modem which changes digital signals to analogue ones or vice versa. Such a device may be wired directly into the user's system, may be built into a television set as occurs with Prestel sets, may be part of an acoustic coupler into which the normal telephone handset is then placed, may be part of a special telephone, or in the future is likely to be a chip which is then inserted into a computer. Any of these systems will be effective, but the acoustic coupler is liable to external interference and therefore likely to receive occasional faulty or corrupt signals.

After the user has connected his system to the telephone circuit in this way, he has then to ensure that his particular receiver has the appropriate decoding arrangement. Some receivers are dedicated to a particular system, as for example Prestel television sets or certain computer terminals, but if a general purpose computer is used appropriate software often has to be obtained. This is necessary if the transmissions need to be interpreted so that the user's equipment can display them. For security reasons, most links with large computers require the use of a password before the user can start interrogating it. Using a computer to act as a reception terminal means that the large computer could be used as a source of computer programs which could be transmitted to the user. This is now frequently practised, and is referred to as telesoftware.

The exception to the foregoing paragraphs is the broadcast teletext system. No connections to telephones are required, only an appropriate television set or add-on unit. A form of telesoftware is also available from this system, requiring a special box attached to an aerial and the computer. The computer can then capture and record any pages transmitted, and if these happen to be computer programs, they too can be stored and then run as normal. Naturally as with all telesoftware programs, the language of the program must be suitable for the computer receiving it.

For both teletext and viewdata special television sets or add-on boxes are required. The add-on boxes link to the normal television set through the aerial socket and do not interfere with the reception of broadcast programmes. In these boxes is the decoder, a computer which changes the broadcast signals or those received through the telephone into the graphics and lettering that appear on the screen. For viewdata they also organize the dialling to the information computer and have a memory system to retain various pages. In the special television sets, these decoders are built into the circuits within the set, and many users feel the quality of the images is better as a result.

The display

For both teletext and viewdata, the system of displaying information on the screen is identical. Each page has a maximum capacity of 24 lines, each of 40 characters. It takes 6720 digital bytes (computer information) to describe each page. Graphics are made up as follows. Each character space can be divided into six boxes, and each box filled with colour. The patches of colour, when joined up, give the appearance of a graphic shape, although it is impossible to create smooth edges. As a result, diagrams have angular borders, and perfect circles are not possible. Seven colours are available for use: white, red, green, blue, cyan, magenta and yellow. Each bit of the screen can be appropriately and separately coloured at the decision of the sender of the information.

As the circuits from the decoder to the tube are separate from those dealing with the reception of the broadcast materials, normal television controls have no effect on the display. The display of teletext or view-data bypasses the colour saturation, brightness and contrast controls. Problems with the clarity of the display are therefore faults in the decoder or more likely with the transmission, with the telephone line connection or the strength of the signal the set is receiving from the aerial. Indeed, most problems with teletext occur because of poor reception through the aerial.

The decoder can withhold part of the display, ie retain it in its memory and release it, or even exchange it, after a timed interval or on a command signal (the 'Reveal' control). Thus, a display can have parts which flash on and off or a graphic can show a part of itself changing position at regular intervals. The command signal facility is useful with games and quizzes: the first display sets the problem; the command signal releases the answers from the decoder and these are superimposed in the appropriate position.

Videotape recorders can be used with videotex sets in the normal way, but cannot record the information display. Viewdata signals can be recorded on to audiotape recorders, like the common cassette recorder, and many of the special television receivers and add-on boxes have sockets for connecting them. Playback of the recorded information display is by a similar route. Other methods of recording the display include photographing it with a camera or printing out the pages in monochrome or colour.

Teletext
Teletext developed from an idea of a BBC engineer who was trying to introduce a subtitling service for the deaf. To solve the problem, he decided to use two of the spare lines being transmitted with the pictures, but normally unseen. Transmission is 625 lines of information to make up each picture, each block of lines being broadcast to the set 25 times per second. However, the picture area is made up of 585 lines, the remaining 40 lines carrying engineering tests and instructions which tell the set how to react to receive the picture. It is two, now four, of these 40 lines which the BBC engineer decided to use for subtitling, and which are now used for all the teletext transmissions. Not more than eight teletext pages can be transmitted every second, so it takes 12½ seconds to transmit 100 pages of information. Both ITV and BBC transmit in the same way. The pages are transmitted in sequence and the selected page is stored and displayed next time it is received by the set. Thus there can be a delay of several seconds before the chosen

page is displayed. As will be clear from figure 23, the information in the BBC and ITV computers is broadcast to the television set. Thus, communication is one-way only, and the whole service is free, that is, it is paid for out of licence and advertising revenue.

Each of the four channels, BBC1, BBC2, ITV and Channel 4, have their own teletext transmissions, first transmitted in September 1974. The BBC service is known as CEEFAX (from 'see facts'), while ITV's service is known as ORACLE, an acronym derived from Optical Reception of Announcements by Coded Line Electronics. To obtain the particular service, the appropriate channel must be tuned in and then the page called. All pages show a very accurate 24-hour clock in the top righthand corner, perhaps a cheaper method of checking the time than ringing the telephone service.

Certain pages of teletext are designed to be superimposed on the picture. The 'Newsflash' page appears as a maximum of five lines within a black rectangle in the bottom third of the screen, when in the teletext mode, the rest of the screen showing the broadcast picture. Similarly, subtitles are superimposed, the writing on a black background, during those programmes for which they have been prepared. The 'Alarm Clock' page also superimposes. Teletext pages only replace the picture or superimpose when the teletext mode is selected. There is no effect at all on the sound reproduction which continues as transmitted by the selected channel, unless it is deliberately muted or the volume control is adjusted by the user.

Some pages have the equivalent of continuation sheets, when all the information cannot be contained within a single one, or a sequence is desired. Up to 20 such continuation pages have been used, but normally the limit tends to be five or six. The existence of such pages is clearly shown in the following ways. In the corner of the page a sign like '2/3' or '2 of 3' appears, indicating that page 2 of a sequence of three pages is being shown. Another system is to show letters 'A, B, C, D, E' with the 'C' for example flashing or in a different colour. This indicates that the third page of a sequence of five is being transmitted. At the bottom of each of these pages a statement usually occurs like 'More in a moment'.

Viewdata

A British Post Office invention by Sam Fedida, the concept was ready in 1974, field-tested in London, Birmingham and Norfolk from September 1978 and went on public access in September 1979. Viewdata is a system by which the television set is linked directly to computers containing large amounts of information through the telephone network. In many countries overseas similar systems are now being developed or the British system is being marketed, particularly in linking computers for management purposes in large commercial enterprises. International standards are being sought, but are full of national and political problems. Undoubtedly, the dream must be a comprehensive international interconnection of viewdata services.

The well-known viewdata systems currently being operated or developed are:

British Telecom network — Prestel
France — Antiope
West Germany — Bildschirmtext
Canada — Telidon
Japan — Captains
Sweden — Datavision
Finland — Telset

The system: From figure 24 it will be seen that the user's television set is directly connected through the telephone network to the Prestel computer. Also having direct access to that computer are the information providers (IPs). The user's television set's decoder, either that within the set or an add-on unit, is wired into the telephone network through a jack socket by British Telecom who thereby commission the set. This means that the user and the set are identified by name and address to the computer for charging, messages, etc. At the same time the keypad is programmed to dial the local computer automatically, although the normal telephone can do this as well. Some keypads have the capacity of storing up to three different telephone numbers so that three different computers may be contacted through a local call. All the computers around the country are interconnected, so that all the pages of information that they carry are nationally available and instantly updated everywhere.

Unlike teletext, Prestel use incurs charges every time it is accessed. These charges are in three parts: the telephone call which forms part of the normal accumulation of telephone units, a charge for contacting the computer and one for the pages viewed. Because of the direct link to the computer, there is no cycling time and pages appear almost instantaneously. Another major feature of the system is that the user can 'talk' back to the computer sending messages to British Telecom, IPs and other users.

135

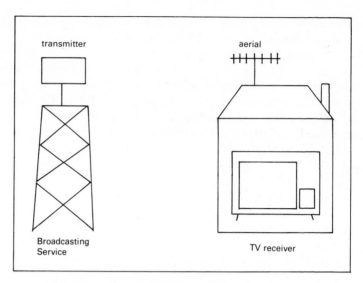

Figure 23. Arrangement for teletext signals

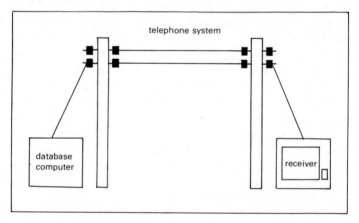

Figure 24. Arrangement for viewdata signals

British Telecom employs a common carrier policy. This means that they provide the network of computers, telephone lines, computer software and central Prestel indexing which guides users to the pages of the IPs. They then rent blank pages to IPs and it is the responsibility

136

of these IPs to fill them, keep them updated and organize their arrangement. Some are called umbrella IPs because they provide pages and often editorial work for many organizations. Apart from ensuring that they do not contravene the law, British Telecom is not concerned at all in the content of the pages or the way in which the IPs make use of the space at their disposal. This strategy absolves British Telecom from any responsibility for controversial content or seeking to achieve appropriate balances, although the selection of IPs from those requesting space does go some way towards being an editorial policy.

Access to Prestel requires certain levels of security. The receiver has to be registered, and this is checked by the Prestel computer each time connection is made. Many users also introduce a password to prevent casual and unauthorized use of their system. Further developments of viewdata have seen the emergence of Closed User Groups and the Gateway. Some information providers felt that their material should only be accessible to a limited number of people, either because the information might be sensitive or because it was restricted to members of a particular company. The part of the database containing this information is therefore only accessible to a few who have a special password in order to be able to use those pages. This group is referred to as a closed user group. Another means of limiting access is to retain the restricted information on a private computer which can be accessed through the Prestel system acting as a gateway to it. Of course, the access through the gateway need not be limited, and members of the general public can use the database if the owner wishes.

EQUIPMENT CARE AND MAINTENANCE

If equipment is to give maximum performance for as long a time as possible, a system of regular maintenance is essential. The frequency of this will naturally depend on use, but as a rule of thumb, there should be weekly checks, monthly cleans and yearly inspections. The last should be done by qualified engineers, and the comments that follow refer to the first two parts of the system only.

In all aspects of care and maintenance, attention should be paid to the manufacturer's instructions, and the operating manual is an important reference point. For instance, the exact replacement type for lamps must be identified. Because of differences between the connectors of the lamp to carriers, the potential for mistakes is reduced, but there are errors possible in putting low voltage lamps into high voltage machines. The method of access to lamps varies between models and the operating manual should describe how this is done. On no account should lamps be changed or the inside of equipment investigated without the mains power being switched off and unplugged.

Care of plugs

Plugs carrying mains electricity to equipment can be a major safety hazard. Physical damage is commonly caused by careless use, and they should be regularly checked for cracks, chips or breaks. It is also necessary to ensure that the cable emerging from the plug is correctly held by the gripper device, as this can become loosened if users pull plugs from sockets by tugging on the cable.

Care of lenses

All lenses and other glass surfaces in equipment are carefully and accurately positioned, so dismantlement for cleaning purposes should only be done if there is no other means of access.

The biggest problems are dust and grease from finger marks. Scratches cannot be eliminated, and if they interfere with effective viewing the lens or glass has to be replaced. Many modern lenses are made of plastic and if they are rubbed with a cloth there is a chance that electrostatic currents are created which appear to 'glue' the dust to the surface. Basic cleaning should consist of wiping surfaces with lint-free tissues or an anti-static cloth. These can be obtained from opticians.

If grease is present, breathing on the surface and wiping with a tissue or cloth may be sufficient. Should this not work, a small amount of spirit may be wiped over the area, but be careful not to allow this to touch glued joints as it may act as a solvent. On no account should dirt be scraped off a lens or glass in case the surface becomes scratched.

If access to the lens is too limited for a tissue or cloth to reach, a soft brush may be used, particularly if linked to a puffer to blow the dust off the surface.

Care of apertures

When film is being projected, the edges of the frame are defined by the edge of the aperture as well as the boundaries around the picture. These are found particularly in cine projectors but also occur in some filmstrip and slide projectors. As any cinemagoer will have noticed, bits of hair or apparently even cobwebs sometimes seem to hang from the top of the picture. These are attached to the bottom of the aperture in the gate (remember the aperture like the picture is inverted on the screen), and they move in the convection currents caused by the heat of the lamp.

Access to the apertures is gained by moving the projection lens out or swinging it to one side. A stiff brush should be used to clean around the edges.

Oiling

Most modern equipment has its mechanical parts permanently lubricated in sealed joints so that there is little need for oiling. However, some operating manuals indicate points where light oil is required. Depending on use it is unlikely that lubrication need be done more frequently than every six months.

Silicone fluid is useful where two surfaces are screwed together, for example between lens holders and carriers. If they should prove particularly stiff and difficult to control, a small amount of this fluid can improve use.

Oil or any other lubricant must be kept away from all film or glass surfaces.

Care of heads

These delicate pieces of ferrite collect dust and deposits from the magnetic coating of the tape, which accumulate and prevent close contact. Regular cleaning is therefore essential. At the same time, the capstan spindle and pinch wheel should be cleaned.

Abrasive tape cassettes can be purchased for use with sound cassette recorders and can be quite effective, particularly for heads. A weekly play through with this tape can keep standards of replay to a high standard but they should be supplemented by the following method every few months.

Methylated spirit should be rubbed over the surfaces. While a cloth can be used for the spindle and pinch wheel, it is advisable to use a stick with cotton wool at the tip (commercially sold as Q-Tips). One should be used to apply the spirit, another to wipe it away. The rubbing motion should be up and down to be most effective. Under no circumstances should any metal be brought into contact with or near the heads.

Videorecorder heads are more delicate than those in sound equipment and often less accessible. Aerosol sprays are available which are suitable for a weekly clean, but again a six-monthly wipe with spirit is useful. It may be necessary for an engineer to do this if access is difficult, as the dirt still accumulates. Abrasive materials must not be used.

Care of styli

The stylus on a record player wears away, and therefore careful inspection is needed to ensure that it does not need replacement. In the case of magnetic cartridges, it is usual for the whole cartridge to be changed, but in ceramic cartridges only the stylus itself has to be replaced. Timers are available which keep track of the extent of use of a stylus.

In its travels along the grooves of the disc, the stylus picks up dust and also pieces of plastic material which should be removed. Dust can be prevented by keeping the discs themselves clean with anti-static cloths, or the occasional use of a dust brush.

Liquids are available for cleaning the stylus. A small amount is placed on a brush which is carefully drawn over the tip. The liquid helps to loosen the material attached to the stylus and the brush clears it away. This is a delicate part of the equipment and the treatment should be gentle. Under no circumstances should the stylus be fingered as grease will be deposited which will make the final condition worse than at the beginning.

Care of headphones, microphones, etc

These require no special treatment to maintain mechanical and electrical quality, but these well-handled pieces of equipment can transfer disease-causing organisms between users. Careful use of disinfectant over those parts of headphones which touch the ears and other handled parts will help to prevent cross-infections occurring. Microphone surfaces may be carefully wiped with cloths impregnated with disinfectant, but aerosol sprays are not recommended.

Fuses

Equipment sometimes carries an internal fuse, and all mains equipment should also be fused at the plug or socket. The fuses used should be correct for the power supply used by the equipment, and this is normally indicated by the manufacturer. As a rough guide the following ratings may be used if no other instructions are given. They apply only to 220-250 voltage mains:

— 3 amp fuse: radio, tape-recorders, record players, all projectors with a lamp rating less than 500 watts.

— 5 amp fuse: television equipment, all projectors with lamps rated between 500 and 1000 watts.

— 13 amp fuse: all other equipment.

Fuses which are part of equipment are of two types, replaceable and reinsertable. The replaceable variety can be removed and changed, and are usually similar in design to those used in mains plugs. Reinsertable fuses disengage from the circuit when they should blow, and may be pushed back in when the fault has been rectified.

Major electrical faults and damage which cause fuses to blow will require the intervention of an engineer. However, a lamp failing in normal use is quite likely to break the fuse, and after a new lamp has been inserted it may be necessary to change the fuse as well.

MANUAL OF PRACTICE

In this section, each type of format and equipment is introduced to explain the operations required to view and/or listen. Because models vary, the detail of the instructions can only be limited, but the principles are the same in all cases. The operating manual that is supplied with the equipment should give further details. A list of sockets and controls that are commonly found are given with a simple explanation of their use.

Filmstrip projectors

1 Identify the format of the filmstrip. Is it single or double frame? (page 67).

2 Check whether the projector is suitable for that format (page 95).

3 Check that the lens is appropriate for the screen and distance. If there is only one lens, check if there is a mains source for the projector the distance from which it will have to project. An extension lead may be necessary.

4 Detach the filmstrip carrier from the projector.

5 Place it on the table so that the side which is to be towards the screen faces downwards.

6 Locate the end of the trailer of the filmstrip and find the last two frames.

7 Look at the frames and orientate the strip until they are arranged as you wish to see them on the screen.

8 Now turn the strip until the bottom left hand corner of that picture is in the top right hand viewing position (see figure 25).

9 Keeping the filmstrip in that position:

In the case of the single frame filmstrip, move the carrier so that it is vertical and attach the end to the upper spool.

In the case of the double frame filmstrip, move the carrier so that it is horizontal and attach the end to the left hand spool.

10 Turning the spool holder clockwise, wind the strip on to it until the beginning is located.

11 Open the frame holder and pull the strip through until the first picture is at the centre.

12 Attach the beginning of the leader on to the front spool or spools.

13 If the spools carry cogs to locate in the sprocket holes, ensure that they do.

14 Close the frame holder.

142

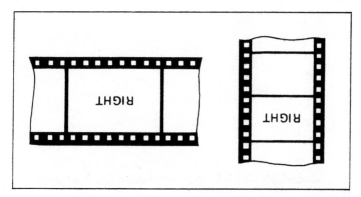

Figure 25. Double and single frame filmstrips orientated for projection

15 Check that the aperture is correct for the filmstrip. A cover or gates may have to be inserted, removed, opened or closed.

16 Re-attach carrier to projector, ensuring orientation as in 9 is maintained.

17 Attach mains lead to power source, point projector at screen, switch on and if necessary switch on power on the projector.

18 Focus, usually by turning outside of lens.

19 To wind on frame by frame, turn the lower (single frame) or right (double frame) spool anticlockwise.

20 On completion of viewing, rewind. Then detach strip from spools and return it to container.

The foregoing applies to a projector used with a front projection screen or with a rear projection screen with a mirror in-between. If it is projected directly on to a rear projection screen, the following changes will occur:

5 Place the carrier on the table, the screen side uppermost.

9 Keeping the filmstrip in that position:

In the case of the single frame filmstrip, move the carrier so that it is vertical and insert end of filmstrip to the upper spool.

In the case of the double frame filmstrip, attach end of strip to left hand spool.

19 To turn double strip, wind on to left hand spool as you face the screen.

Slide projectors

For convenience of loading, slides should be 'spotted'. To do this, place the slide on the table orientated in the way you wish to see it on

143

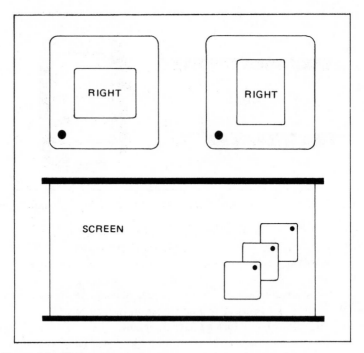

Figure 26. Slides with spots

the screen. The spot should now be placed on the mount on the bottom left hand corner (figure 26).

In all projectors using front projections screens or rear projection screens via a mirror, the slide is inserted in such a way that it enters the light path between lamp and lens orientated with the spot in the top right hand corner as viewed from the rear of the projector.

To set up the projector

1 Locate the mains power point which is to be used.

2 From the distance between projector and screen and the size of the screen, select the appropriate lens (if necessary, see figure 13).

3 If there is only one lens, check whether it is possible to locate the projector at an appropriate distance, even with an extension lead.

4 Place the projector on a stand and adjust the screen to correct distortions. To check this accurately, insert a test slide and focus. The horizontal level of the projector is also normally adjustable by turning or lowering the feet.

To insert slides

1 The slide carrier is usually one of three types:

(a) A side to side carrier (see figure 27.1) used with manual projectors.

(b) A straight tray (see figure 27:2) used with semi and fully automatic projectors. These vary in the degree to which they are enclosed, and usually take up to 36 slides. A circular tray which is held in the vertical is a possible substitute as it carries up to 80 slides.

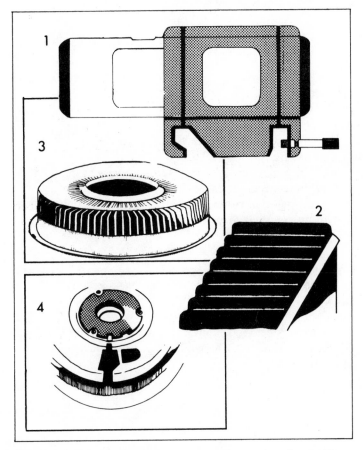

Figure 27. Slide carriers/magazines: 1=side to side; 2=straight tray; 3=circular magazine for gravity feed; 4=bottom plate of above magazine in correct place for loading

(c) A circular tray is used horizontally (see figure 27:3) with fully automatic projectors. Before loading, check that the rotating plate underneath is locked in the right position (see figure 27:4).

2 Slides should be inserted with the spot on the top right hand corner.

(a) Attach carrier to projector and insert slide.

(b) Load the tray and push it into position.

(c) Load the tray and place it firmly on the projector, aligning the slot on the tray with the red spot on the projector.

To project

1 Switch on mains supply and if necessary the power switch on the projector.

2 Introduce the first slide into the light path. In manual projectors, this is done by sliding it across; in semi automatic projectors, by pushing in the lever; in automatic projectors, press the forward button either on the projector or on the remote control device.

3 Focus by rotating the lens holder in its carrier or turning the appropriate control.

4 When removing carrier at the end of the viewing, ensure that all slides are removed from the light path.

In a rear projection system without a mirror, the slide is inserted with the spot top right as you face the projector and away from the screen.

Controls

The following controls are sometimes found on projectors:

(a) On/off for mains power.

(b) Focus control.

(c) Brightness high or low. Always use low level lighting if acceptable as this increases lamp life. This control may be a switch or an exchange of an external attachment.

-◯- sign means low.

⭆◯⭅ sign means high.

(d) Reverse for automatically returning to previous slide.

⬇ is the usual sign.

146

(e) Forward for automatically moving on to the next slide.

 ↑ is the sign

Ⓣ is seen also, the outside arrow indicating that not only is this the forward control, but also releases the change action so that the tray can be moved freely either to a new position or off the projector.

Microform readers
1 Before viewing, check that the magnification from available lenses is appropriate to the reduction ratio of the microfilm.
2 Check that the reader is plugged into the mains supply which is switched on. If there is a mains power switch on the reader, this is better switched on after the microfilm has been fixed to the equipment.

Roll-film readers
3(a) Open reel readers. The spool of film is normally attached to the left-hand holder, the loose end pulled through the gate and attached to the right-hand spool. Because of the extensive variations between different readers in the arrangement of prisms and mirrors, the orientation of the film spool cannot be generally stated. If there is no indication on the reader, then trial-and-error is the only technique.

(b) Cartridge. The cartridge is normally attached as shown on the reader to the left-hand side, and the film either hand led or wound through the gate in the light path to be attached to the open spool on the right side.

(c) Cassette. The cassette must be suitable for the reader. Placing the cassette on the reader is usually an obvious procedure, two spindles sticking up to receive the container. The film channel is on the side furthest from the user. The upper surface is usually either marked with arrows, a label, an impressed word in the case, or it is clear because it can only be placed on the reader one way round.

4 Turn on the mains power.

5 Focus by turning lens or adjusting control marked accordingly.

6 To move frames:

(a) A crank may be attached temporarily or permanently to each reel for hand turning.

(b) A single crank in the front or at the side of the reader through gears turns both reels simultaneously.

(c) A motorized drive turns the reels mechanically at a varying speed.

Microfiche readers

3 If there is a tray, open it usually by pulling it towards you. In some models, the tray has to be opened by winding it out or using a lever.

4 Inserting the fiche. Place the fiche on the bottom of the open tray; the eye-legible heading is commonly on the user's side, but it may face upwards or downwards depending on the mirror system.

If there is no tray, the fiche may be inserted with or without a plastic carrier in a slot. It is almost invariably inserted with the eye-legible heading downwards.

5 Identify frame to be viewed, perhaps using the contents list on the first or last frame.

6 Guide fiche to position using grid system or in its absence by trial and error.

7 Adjust focus by turning lens or external control.

Controls

The following controls are sometimes found on readers:

(a) Image rotation to change the orientation of the frame.

(b) Lens change which may be a lever.

(c) Roll film scan to raise or lower the frame.

(d) Tilt adjustment which may adjust the front legs of the reader to tilt it for a more acceptable viewing angle. This may only change the angle of the screen.

(e) The working of the print operation on a reader-printer should be determined from the manual or instructions on the equipment.

Cine projectors

Open spool projectors

1 Select position for the projector with relation to the mains power supply, the size of the screen and the lens available.

2 Attach to mains power supply.

3 Fix spool to front reel holder, the loose length of film hanging from the front (screen-side) edge of the spool. The sprocket holes on a sound film should be on the right when looking towards the screen.

4 To lace the projector:

(a) Manual lacing: Open covers to sprocket drive wheels, and move aside the lens. Follow the path indicated in the projector ensuring there are loops above and below the channel behind the lens. Attach to take-up reel and close covers to drive wheels and lens.

(b) Channel lacing: Open the channel, usually by a lever. Thread film through the channel, attaching end to take-up reel. Close the channel.

(c) Self or automatic threading: Trim end of film using attached clipper. Turn on power to motor drive and feed into first sprocket drive channel. When sufficient leader emerges from end of threading channel, stop motor and attach to take-up reel.

5 Check that claws are engaging sprocket holes at gate by turning 'inching' or 'animation' control. The film should move up and down channel.

6 Plug in external loudspeaker if required to socket marked. Place speaker in suitable position.

7 Turn on motor and lamp into forward movement. As film is projected, adjust focus by turning lens holder or an external control. Adjust height by raising or lowering legs at the front of the projector.

8 Turn on amplifier and adjust sound volume to a suitable level.

9 Rewind film by switching to stop and then rewind or reverse. Stop when number 3 appears projected. Switch off amplifier, lamp and motor in that order.

10 To project for viewers, switch on amplifier first, then motor, then lamp.

11 At end of viewing, rewind the film back on to original delivery reel. To do this, the film should have been completely driven through the projector. Turn off the amplifier, lamp and motor. Attach loose end of the film directly to the front reel, passing on the projector side of it. Engage the rewind gear by the marked control and switch on reverse.

Cassette projectors

1 Select position for the projector with relation to the mains power supply, the size of the screen and the lens available. As many of these operate with a fixed rear projection screen with a mirror, only the first point may be relevant.

2 Hold cassette with part marked top upwards. In most cases, these are inserted vertically into the projector.

3 Insert cassette into projector, the film edge nearest the lens. The cassette has to be firmly pushed into place, and usually clicks into position. The first click may not indicate complete insertion.

4 Turn on mains power and switch on motor. Lamp lights instantly.

5 Focus by adjusting lens and position the projector so that the

image fills the screen as far as possible. If there is sound, adjust volume to a suitable level.

6   Observe film and turn off when picture shows titles. Being a continuous loop, the film cannot be rewound.

Controls

The following controls and sockets may be present on the projector.

(a) Forward (with motor) causes film to pass through projector path without light. Forward with lamp causes lamp to illuminate the projector.

(b) Reverse (with motor) causes film to pass backwards through projection path without light. Reverse with lamp causes lamp to illuminate the backward projection.

(c) Rewind causes a gear to be engaged to increase the motor speed. This should only be used when the film is out of the projection path, and should be disengaged when rewinding is complete.

(d) Still frame causes projection to stop with a single picture illuminated. It may be necessary to turn inching (animation) control to move the shutter to let light pass. Refocusing may be needed.

(e) Framing control moves the position of the aperture to cover black frame lines which may be visible.

(f) Inching (animation) causes the film to be wound manually through the projection path for inspection of individual frames.

(g) External speaker ( ) is the socket to which an extension speaker may be attached.

(h) Microphone ( ) is the socket into which a microphone may be inserted for voice over commentary. Before doing this, the impedances should be checked.

(i) Bright/low adjusts light output from the projector lamp.

(j) Opt/mag control selects the appropriate sound reproduction method.

(k) Volume, treble, bass control the amplifier and the quality of sound.

Soundtape recorders/players

Recorders/players may be battery or mains operated. Recorders/players may contain their own amplifier and speaker or require equipment to be added to provide these. Appropriate parts should be at-

150

tached if necessary. Turn on mains supply and power switch on recorder/
player. Set odometer to zero if it is to be used.

Open reel equipment

1 Place tape on left-hand spindle, the loose end of the tape coming
from the outside or left of the spool.

2 The tape should be laced across the heads and attached to the
empty right-hand spool. If the tape has a metal strip, this should be
just to the right of the pinch wheel. In some machines, it may be
necessary to release the brakes by turning a lever to 'free'.

3 If track or speed selection is necessary, adjust the appropriate
control.

4 Turn volume control to estimated level. There may be separate
volume controls for different tracks.

5 Switch on 'play'.

6 Modify volume, treble and bass controls as necessary.

7 At end of playing, switch to 'stop'.

8 To remove tape, switch 'rewind', then 'stop' when rewinding is
complete; remove tape.

Cassette and cartridge equipment
(Read cartridge for cassette except at stage 7.)

1 Open cassette compartment. Various methods may be used. A lid
may be lifted; a control pressed (possible markings: 'cassette', 'eject')
to reveal a slot; a slot may be apparent.

2 Insert cassette into compartment. Usually the side to be played is
uppermost. The tape should be towards the heads. If inserted into a
slot, the cassette usually clicks into position. A cassette carrier may
have to be pressed down into position.

3 Turn volume control to estimated level.

4 Switch on 'play'.

5 Modify volume, treble and bass controls as necessary. There may
be separate controls for different tracks if stereo is being played.

6 At the end of playing, switch 'stop'. This may be the first pressure
of the control marked 'eject'.

7 The cassette may be removed at this point or rewound by pressing appropriate control. Note that a cartridge cannot be rewound.
Removal may be a reverse of the operations in one, although an 'eject'
control is likely to be present to partially release the cassette or cartridge.

Controls

The following controls or sockets may be present on the recorder/player.

(a) Play (▶).

(b) Fast forward (▶▶) causes tape to move at speed in a forward direction.

(c) Rewind (◀◀) causes tape to move at speed in a reverse direction. The odometer should operate accurately with both this and fast forward.

(d) Pause (■) causes the tape to stop and hold the position. If used during recording, there should be no audible sound made.

(e) Record (a red mark or colour is standard) changes mode of recorder.

(f) Channel means track both for selection of one being played and volume.

(g) Microphone (◯) refers both to a socket for plugging in and the controls for level of recording.

(h) External speaker (◁) is the socket(s) for connection of this equipment.

(i) Headphones, headset (◠) is the socket for connection of this equipment.

(j) Aux, gram or other equivalent words indicate sockets into which other equipment is plugged for recording on tape.

(k) CrO_2 (chromium dioxide) is the control which must be operated when this type of tape is being used in cassette recorders. Increasingly this difference is recognized automatically by the equipment.

(l) Restart is used particularly if the tape pause cue tone has caused the cassette to stop. This will also restart the machine after it has been stopped by the assigned control.

Tape-slide equipment

Some of this equipment is supplied with the tape recorder, synchronizing device and the slide projector already connected. In which case move from stage 1 to stage 4.

1 Check the mains supply is in an appropriate place, and insert plug. In the case of multiple equipment, two or three power sources may be required or a multi-access socket used.

2 Link synchronizing device to tape recorder and slide projector.

Access to tape recorder will be indicated as it must be a specially made machine, while the plug to the projector is to the remote control socket.

3 Load slides and insert tape.

4 Check synchronizing device is in the playback mode. As 'red' almost always refers to record, this colour should not be indicated.

5 Turn on mains power on each part of the system.

6 Insert first slide into projector and focus. According to recommended standards, the first cue tone on the tape should change first to the second slide. However, in some programmes the producers have used it to introduce the first slide and users should be aware of this.

7 Adjust the volume on the tape recorder to an estimate of the appropriate volume. In most programmes the first slide is accompanied by introductory information or music so that final adjustment can be used then.

8 Play the tape. If the programme is to be used by one or two users only, headphones should be inserted first.

Controls
The controls found on this equipment are the same as those on separate tape recorders and slide projectors listed earlier. Synchronizing devices have a control to select record or playback but rarely any other. On a few machines it is possible to select the appropriate relays to recognize the different standards of cue tones (see page 117) and therefore choose the one used with a particular programme.

Videotape recorders/players

1 Place the receiver or monitor and videotape recorder in a suitable position so that there is no danger from their being knocked over. Mains supply should be at an appropriate distance, usually two separate sockets or a multi-access junction box being necessary.

2 Link recorder and receiver/monitor together. This may be through a video out to video in socket, or direct to the aerial input on the receiver.

3 (a) Open reel systems: Lace tape on recorder. Follow the plan on the recorder carefully, particularly around the drum carrying the heads as the path here varies between different models. The tape should be tight, tension levers helping to sustain this, and the end fixed to the take-up reel on the right. The controls should be set at 'stop' or 'free'.

(b) Cassette or cartridge: Before inserting the container it is

153

usually necessary to open the appropriate slot. This may be as simple as holding open a lid or moving a lever or control to raise the slot. The lever in this case is commonly marked 'eject'. The container is almost always inserted with the tape directed away from the user. Before inserting a cassette, look underneath the container and remove any tension-retaining wheel, which will incidentally fall out easily. This should be replaced after use before returning the cassette to its box. The lid should be closed or the slot pushed back into the equipment by hand or by means of the lever.

4 Press odometer button to zero the digits.

5 Switch on mains supply and the power input to each machine.

6 Adjust volume level on receiver/monitor to an estimated level. Similarly adjust any tone (bass/treble) controls.

7 (a) Open reel equipment: Switch control to play.

(b) Cassette or cartridge: Switch control to play. There will be a pause while the tape is partially withdrawn from the container and wound around the heads. On some equipment a red light glows while this takes place, turning off or to green when the programme play starts.

8 Some adjustments to sound and visual tuning may be required, removing visual distortions or the density of the colour.

9 When the viewing has been completed, switch controls to 'stop' first. In the case of open reel and cartridge, 'rewind' has to be engaged next until the tape has returned to the delivery wheel; finally return to 'stop' and remove videotape. Cassettes may be withdrawn without rewinding, but there is a delay between the control 'stop' and 'eject' while the tape is unwound from the heads and is returned to the container. This is not the same as rewinding as the cassette will start playing again at the same point as that at which it stopped if 'play' is engaged. When the tape has returned to the cassette, the eject control or lever is operated to retrieve the container.

Controls

The following controls may be present on the videotape recorder/player:

(a) Play is the control for forward (▶).

(b) Fast forward causes the tape to move forward at speed (▶▶).

(c) Rewind causes the tape to return to its delivery reel at speed (◀◀).

(d) Stop causes the programme to stop.

154

(e) Pause may cause the programme to stop with a single picture being transmitted (also known as stop frame), or on some machines it is used to hold the tape wound around the heads but with no transmission to the receiver/monitor.

(f) Tracking is turned to eliminate banding on the picture if this is caused by mistracking of the heads.

(g) Skew is turned to eliminate distortion at the top of the picture.

(h) Channel 1, 2, Mix gives alternative positions for sound recording differentiation. Normally this is held at 'mix'.

(i) Record must be applied simultaneously with the 'play' control.

Record players

1 Place in an appropriate position for the mains power electricity. If it is only a turntable deck, it requires an amplifier and speakers which must be attached.

2 Inspect disc to identify the speed, and select that on the player. At the same time ensure that the stylus and cartridge are suitable.

3 Adjust volume and tone controls to appropriate levels.

4 Place disc on turntable.

5 Switch on power supply.

6 Lift arm either manually or by a control.

7 Move arm over disc to point immediately above place where user wishes to start. The turntable should now be turning.

8 Lower arm either manually or by a control.

9 At the end of play, the arm returns to its rest which causes the turntable to stop.

Controls

(a) Reject is used to stop a disc playing in the middle. The stylus is lifted and returned to its rest.

(b) Speed selector, usually giving an alternative between 33-1/3 and 45rpm, should only be operated when the turntable is stationary.

(c) Arm lift (▼) and arm lower (▼).

(d) Graded control for arm weight, which is located at the rear end of the arm, should be adjusted to manufacturer's recommendations, usually with a measuring device under the cartridge.

(e) Balance for stereo channels alters the relative volumes between left and right speakers.

155

Microcomputers

1 Place in an appropriate position for mains power electricity. The computer may have a separate power unit between it and the mains or this may be built into the machine. The television set also needs to be connected to the mains, and any backing store, cassette or disk drive, may also require a power supply. If the backing store and/or the set is an integral part of the computer, steps 2 and 3 do not apply and only one mains connection is needed.

2 Connect the backing store to the computer through appropriate leads into both pieces of equipment.

3 Connect the computer to the television set. If the set is a monitor, the connection should be to the video socket if the computer has a video output. If the set is a receiver, the computer connects to the aerial socket.

4 Switch on mains electricity and power at the computer, television set and backing store.

5 Place the cassette in the player, closing the lid and setting the volume. If using a disk drive, insert the disk and close the door.

6 Instruct the computer to load the program from the backing store. The way this is done depends on the computer operating system and must be extracted from the machine's manual. Sometimes the computer controls the motor of the cassette recorder and the user does not have to switch it on. The computer always controls the disk drive.

7 Run the program.

Controls

In general the keyboard provides all the controls for the computer, and the instruction manual(s) should be consulted to determine which keys or combinations of keys are required to produce the relevant commands. These arrangements are specific to the machine and the programs that are being run.

Part 4

THE USER AND THE MATERIALS

INTRODUCTION

So far, our consideration of the user of NBM and the materials themselves has focused on them as separate entities, identifying needs and
characteristics. Bringing them together within the library raises a
number of issues which are the subject of this chapter.

First, the librarian has to acquire the materials. This involves amongst
other problems, identifying various sources of supply. Having acquired
them, consideration has to be given to cataloguing, classification and
indexing so that the user can find what he needs from the collection. A
manual of practice is introduced after this section to give clear guidance
on procedure. Making materials available also means that the librarian
has to store them, and this is dealt with later in the chapter. Finally,
the issue of copyright is discussed because some users may wish to
obtain duplicates. The legal constraints on copying NBM are not the
same as those for books.

ACQUISITION OF MATERIAL

A library is often judged on the quality and quantity of its stock. Indeed, librarians often complain that their collections are assessed by what they do *not* have, rather than by what is on the shelves. A professional librarian should have the expertise to be able to create a collection of materials that will satisfy the diverse requirements of most clients. Part of this expertise lies in the knowledge of the current bibliographical organization of non-book materials. (No attempt is made here to establish methods of assessing the needs of library clients.)

The pattern to be adopted is as follows; each step is described in detail in this chapter:

1 Identify what exists
2 Decide by means of evaluative tools what to preview
3 Obtain the documents
4 Preview
5 Decide what to purchase or hire
6 Consider the need to let clients know the reasons for selection or rejection of documents
7 If the materials to match the need do not exist, consider producing the material within the library.

Before following this pattern, it will be necessary to consider the problems hampering acquisitions. These may be traced to those deriving from publishers, those from distributors, or problems due to the lack of bibliographical control.

Publishers

In chapter two the complexity of production of NBM was mentioned and publishers of it were considered in their national, local, institutional and individual aspects. It is extremely difficult to obtain statistics about the number of companies and individuals involved in NBM production. However, some general points may be made. Nationally, there are a vast number and range of individuals, associations, institutions and companies producing NBM for sale or hire. Some indication of the complexity may be gained from the brief survey that follows.

Film production can be divided into two main parts: the 'theatrical' cinema which shows mainly 35mm film, and the 'non-theatrical' area of 16mm and super 8mm film and videorecordings. The 'non-theatrical' is the major interest here and includes feature films, cartoons, documentaries, training and educational films. These are usually distributed for hire or sale through film libraries. These films may be produced by the film giants such as Twentieth Century Fox, industrial companies such as British Petroleum, broadcasting institutions like the BBC, and organizations such as embassies and professional associations. There may be limitations on who can use them and where they may be shown, some of these are a result of local booking conditions, copyright, company policies and medical restrictions. A similar pattern may be perceived for the production of videorecordings. However the distribution pattern also involves many smaller outlets for example, garages, local bookshops such as Heffers of Cambridge as well as 'high street' video shops.

Similarly the production of sound recordings can be divided into two main parts: the commercial record and cassette industry, and semi-commercial institutions. The former is extremely well organized by large companies such as EMI and RCA. Current output is controlled in a similar pattern to book publishing by trade publications such as *Music master* and catalogues. The semi-commercial side is not so well organized and includes institutions such as the Institute of Chartered Accountants, industrial companies such as Scottish & Newcastle Breweries Ltd, and commercial concerns like the British Life Assurance Trust for Health and Medical Education.

The publishing of microcomputer software is very diverse. Commercial provision includes book publishers such as Longman, Thomas Nelson, traditional computer companies such as APPLE and Atari, and small one-man providers such as JSD Software of Northumberland. Colleges and schools have produced software that has gained national recognition, for example Chelsea College, Hatfield Polytechnic, and King Edward VI Five Ways School.

This software may be bought direct or through local specialist distributors. The BBC Acornoft and Sinclair Spectrum material is available in local bookshops. However, material is also distributed through telecommunications. For example, MICRONET 800 is available via Prestel and the BBC has a teletext software service for the BBC micro.

The publishing pattern of other non-book materials is more diverse. It is impossible to impose a coherent structure in this area. There are a number of commercial companies who produce NBM and have established large lists, such as Educational Productions and the Slide Centre. Industrial companies have also produced materials, for example, British Gas, the National Coal Board, and ICI. There has often been close cooperation with the commercial companies to produce an item; thus Michael Benn and Associates produced *Airports: a multi-media resources pack* with the British Airports Authority, BP Educational Service and the assistance of Bath University School of Education. Professional associations have also contributed in this area, for example the Institute of Supervisory Management and PIRA. Book publishers have also become involved — Longman/Common Ground Filmstrip, Macmillan, Heinemann.

On a local scale, the picture becomes even more complicated. Local producers of NBM are perhaps more prolific within the educational sector. The largest producer in the UK is probably the Open University, where NBM devised originally for students has roused such interest from other institutions that its soundtapes and films have now been made available to any purchaser. Open University Educational Enterprises has been established as a publishing firm to market Open University publications and also other relevant educational materials. The Schools' Council has been prominent in producing teaching materials, which have been widely distributed.

However, it is productions made within individual institutions that perhaps best illustrate the difficulties. All sections of education from primary schools to polytechnics have produced materials designed initially for their own internal students. There is always the possibility that these may be valuable in other institutions, and there is no single method of publicizing such material. Some areas have established area resource organizations which have produced locally inspired material and sold them to local schools. A few of these, indeed, are now selling to the national market.

Art galleries and museums are also major producers of slides, postcards and posters of their exhibits. Again some of these have realized the potential value of a wider market and arranged national distribution. The National Portrait Gallery, London slide sets for example are distributed through The Slide Centre.

There are also commercial producers who have concentrated on their local market, such as slides of local views, and some public libraries have produced a great deal of valuable publications in the local history field.

Distributors
Many of these producers also distribute their own materials, and this can cause problems for the librarian used to dealing with one or two library book suppliers. There is no equivalent to the bookshops in this

field, although some NBM such as portfolios or those published by book firms, may be obtained from bookshops. There are well-established library suppliers for sound recording such as the Long Playing Record Library which will provide discs and cassettes together with library stationery and catalogue cards. The demise of the Audio Visual Library Service has been compensated to a limited extent by T C Farries & Co Ltd. of Dumfries. The Slide Centre has established its position as a distributor of filmstrip and slides for a number of other companies as well as its own productions.

Chivers the library book suppliers also provide videorecordings to libraries. Videorecordings and motion pictures are also provided via film libraries. There are over 150 film libraries and each has its own catalogue and distribution system. The National Audio-Visual Aids Library offers for hire a wide selection of educational films and also sells 16mm films, videotapes, filmstrips, slides, overhead projector transparencies, wallcharts etc.

The librarian used to obtaining books on approval will find more difficulty with NBM. The fragility of some material has caused a few publishers to insist on the library paying for any material which is damaged during preview. The dishonesty of some librarians, who have copied the material and returned the original, has resulted in some distributors refusing to supply material on approval. Indeed some small publishers will only supply material after payment and not to an order alone. As one remarked privately: 'why should we give you an interest free loan?' The problems associated with piracy of computer programs have resulted in many commercial providers refusing to provide these on approval. They will, however, often allow the library to make one copy for security purposes.

Bibliographic control
The diversity of production and distribution agencies creates problems for the librarian in identifying available materials, and this is further aggravated by the absence of any one bibliographical tool to cater for all the current output. It is well to remember that there are many more book publishers and book publications than exist in the field of NBM, but books enjoy an established and comprehensive distribution network. A single volume, *British books in print*, enables the librarian in the UK to identify a majority of the book publishers' output. This work lists 345,000 titles from more than 9000 publishers, and copes with 43,000 new titles each year, the microfiche edition updating this information

monthly. The *British national bibliography* enables the librarian to establish the existence of the great majority of books published since 1950 via an author, title, series and subject approach, and is also available via online computer access.

However, the equivalent of these works does not exist for NBM, and information about these materials is usually dependent upon the publishers' own publicity systems. As has already been pointed out, there is no legal requirement for the deposit of NBM at the British Library or anywhere else, and so it is difficult to establish a 'British National NBM Bibliography'. Of NBM, film is perhaps the best organized, with the *British national film catalogue*, although even this does not include the complete film output of the UK. The local producers are scarcely organized, although there has been some attention in the educational fields with HELPIS.

At a national level the most exciting development has been the *British catalogue of audiovisual materials*. This resulted from the British Library/Inner London Education Authority Learning Materials Recording Study and was published in 1979 with a supplement in 1980. It includes the more common types of audiovisual materials, but excludes 16mm films, videorecordings and musical sound recordings. However, it is still dependent upon access to collections such as the ILEA Central Library Resources Service. The bulk of the records in the Supplement are the result of the 'direct reporting' by publishers of information on their products. It is to be hoped that a more satisfactory method can be used for future editions of the catalogue. The data are available on BLAISE-AV.

In summary, while there is an excellent bibliographical system for published books, and a well-tried distribution network, there is no system for NBM, merely hundreds of separate publishers' catalogues and lists. The librarian faced with this requires perseverance, luck, and an occasional prayer!

Steps 1, 2, 3: identifying available material, evaluating from printed sources and obtaining documents: These three steps will be considered together. Although bibliographic organizations and tools are listed separately below, there is a considerable overlap between them. The following section does not attempt to list all the available sources of help but points out a general pattern and some of the major examples.

(a) Bibliographic organizations

This section describes a range of organizations that a librarian may look to for help and advice. It is not a complete listing and for further details a useful source of information is the *International yearbook of educational and instructional technology 1982-83* Kogan Page, 1982.

Any librarian in the United Kingdom would almost certainly first turn to the British Library for information concerning bibliographic organization. The British Library is empowered to take a central role in NBM organization, and it funded fundamental research in this area.

However, the major impetus for development in this field has come from a body outside the library scene, namely the Council for Educational Technology.

Council for Educational Technology for the United Kingdom (CET)

This was established in 1973 by the Secretary of State for Education and Science to replace the National Council for Educational Technology founded in 1967. Its policy is to advance the practice and theory of educational technology. While its concern necessarily lies with the educational sector, in undertaking the task of gathering and disseminating information on all aspects of NBM it has funded research into their bibliographic organization. Notable publications as a result of this interest have included: Gilbert, L A and Wright, J *Non-book materials: their bibliographic control* NCET, 1971 (working paper no 6); Library Association (Media Cataloguing Rules Committee) *Non-book materials cataloguing rules* NCET with the LA, 1973, (also known as the LA/NCET rules); Fairfax, O, Durham, J and Wilson, W *Audiovisual materials: development of a national cataloguing and information network* CET, 1976 (working paper no 12).

The *British catalogue of audiovisual materials* was produced in collaboration with the British Library. The organization has funded considerable work on the use of Prestel and also microcomputers in libraries. This includes Gilman, J A *Information technology and the school library resource centre* CET, 1983.

The council's involvement with 'user specification' and a variety of bibliographies is mentioned elsewhere.

Without the efforts of this particular organization the developmental work in the national bibliographic organization of NBM would probably not yet have begun. Further information about it can be obtained from the journal *CET news.*

Its counterpart, the Scottish Council for Educational Technology, which incorporates the Scottish Central Film Library, should also be noted; its services include a 'software preview service', and an excellent information and bibliographic service on NBM and its equipment.

Educational Foundation for Visual Aids (EFVA)
This sponsors the National Audio-Visual Aids Library and Centre (Paxton Place, Gipsy Road, London SE27 9SR), and its several departments are:

Technical Sales and Service Departments which supplies, maintains and repairs audiovisual equipment through regional and area centres. This is particularly aimed at Local Education Authorities.

Training Department which offers advice and courses on the application and potential of audiovisual media in teaching and training.

Publications Department which provides the varied publications available from EFVA. Unfortunately, it has limited funds and has been unable to update the excellent subject catalogues of *Audio-visual aids: films, filmstrips, transparencies, wallcharts and recorded sound*. However, it has updated *16mm films in the National Audio-Visual Aids Library: a subject catalogue* EFVA, 1976 with *Supplement*, 1977-78, 1979-80, and 1980. A specialist catalogue of the *Film library for teacher education, 1982-84* is also available.

National Audio-Visual Aids Library which provides a large collection of educational and training films for loan. There is a special film hire scheme in operation which is available as an institutional subscription. Videocassettes such as the *Master class* series are also available. Filmstrips, slides, kits, ohp transparencies are also available for purchase.

Training and Educational Systems Testing Bureau
The demise of EFVA's Experimental Development Unit for testing NBM has resulted in a privately funded organization (located at Vauxhall School, Vauxhall Street, London SE11 5LG) taking on this work. It tests NBM equipment for satisfactory standards of performance, safety and ease of handling. The results are available to education, industry and business through TEST Bureau Technical Report. These are distributed every two months together with a newsletter *Technical news*. The equipment surveyed includes projectors, televisions, cassette recorders and microcomputing equipment.

Microelectronics Education Programme (MEP)
This is the agency sponsored by the Departments of Education and Science of England, Northern Ireland and Wales to encourage curriculum

work in schools to develop understanding and use of microelectronics and computers. Set up in 1980, its directorate is based at Cheviot House, Coach Lane Campus, Newcastle upon Tyne, NE7 7XA. However, MEP supports information centres in each of its fourteen regions where callers or enquirers can obtain details about materials and computer programs. In addition there are four information centres for special education called SEMERCs. Each region also publishes a newsletter containing reviews, comments, lists of materials and references to work in progress. Also available are specially written information sheets about hardware, programs, microelectronic techniques, curriculum papers and national activities.

MEP publishes books through the Council for Educational Technology, and many other materials, videotapes, tape-slides, computer programs, curriculum materials and hardware devices through a wide variety of commercial publishers and firms. It also works on joint projects with organizations like BP, BBC, and the Independent Television Companies.

Together with the British Library, MEP has sponsored the work of SoCCS to develop cataloguing rules for computer programs. It is a co-sponsor of CEDAR which maintains a database of programs for computer-assisted learning for use in all levels of education.

British Film Institute (BFI)
This is the major source of information concerning film in the UK and was established in September 1933 'to encourage the development of the art of the film, to promote its use as a record of contemporary life and manners, and to foster publication, appreciation and study of it from these points of view'. The development of television resulted in the institute also deciding 'to foster study and appreciation of films for television programmes generally, to encourage the best use of television'. However, while the majority of its services are still geared to demands for film it is clear that television is a growing interest.

Anyone over the age of sixteen may become a member or associate, and corporate membership is available to educational establishments and film societies. The *National Film Theatre* on the South Bank, London, offers a wide range of programmes, and has helped to establish a number of regional film theatres.

The *National Film Archive* is the national collection of film, and tries to cover any film shown or programme transmitted in Great Britain. It has more than 23,000 titles, and one million still photographs;

the latter can be duplicated for purchase. It adds some 1500 recorded features each year. It also has a TV off-air recording scheme which includes such programmes as BBC's *Nationwide*. Some 1000 TV programmes are added each year. The archive is developing a computer-based record-keeping system which will allow the production of computer-typeset catalogues. The *National Film Archive catalogue* Vol. 1 *Non-fiction films* was published in 1980.

The Institute's *Programming Unit* provides advisory and booking services to over 30 public exhibition venues throughout the UK and coordinates *Films and TV drama on offer*.

The *Information Division* is a collaboration of six departments and it exists 'to collect, hold and disseminate information of all kinds about film and television and to promote educational and cultural activities'. The book collection, it is claimed, includes almost everything published in English on film and television. Other documents include scripts, current and extensive back runs of periodicals, press books, newspaper clippings, and documentation relating to individuals. Its major publication is the *British national film catalogue* (BNFC). This, published from 1963 onwards, is a quarterly record of British and foreign films available in Great Britain. There are two main sequences, non-fiction films and fiction films. Features (covered by *Monthly film bulletin*) and newsreels have been excluded since 1969. Classified by subject, with alphabetical indexes under subject, title, distributors, actors, sponsors, technicians and production companies.

The *Stills, Posters and Designs Department* has an extensive collection of stills, colour transparencies and sketches. The records have been computerized to produce a printout for publication of a catalogue of stills, posters and designs.

BFI Publishing has produced books on film theory, a reader for the Open University course *Popular television and film*, and even a BFI Calendar.

Other of its publications include *Sight and sound* (which is concerned with the aesthetic aspects of film), and *Monthly film bulletin*, (which reviews all feature films and some shorts and gives basic information about the film: credits, plot synopsis and a critical assessment).

National Sound Archive

The main objective of this organization (formerly the British Institute of Recorded Sound) is to preserve sound recordings of all kinds — music of all countries and periods; literature and drama; language and dialect;

speeches and historical events; wildlife sounds. The Archive is located at 29 Exhibition Road, London SW7. It provides a free listening service by appointment. Total reference stock in 1982 comprised more than 400,000 discs of all kinds, more than 20,000 hours of recorded tape and a unique collection of non-commercial cylinders.

The extensive library concerns itself with discs, including record catalogues of all periods and countries and about 100 periodical titles. The majority of British record manufacturers present new records as they are published. There is a half-yearly journal, *Recorded sound.*

During 1983 the British Institute of Recorded Sound became part of the British Library. Its Director is answerable to the Chief Executive of BL.

British Library of Wildlife Sounds (BLOWS)

A department of the National Sound Archive whose eventual aim is to have a copy of the complete vocabularies of all sound-producing animals of the world, along with all the major, individual, seasonal and geographical variations. The collection relies on commercial recordings, the BBC sound archive discs, and privately made tape recordings. Closely linked with other wildlife sound libraries, it has assumed a special responsibility for those recordings made in Britain, by British recordists anywhere, and in the Antarctic. It is a reference collection, but some copies of tape recordings can be supplied for 'genuine scientific purposes'.

British Universities Film and Video Council

Founded in 1948, 'Its objects are to encourage the production, application and study of audiovisual media, materials and techniques for degree level teaching and research in institutions of higher education in the UK, and to provide a forum for the exchange of information and opinion in this field'. The Council is based at 55 Greek Street, London WIV 5LR.

The *Audio-Visual Reference Centre* offers a unique preview and research facility for audiovisual materials produced in universities, polytechnics and other institutions of higher education. It runs an information service which consists of a small reference library, a file of appraisals on NBM for its members, and an enquiry service. Its *Newsletter* is published three times per year and gives details of new releases and information about conferences, publications, etc.

The Slade Film History Register includes copies of all British newsreel issue sheets as well as information on collections of archive film and television in the UK and overseas.

Publications include: *Audio-Visual materials for higher education,* 1979-80 and the update edition 1981-82. These list 3,530 items which include documentary and non-fiction films, videotapes, sound tapes and tape-slide programmes currently available in the UK. They have been appraised for use in degree level teaching or research.

Higher Education Learning Programmes Information Service Catalogue (HELPIS) 7th ed, 1982-83. This lists 2,000 items made in universities, polytechnics and other institutions of higher education in the UK. (This is only material for degree-level teaching or research which may have applications outside the producing institution.)

The *Researcher's guide to British film and television collections* is an invaluable directory to archival collections of film and television material.

In the USA particular note must be made of the Library of Congress, the National Information Center for Educational Media (NICEM), and Educational Products Information Exchange (EPIE) Institute as national bibliographic agencies.

Library of Congress
Compared to the British Library this organization has produced a wealth of bibliographic tools, even though NBM does not have a very high priority in the overall objectives. However, the Library of Congress does have one of the largest collections of NBM in existence. It has some ten million prints and photographs, 250,000 reels of motion pictures, 500,000 sound recordings, and over three million microforms. Its catalogues include *Motion pictures and filmstrips 1953-5, 1958-62, 1968-72.* This excludes microfilm, and has been superseded by *Films and other materials for projection 1973-* (three quarterly issues pa, with annual and quinquennial cumulations) which now includes transparency and slide sets. For earlier materials on film, information is supplied in Niven, K R *Motion pictures from the Library of Congress paper print collection 1894-1912* University of California Press, 1967. It has also produced *The George Kleine Collection of early motion pictures in the Library of Congress: a catalog* LC, 1980. This lists approximately 3000 films, and the Library of Congress will supply prints of restored films.

Sound recordings are listed in *Music and phonorecords 1953-72,* which includes musical and non-musical sound recordings, as well as libretti and books. It has been brought up-to-date by *Music: books on music and music recordings 1973-* , which includes Library of Congress printed cards and the cards of cooperating libraries.

Photographs of prints are catalogued by Beall, K F *American prints in the Library of Congress: a catalogue of the collection* the Library/ Johns Hopkins Press, 1970 (contains entries for 12,000 prints from over 1250 artists) and Vanderbilt, P *Guide to the special collections of prints and photographs in the Library of Congress* the Library (Reference Department), 1955.

National Information Center for Educational Media (NICEM)
As the result of research by the University of Southern California's Department of Cinema this databank of computer records for a large range of NBM in the USA was established at USC, University Park, Los Angeles, CA 90007. It holds some 500,000 entries and also has information on publishers and distributors. Information is supplied to the center by the Library of Congress, by publishers, distributors and libraries. Indexes are supplied in printed and microform catalogues. These indexes are by form, for example, *Index to 16mm educational films* and also by subject as in *Index to vocational and technical education.*

Library users can also use the data bank as a cataloguing service by adding extra information to establish a personal catalogue of their holdings.

Educational Products Information Exchange (EPIE) Institute
A major source of information concerning NBM in education, EPIE Institute (475 Riverside Drive, New York, NY) is an independent non-profit making agency. Its work includes an Educational Equipment Testing Laboratory, information on the use of equipment, research into the selection and use of NBM in education, training programmes and a publications output. Its publications include *EPIEgram: materials*, which focuses on the needs of users of NBM materials, and *EPIEgram; equipment* which considers a wide variety of equipment. EPIE reports analyse in great detail materials and equipment and include client evaluations.

Libraries
The growing interest shown by librarians in NBM has resulted in the establishment of a number of collections that are excellent examples

for those beginning in this field. A selection is given below, and case studies of libraries involved in NBM are regularly presented in the periodical *Audiovisual librarian*.

Birmingham Public Libraries, Visual Aids Department: A loan service for illustrations, posters, wallcharts, slides and filmstrips. The Central Library also has a record and cassette library, art posters and 'Art packs for schools', and special collections of Edwardian and Victorian photographs.

Dundee College of Education: An outstanding example of the development of a learning resources unit and its implications for librarians. Details of it are to be found in Lickley, A *Towards individualized learning in teacher education* CET, 1977, and *College with a difference* CET, 1978 (cine film). A regular catalogue lists the NBM produced by the college lecturing staff and the learning resources department.

Centre for Information on Language Teaching and Research (CILT) (20 Carlton House Terrace, London SW1Y 5AP): Concerned with modern languages and their teaching. Has some 25,000 books plus audiovisual and recorded language teaching materials. Provides listening and viewing facilities. Publications and library of interest to all librarians not just those concerned with modern languages.

London Borough of Camden, Libraries and Art Departments: Has one of the largest audiovisual collections in a public library.

Brighton Polytechnic: Superb example of an integrated library and learning resources system. Library media services has brief to: purchase NBM; provide off-air recording of radio and television programmes; provide information services on NBM; analyse effectiveness of NBM in teaching and learning.

Advisory Unit for Computer-based Education (Endymion Road, Hatfield AL10 8AU): Major centre for the development of computer materials for education. Provides a catalogue of programs for school use.

Inner London Education Authority Central Library Resources Service: Centre for Learning Resources (275 Kennington Lane, London SE11 5QZ): Amongst its many services provides a reference library and information service of some 40,000 items including textbooks, slides, filmstrips, sound recordings, transparencies and wallcharts. ILEA also has a film video library.

Wiltshire County Library, Children's Library Service: supply 'information and inspiration in a variety of media: books, records, filmstrips, videorecordings, slides, wallcharts, tapes, models.' An exhibition stock, project collections and a circulation service of framed prints. Imaginative development of the potential of documents closely linked to their clients' needs.

Gateshead Public Library: Leading exponent of the use of Prestel for community information. Special scheme linked with local supermarket for the ordering of goods by OAPs using library Prestel sets.

Vendors

Economic factors are important reasons for librarians to choose one or two reliable suppliers of library materials. Such suppliers are numerous for books (they readily supply material with library markings and stationery incorporated). There are a number of suppliers of sound recordings, for example the Long Playing Record Library Ltd, who will process the sound discs and also supply catalogue cards. In the field of slides and filmstrip the Slide Centre is an invaluable source and their annual catalogue an essential tool for the librarian. The best-known supplier of NBM in the UK was Audiovisual Library Services Ltd. Unfortunately, the firm now only offers a packaging service for library materials from its parent body Dunn & Wilson. A spoken word cassettes and language courses service is still available from AVLS. A new firm T C Farries & Co Ltd (Irongray Road, Lochside, Dumfries) now offers an NBM service. It has produced an *AV catalogue* which is arranged in Dewey classified order. Items are supplied in publishers packaging plus library servicing. Such vendors are more common in the USA with its larger market and the annual publication *Audiovisual market place* (Bowker) gives many examples.

However, just as the library relies on bookshops as well as library suppliers so the librarian must be aware of the smaller firms supplying specialist services for the various forms of NBM. Some examples of these are the Institute of Tape Learning which supplies tape recordings that are used in the subliminal mode, that is on the threshold of sleep; Studio Two for models of dinosaurs; Camera Talks Ltd for filmstrips designed in particular for the needs of doctors and nurses; and Contemporary Films Ltd for films of East European and Third World countries. Library videorecording suppliers include Chivers Ltd, and Wynd-up video. There is no general supplier of computer materials although software for the Sinclair and BBC machines is available through the bookshops of W H Smith.

Further details of suppliers are given in the Printed Sources section which follows, but the librarian involved in this area must be prepared

172

to search through lists of distributors and advertisements in periodicals to obtain up-to-date details of the suppliers of specialist aspects of NBM.

Exhibitions
New developments in equipment, and the opportunity to see a wide range of NBM, make it essential to attend exhibitions. Local equipment suppliers regularly hold exhibitions, and at a national level there are a wide range: the Audiovisual Exhibition and Conference, which deals with NBM used in training and sales; Education, Training and Development which is a focal point for education and training in the UK and shows the latest developments in the full range of equipment and services; Photography at Work; Audio Fare for Hi-fi equipment and materials; and Personal Computer World Show which is the major exhibition of microcomputers. Details of these exhibitions may be found in periodicals such as *Audiovisual librarian*, *Audiovisual* and *Personal computer world*.

Personal contact
Close contact must be made with other librarians and specialists involved in this field, with experts from local radio and television stations, and local film and photographic societies. Area resource organizations enable libraries to share the problems of selection and there is a Standing Conference of Area Resource Organizations (SCARO). Further details may be obtained through CET and their information officer. The regional centres for the Microelectronics Education Programme will also provide details of microcomputer experts within their region. In certain areas local self help groups such as SHEMROC (Sheffield Media Resources) will also provide details of local experts in a variety of NBM materials. *Personal computer world* has a regular feature on computer clubs such as Computer Town UK. However, it is to the professional associations that librarians will turn most readily for help and advice. In the UK the Aslib Audiovisual Group and the Library Association Audiovisual Group have been most prominent in establishing workshops and conferences.

In the USA the American Library Association have established standards for resources through such bodies as the Audiovisual Committee of the Public Library Association.

(b) Printed sources
This section is divided into the following divisions: General; Paper; Still pictures; Moving pictures; Sound recordings; Realia/specimens; Micro-computing. There is some overlap between these, and reference should also be made to the sources available from the various bibliographic organisations which have been mentioned above. Both American and British printed sources are listed here, but it must be stressed that no attempt has been made to give a complete listing; these are only examples to explain a general pattern of searching.

General
The development of large online computer data bases offers the possibility of a comprehensive listing. BLAISE-AV offers the potential for a UK listing, and the possibility of further computerization of the British National Film Catalogue and the closer links established to the National Sound Archive by the British Library holds out the promise of national online service for NBM. The developments of the OCLC service in the USA and UK similarly offers the librarian access to over seven million records which include a high percentage of NBM published.

Particular reference should be made to the sources mentioned under the various organizations. The major guide to bibliographic sources is: Andrew, J R *Non-book materials and the librarian: a select bibliography* 2nd ed, Aslib Audiovisual Group, 1972. This covers books, pamphlets and periodical articles written in English since 1965, on all aspects of the librarianship of NBM. Supplements are carried in each number of *Audiovisual librarian* 1- , 1973/4, a quarterly journal jointly published by the Library Association Audiovisual Group and Aslib Audiovisual Group. It is an invaluable source for news of developments and reviews of books and NBM on the subject of audiovisual librarianship. It also contains news of microcomputer equipment and materials. Also note Sive, M R *Complete media monitor: guide to learning resources* Scarecrow Press, 1981; *Educational media yearbook* Libraries Unlimited, which is an annual publication which includes a 'mediagraphy' which lists print and non-print sources.

One of the pioneer works is by Croghan, A *A bibliographic system for non-book media: a description and list of works* 2nd ed, Coburgh, 1979. It is essential reading and contains a wealth of sources both British and North American. The most useful general handbook is Henderson, J and Humphreys, F *Audiovisual and microcomputer handbook* Kogan Page, 1980- .

Periodicals are, of course, essential to keep up to date for the calendars of events they provide, and their reviews of new NBM and equipment. *Audiovisual* (MacLaren 1972-) is monthly. It is a valuable source for new developments in equipment and NBM use in industry and commerce. Its annual supplement is known as the 'Directory', listing equipment manufacturers, production services, and NBM publishers. Trade names are included. *The booklist* (American Library Association 1905-) has reviewed NBM regularly since 1969. *Material matters* (Hertfordshire Library Service, County Headquarters, Hertford, SG13 8EJ) is issued nine times per year. It reviews the full range of NBM for children up to school leaving age. The *Times educational supplement* (Times Newspapers, 1910-) has a resources section, NBM and equipment reviews, and current awareness. These reviews are *not* listed in the *Times index.*

Comprehensive listings do not really exist. The available catalogues listing all types of NBM do not have the complete coverage required. The nearest to a national bibliography of NBM is the *British catalogue of audiovisual materials* from the British Library 1979 plus supplements, and the catalogues from the National Information Center for Educational Media. However, both are descriptive and the librarian must look elsewhere for evaluation. Useful sources for this are *International index to multi-media information* (Audiovisual Associates, 1974-). Quarterly; formerly *Film review index 1970-1973*. This cites references to all forms of NBM material in over 100 North American and British publications. Citation includes review source. Indexed via title, series, subject, author, producer, distributor and reviewing publications; uses a MARC-based system. *Media review digest* (Pierian Press, 1974-) is the successor to *Multimedia reviews index 1970-1973*. It is an annual index to and a digest of reviews, evaluations and descriptions of NBM appearing in a variety of periodicals. Also note *Instructional innovator* formerly *Audiovisual instruction* that has regular features on computers (Association for Educational Communication and Technology, 1956-) of which there are eight per annum. It contains reviews of bibliographic tools and describes new equipment.

Directories and yearbooks are invaluable sources for technical details, addresses of manufacturers, publishers and specialists, and to find out current work in the NBM field. The British librarian does not have access to a general NBM directory, and would benefit from the equivalent of *Audiovisual market place: a multi-media guide* (Bowker). Annual, lists American and Canadian publishers of NBM, associations, equipment manufacturers, cataloguing services, library suppliers, etc.

Publishers' catalogues are invaluable for a librarian who wants to have a complete coverage of NBM materials. Two of the most important are those from (a) The Drake Group of Companies which includes Educational Productions Ltd (212, Whitchurch Road, Cardiff CF4 3NB) supply a wide variety of forms and subjects. They are major producers and their catalogues are a necessity. Apart from their own material they stock material from Story Teller Tapes, Youth Hostel Association, Design Council, Schools Council, Historical Association, Language Master Programmes, Lincolnshire Educational Television Centre, and sound cassettes on 'Librarians speaking'. (b) Fergus Davidson Associates Ltd, 376 London Road, West Croydon, Surrey, CR0 2SU. A wide range of NBM is distributed for some twenty publishers, including a number in North America. Particularly useful for the catalogues of Encyclopedia Britannica Corporation, and the National Film Board of Canada, provide an excellent record and cassette guide to over 30 publishers including Ivan Berg Cassettes, Seminar Cassettes Ltd, and the Scripture Union, as well as Educational Films of Scotland, International Tele-Film Enterprises, and Chatsworth Film Distributors Ltd.

The Open University has developed an international reputation as a supplier of learning resources and its catalogues should be in most libraries. Open University Educational Enterprises, 12 Cofferidge Close, Stony Stratford, Milton Keynes, MK11 1BY is the address for purchase of all Open University productions.

Guides to publishers' catalogues do not provide complete coverage, and subject access is particularly difficult. Three examples are *Index to instructional media catalogues* Bowker, 1974. This is a guide to 650 American publishers of NBM. Subject index and also details of equipment and service are included. *World AV programme directory*, compiled by The Videofilm Centre and published by Bowker. This is a microfiche collection of publishers' catalogues. There are three supplements per year. There is also the *Educational media catalogs on microfiche* Olympic Media, 1983, which is an American publication. *Treasure chest for teachers: services available to teachers and schools* the Schools Publishing Co is an invaluable source of information concerning materials available from societies, associations, embassies, commerce, industry, museums, art galleries, and commercial publishers, and is particularly useful for addresses, and includes subject indexes. A useful listing is *AVSCOT checklist of UK audio-visual software producers* The Scottish Branch of the Audiovisual Group of the Library Association, 1981.

Museums and art galleries are prolific publishers of NBM and two essential guides are Roulstone, M *The bibliography of museum and art gallery publications and audiovisual aids in Great Britain and Ireland* Chadwyck-Healey, 1980, which contains more than 15,000 publications and audiovisual aids from over 1000 museums and galleries. The majority of them are not listed in any other bibliography. NBM include posters, slides, films, discs, tapes, models and reproductions. Paul Wassermann has edited *Catalog of museum publications and media* 2nd ed, Gale, 1980, index and directory of publications and audiovisuals available from US and Canadian museums and art galleries.

There is no one comprehensive specialist subject source guide, though a wide range of tools is available, including the catalogues of specialist subject publishers and subject bibliographies. The British Universities Film and Video Council is perhaps the major supplier of such guides for higher education. A further problem is the wealth of subject material that is unpublished, but available through exchange or special arrangements. General subject guides include the Higher Education Learning Programmes Information Service Catalogue (HELPIS) 7th ed, 1982-83, BUFC, 1982. It lists some multimedia produced by universities and polytechnics, to encourage exchange of materials.

Specialist subject guides are numerous and include the following: *Guide to audiovisual material for the construction industry* Building Centre Trust, 1982; Malley, I *Catalogue of United Kingdom audiovisual media suitable for use in library instruction courses* 2nd ed, Loughborough University of Technology Library, 1980; Mehlinger, H D *Unesco handbook for the teaching of social studies*, Croom Helm, 1981; the series produced by the City of London Polytechnic which includes *Media resources on 'Industry for lecturers'* 1980; *Inequalities for lecturers* 1980; *Town and country planning for lecturers* 1981. An up-to-date guide to information on China is Mary Sive's work *China: multimedia guide* Neal Schumann, 1982. Medical material is covered by the *Graves medical audiovisual library* (Holly House, 220 New London Road, Chelmsford, Essex CM2 9BJ). There is a catalogue for this postal service of medical and paramedical NBM. A regular newsletter is available for subscribers. A useful work for people concerned with the new technology is Maddison, J *Information technology and education: an annotated guide to printed, audiovisual and multimedia resources* Open University Press, 1983. This contains over 1500 references to printed works, some 400 films, and over 300 educational packs.

Specialist subject publishers include the following: The British

177

Council, Design, Production and Publishing Department (65 Davies Street, London W1Y 2AA). They produce 'Literature study aids' for the student of English literature. As well as books they produce tape-slide programmes, for example on 'British books and libraries', and 'Microcomputers in schools'; videorecordings, for example on the 'Overhead projector' and sound cassettes, for example a series of inter-views of leading British novelists and dramatists. British Petroleum Educational Service (P O Box 5, Wetherby, West Yorkshire LE23 7EN) provides a 'Resources catalogue for schools and colleges'. This includes a wide range of material on oil, road safety, energy, travel and environ-ment. There are BP Preview Centres on a regional basis for this mat-erial. Material can also be ordered via Prestel. Details are also available of their work on computer programmes, eg conservation and marketing. The Chemical Society, Education Division, Educational Techniques Subject Group (Burlington House, Piccadilly, London W1V 0BN) aims to produce materials for use in chemistry education in schools, uni-versities and polytechnics. 'Chemistry cassettes' present authoritative accounts of various aspects of chemistry, prepared and spoken by distinguished chemists. Details are also available of CALCHEM materials and it is planned to put them in a suitable form for microcomputers.

The Historical Association (59a Kennington Park Road, London SE11 4JH) aim to stimulate public interest in all aspects of history. Slide sets are produced in collaboration with Educational Productions, 16mm films using only original newsreel material from the 1930s in collaboration with Macmillan Education. The Town and Contry Plan-ning Association (17 Carlton Terrace, London SW17 5AS) publishes a monthly *Bulletin of environmental education* (BEE) which is a mine of information of materials on the environment.

Equipment: Details of equipment may be obtained via the manufac-turers' publicity material, the annual distribution lists, and periodical advertisements. Directories and yearbooks will also give lists of equip-ment and their manufacturers' addresses. A general source is: *Audio-visual and microcomputer handbook: SCET guide to educational and training equipment* Kogan Page, 1982. It is designed to help both the expert and the beginner to find their way through the morass of conflict-ing information, advice and advertising which exists with regard to audiovisual equipment and services. It also lists software producers and distributors and training courses, and is an essential handbook for every library. In the USA the *Audiovisual equipment directory* (National Audiovisual Association) is essential reading.

Criteria to judge equipment by may be obtained from standards and specification sources such as USPECS, CET. Evaluation of equipment can be located in general periodicals such as *Audio visual* and in specialist periodicals for the various forms. The Training and Educational Systems Testing Bureau issues reports on equipment and these include the full range of audiovisual hardware including microcomputers. Note also the services of the Educational Products Information Exchange in the USA.

The Consumers' Association also evaluates equipment in its periodical *Which?* (1952-). However, these should be treated with caution as they are judging for domestic rather than institutional usage. Whether a cassette tape recorder can survive a fall of three feet on to a concrete floor is perhaps more important than the question of its control knobs being aesthetically pleasing!

Paper

Paper as a medium for NBM includes a wide range of forms — wallcharts, portfolios, posters, art reproductions, games, programmed learning materials. There is no comprehensive source to guide one in the quest for this material. Wallcharts, posters and art reproductions tend to overlap, and there are numerous shops selling these forms.

One comprehensive listing of educational wallcharts, now sadly dated, is *A catalogue of wallcharts*, 7th ed, EFVA, 1972. This consists of a subject-arranged list of charts and flannelgraphs suitable for use in schools, without evaluations. There is no comprehensive up-to-date guide to wallcharts although note the entries in the *British catalogue of audiovisual materials*. Similarly the guides to art reproductions are dated. An international listing of art reproductions comes from Unesco: *Catalogue of colour reproductions of paintings prior to 1860*, 8th ed, 1968, and *Catalogue of reproductions of paintings, 1860-1973*, 10th ed, 1974. These carry beside each entry a small black and white reproduction, together with information on printer, publisher, and price. There is also an index of artists, publishers and printers. A comprehensive source is *Art index* H W Wilson, 1929- , which includes listings of reproductions in art periodicals and museum publications. There is also a specialist publication *Reproductions* 4th ed, Haddahs Fine Arts, 1982.

Audiovisual Library Services have a stock catalogue *Wallcharts, posters and prints* which includes material from the *Sunday times*, British Museum, official Olympic posters and a number of the major publishers.

There are numerous publishers' catalogues, three examples being:

Sports Posters (61 Chandos Avenue, Whetstone, London, N20) which has a large display of material which reflects their name. Educational Graphics (43 Camden Passage, London N1) have a very wide range including art reproductions. The Pictorial Charts Educational Trust is based at 27 Kirchen Road, London W13 0UD.

There are a number of suppliers of games. C Elgood Associates Ltd (21 Cork Street, London W1X 1HB) produce a wide range of business games and training exercises. The Society for Academic Gaming and Simulation in Education and Training (Centre for Extension Studies, University of Technology, Loughborough, Leics LE11 3TU) publishes a quarterly periodical *Simulation/games for learning* Kogan Page, 1971- , and members also receive SAGSET news, which includes current information and reviews of games, simulations and books.

Programmed learning is covered by the Association for Educational and Training Technology, whose *International yearbook of educational and instructional technology*, Kogan Page, 1972- , has a major listing of programmed learning centres in the UK.

Portfolios are numerous and the most famous publisher is Jackdaw Publications Ltd of 30 Bedford Square, London WC1B 3EL. The form has been adopted by a number of producers.

Still pictures

These include photographs, slides, filmstrips, overhead projector transparencies, and microforms. Many of the sources also include illustrations collections. There are a number of commercial picture libraries, the finest in the UK probably being the BBC Hulton Picture Library which contains over six million photographs, drawings, prints, etc. However, picture libraries charge for their services and anyone interested in using this form is advised to look at Harrison, H P *Picture librarianship* Library Association, 1981, and also British Association of Picture Libraries and Agencies *BALPA Directory: a list of members, a subject index and a practical guide for libraries and their users* BALPA, 1981. Bradshaw, D N and Hahn, C *World photography sources* Bowker, 1983, covers over 2000 collections and indexes them alphabetically, geographically and via subject.

The major guide to British collections is Wall, J *Directory of British photographic collections* (Royal Photographic Society, 1977). 'Every kind of photographic collection has been the subject of this enquiry . . . from the discovery of photography to the present day'. Arranged in main subjects with subject, owner, location, title and photographer indexes.

One of the most useful publisher's catalogues for slides and film-strips is that of the Slide Centre Ltd, 143 Chatham Road, London SW11 6SR. This invaluable catalogue includes slide and filmstrips, some with sound commentaries, from Ladybird, Diana Wyllie, Mullard, Health Education Audiovisual, Longman/Common Ground, Wood-mansterne, Focal Point, Students' Recording, BBC Radiovision, Walt Disney, and also their own Slide Centre slidefolios.

Other publishers include Camera Talks Ltd, 31 North Row, London W1R 2EN, which produce filmstrips aimed in particular at the needs of doctors, midwives, nurses and health inspectors. Also non-professional topics such as 'Crime prevention' and 'Sex and education'. Educational Audio Visual Ltd are American in origin (Pleasantville NY 10570). UK distributor: Mary Glasgow Publications Ltd of Brookhampton Lane, Kineton, Warwick CV35 0JB. They produce sound filmstrips and are particularly strong on social studies, world history and music. Visual Publications, The Green, Northleach, Cheltenham GL54 3EX sell slides, integrated media kits and sound filmstrips. Two subject specialities are fine and applied arts and sciences, in particular earth sciences. (In USA: 716 Center Street, Lewiston, NY 14092.)

Major slide library catalogues are those of the Design Council, whose *Slide library catalogue* (1973) fulfils the aim of the council which is to encourage good design by photographing objects in its own collection which meet this criterion, and also objects it does not possess. The *Design Centre Selection, 1981-82* is a photographic record of some 7000 British made goods and is available on microfiche. The Victoria and Albert Museum, National Art Slide Library, has more than 500,000 slides listed in subject catalogues. The majority of catalogues are available only on site, but there are shorter listings available for borrowers. Slides may be borrowed free of charge, in person or by post, by any resident in the United Kingdom.

Photographs are available from a number of firms, for example the Photographic Gallery, 8 Great Newport Street, London WC2 7JA, where the stock includes the original work of photographers and post-cards of Victorian photographs. Aerofilms Ltd, of Gate Studios, Boreham Wood, Herts WD6 1EJ publishes the *Aerofilms book of aerial photographs* (1971). It holds photographs from the Victorian age to date, but this firm specializes in aerial views from the 1920s to the present. Over 500,000 aerial photographs are for sale. Suppliers of overhead projector transparencies are listed in the *Audio visual and microcomputer handbook* and major publishers include Audiovisual

181

Productions (Hocker Hill House, Chepstow, Gwent NP5 ER) for a wide variety of subjects. Anvis Visuals Ltd, The Model Making Business, Mill Street Studios, Bridgnorth, Shropshire WB15 5AG specializes particularly in engineering subjects, and Fordigraph Division, Offrex Group Ltd, Offrex House, Stephen Street, London W1A 1EA distributes US material on a wide range of subjects.

Cameras and projectors are reviewed in the general equipment sources. The specialist periodicals include the *British journal of photography* (Greenwood, 1860-). A specialist yearbook is the *British journal of photography annual* (Greenwood, 1964-) which includes a picture section, feature section and a formulae section. A regular item 'Epitome of progress' lists current developments in equipment.

Microform materials are covered by *Guide to microforms in print* Mansell, which is in two parts. Part 1 is arranged by subject/title. Part 2 is a subject arrangement. It excludes theses and dissertations. A companion volume is the *Subject guide to microforms in print* (NCR Microcard, 1962-). *International microforms in print* is a guide to microforms of non-US micropublications (*Microform review*, Mansell, 1974-). It includes 'monographs, journals, newspapers, government publications and different types of archival material'. University Microfilms (Ann Arbor, MI 48106; 18 Bedford Row, London WC1R 4EJ) has approximately 11,000 titles of serial literature available.

Specialist periodicals include *Microform review* Jan 1972- , a quarterly journal containing reviews and evaluations. The National Reprographic Centre for Documentation puts out *Reprographics quarterly*, a journal of a national information service for the materials and equipment for micrography and reprography. Contains reviews and micrographic abstracts.

Specialist directories include *Microform market place,* an international directory of micropublishing (Mansell, 1974). Contains full listing of organizations and their publishing programmes.

A current microfiche publishing programme of great value to media studies is that of Chadwyck-Healey Ltd, 20 Newmarket Road, Cambridge CB2 1NB. This publishes the BBC radio 6pm news broadcasts, together with printed name and subject indexes. Annual subscription begins at January 1 1978. Other publications on microfiche from this firm include *BBC radio: Author and title catalogues of transmitted drama, poetry and features 1923-1975* and *BBC television: Author and title catalogues of transmitted drama and features 1936-1975*, together with chronological list of transmitted plays.

182

Equipment is evaluated in *Guide to microform readers and reader-printers* 3rd ed, G G Baker, 1977. This firm also produces a *Guide to microfilm readers and reader-printers* 4th ed, G G Baker, 1979.

Moving pictures
The sources for this section have been divided into cinefilm and video-recording, although there is considerable overlap between the two, and many cinefilms are also available as videorecordings. Bibliographic tools published by the British Film Institute, BUFC, Library of Congress, NICEM and the Educational Foundation for Visual Aids should also be consulted. One of the most important reference books is that produced by the American Film Institute *Catalog of motion pictures; including feature films, 1921-1930* 2 vol, Bowker, 1979.

As far as *cinefilm* is concerned, there are numerous film hire libraries, but perhaps the major source is the British Film Institute's *Distribution library catalogue* (1978). This has a critical text and sources of information on all the 2700 titles available from the BFI. Also of value is the *Films and TV drama on offer* (1982), and *Films and videograms for schools* (1983) lists over 1500 films and videocassettes. Other major film libraries include the Central Film Library, Chalfont Grove, Gerrard's Cross, Bucks SL9 8TN. This specializes in 16mm films and video-cassettes produced or acquired by the Central Office of Information, distributed for non-profit showings. The catalogue (1977) includes general, educational and industrial material. Concord Films Council Ltd, 201 Felixstowe Road, Ipswich, Suffolk IP3 9BJ, are specialists in films of controversy and concern, for example, adoption, nuclear weapons, world poverty. Their catalogue lists over 2500 titles including videocassettes. Founded by members of the Quakers, it also provides a distribution service for over 100 charities. Contemporary Films Ltd, 55 Greek Street, London W1V 6DB, has feature and documentary films, worldwide. It is particularly strong in East European and Third World countries. Guild Sound and Vision Ltd, Woodston House, Oundle Road, Peterborough PE2 9PZ, are probably the biggest commercial distributors of audiovisual educational programmes in the world outside the USA, and have a large film sale and hire business.

Companies which market their own films include BBC Enterprises, Room 503, Villiers House, The Broadway, Ealing, London W5 2PA. Their film and video output is available for purchase from this address. The hiring of BBC materials is through BBC Enterprises Limited Film Hire at the same address as Guild Sound and Vision. Some material is also available through Concord Films Council Ltd. Other companies include Macmillan Education Ltd, Houndmills, Basingstoke, Hampshire RG21 2XS (standard and super 8mm film loops); Video Arts, Sales Dept, 2nd Floor, Dumbarton House, 68 Oxford Street, London W1N 9LA (16mm film, videocassette). Amusing, but practical, films on management problems; Weston Woods Studios Ltd, 14 Friday Street, Henley-on-Thames, Oxon RG9 1PZ (filmstrips and cinefilms of children's stories. An essential address for the children's librarian). (In USA: Weston, Conn 06880.)

A number of industrial concerns also distribute films, for example British Petroleum Film Library, 15 Beaconsfield Road, London NW10 2LE. They make available films on loan to commercial and industrial firms, educational institutions, public libraries, film societies, scientific, technical and cultural societies, international institutions and organizations of all kinds. The Central Electricity Generating Board, Sudbury House, 15 Newgate Street, London WC1A 7AU, produces films on all aspects of electricity, including atomic energy.

There are a number of subject guides, for example *1982/83 films and video catalogue* Mental Health Film Council, 1983. Lists over 600 items from 70 distributors. Royal Anthropological Institute Film Library Catalogue (56 Queen Anne Street, London W1M 9LA). The Educational Film Locator (Bowker, 1980 USA) lists more than 40,000 films and provides a subject and audience level index. A wide range of films on the mining and use of metals is indicated in *Film & Video Catalogue* 3rd ed, Institution of Metallurgists, 1980.

Specialist periodicals include *Film news: international review of non-theatrical film, video, filmstrips, A V materials, and equipment* Open Court Publishing 1939- . *Monthly film bulletin* British Film Institute, 1934-) reviews feature films and shorts. Includes credits, a synopsis of the plot, and an evaluation. *Movie maker* (Model and Allied Publication, 1967-) reviews new products and tests equipment. *Screen digest* (Screen Digest Ltd, 1971-) gives 'monthly news, summaries and intelligence' on cinefilm, television and videorecording. Regular background supplements including video cassette systems, industrial films and cable television.

Equipment for cinefilm and videorecording is evaluated in the general equipment sources and the specialist periodicals.

Comprehensive guides to *videorecordings* are now appearing. Many deal only with the entertainment aspect of the format. A more general source is *Video index* (Link House) which lists new releases and back issues under the headings: movies; music; children; sport; general; foreign; adult. It also lists distributors and also the distributors of specific labels. *Which video* (Argus) evaluates equipment and software. Educational Video Index Ltd (42 Farringdon Street, London EC4A 4AN) lists some 25 producers of video materials in their catalogue. *Video source book − UK* (Distributed by Bookwise Video, Langham Trading Estate, Catteshall Lane, Godalming, Surrey GU7 1NG) is a major source for video materials. The loose leaf handbook *Video production techniques* Kluwer Publishing Ltd, is an important updating service for the video producer.

It is important to remember that cinefilm and videorecordings are increasingly being listed by the same bibliographical tools and the references under cinefilms should also be considered.

Videodiscs are a newer source and bibliographical tools are starting to appear. Note Sears *Video discs: a history and discography* Greenwood Press, 1981. The first general guide is *Internationale Bildplatten Katalog* which lists some 1000 titles, published by Schule Schone, Markgrafenstrasse 11, D1000 Berlin 61, Germany.

Sound recordings
The bibliographic sources for musical recordings are relatively well organized compared to other non-book maerials. It is the non-musical recording that presents perhaps the greatest problem. The reference tools published by the Library of Congress, NICEM, BUFVC should be consulted. The National Sound Archive unfortunately does not publish a catalogue; however, it does produce a quarterly periodical, *Recorded sound* (1961-), which contains discographies and articles on historical recordings. The indispensable retrospective listing for recorded music is compiled by Clough, F F and Cuming, G J *The world's encyclopedia of recorded music* Sidgwick and Jackson, 1952. (WERM) 2nd supplement, 1953, 3rd supplement 1957. This work covers all electrically recorded music up to 1953.

There is no comprehensive listing for non-musical recordings although a useful source is *The gramophone* annual publication *Spoken word and miscellaneous catalogue. The new Penguin stereo records and cassette guide* Penguin, 1982 is an indispensable source for creating a new record collection. It evaluates over 3500 classical music recordings. Its counterpart for popular music sound recordings is the *New Rock Record* Blandford Press, 1981, which lists some 30,000 LPs.

A wide range of publishers' catalogues is available, some describing
185

only tapes or only discs, while other firms are now publishing both. Popular music has a trade list: *Music master* (John Humphries, 1974-). This is an all-industry master record catalogue of popular LPs. Specialist sound disc publishers include: Argo (1 Rockley Road, London W14 ODL) for spoken work, folksong and some reissues of BBC material. Collet's (Dennington Estate, Wellingborough, Northants NN8 2QT) specializes in Russian language and literature. Discourses (35 Crescent Road, Tunbridge Wells, Kent) has sound discs and tapes on a wide range of music subjects, but also produces and publishes the 'British bird' series for Shell. Topic Records Ltd (27 Nassington Road, London NW3 3TX) publishes folksong and folk music.

Cassette publishers include Audio Learning (Sarda House, 183-189 Queensway, London W2 5HL) which have a large range of sound cassettes on several subjects. Seminar Cassettes (218 Sussex Gardens, London W2 3UD) produce discussion tapes including *International report* a series on current controversies. Discussion guides are also available. Sussex Tapes (Sussex Publications Ltd, Devizes, Wiltshire SN10 1BR) publish recordings of debates between notable academics. Subjects include English, history, sociology, mathematics, chemistry. This material is also available through their subscription library.

Subjects specialist publishers include: Waterlow Cassettes (Maxwell House, Worship Street, London EC2A 2EN) which produce sound cassettes aimed at business and the professions. Holdsworth Audio-visual (18 Malbrook Road, London SW15 6UF) produce materials on interviewing, management techniques, etc.

There are periodicals in sound cassette form: *Personnel training bulletin* (Didasko, Didasko House, Station Road, Warboys, Huntingdon, Cambridgeshire PE17 2BR). On the popular musical front there is SFX (SFX Publications Ltd, Brettenham House, Lancaster House, Lancaster Place, London WC2) and CET have set up a number of tape archives for local radio productions. Details of these may be received from CET.

Reviews of recordings and equipment can be located in the specialist periodicals, for example *Cassette scrutiny* which is a one-man operation by Michael Greenhalgh and can be obtained from the editor at Ealing College of Higher Education, School of Library and Information Studies, St Mary's Road, Ealing, London W5 5RF. It is issued quarterly and reviews spoken word and music cassettes and also technical innovations. *The gramophone* (General Gramophone Publications, 1923-) is a monthly periodical which reviews sound discs and equipment, and new record and cassette releases. Its *Classical records catalogue* (1953-) comes out quarterly, and lists LP records and tapes currently available in the UK. The *Popular record catalogue* (1955-) is six-monthly, and covers light, popular, variety, dance, swing and allied music. The *Spoken word and miscellaneous catalogue* is annual, and indexes documentary, children's, foreign languages, instructional, and sound effects publications. *Schwan record and tape guide* is an American publication for currently available records and tapes.

Indexes to reviews include the American *Annual index to popular music record review* (Scarecrow Press, 1973-) and *Index to record and tape reviews: a classical music buying guide* Chulaian Press.

Guidance on equipment can be obtained from specialist periodicals and yearbooks such as *Hi-fi yearbook* (IPC, 1956-), which has articles on how to select equipment, and lists its recordings of the year. There is also an information section on sound equipment, and a directory of brand names, makers and suppliers. A more specialist guide is *ASCE Directory: products, manufacturers and distributors of audio equipment in UK* published by the Association of Sound and Communications Engineers.

Realia/specimens
Given tenacity, a scale model of almost anything can be located. Plastic model kits can be purchased from many manufacturers, especially, in the UK, from Airfix Ltd. There are no comprehensive reference sources to suppliers in the UK, but diligent attention to advertisements in periodicals can prove fruitful. The following publishers are given as examples. Educational and Scientific Plastics Ltd, 76 Holmethorpe Avenue, Redhill, Surrey RH1 2PF, specialize in models of the anatomy, skeleton, etc. Soho Gallery Ltd, 28-32 Shelton Street, London WC2H 9HP, puts out art prints, but also supplies ALVA museum replicas which are cast from works in internationally known museums. Stuart Turner Ltd, Henley-on-Thames, Oxon RG9 2AD, specializes in model engineering construction. Griffin and George (285 Ealing Road, Alperton, Wembley, Middx HA0 1HJ) also produce moulded models and cut out card models. Studio Two Educational (6 High Street, Barkway, Royston, Hertfordshire SG8 8EE) provides a wide range of NBM but of particular interest are their plastic kits and cardboard replicas of prehistoric animals and Egyptian artifacts.

Some museums also supply models; for example the British Museum produces (amongst many other items) a cut-out model of the king's helmet from the Sutton Hoo ship burial.

An American guide which offers some useful insights into the use of realia in libraries is by Hektoen, F H *Toys to go: a guide to the use of realia in public libraries* Chicago, American Library Association, 1976.

Microcomputing software and equipment

The librarian who has to acquire microcomputer software does not have an easy task. The bibliographical control of this format has yet to be established and it is difficult to identify sources of information which are accurate and unbiased. The wide range of equipment and computing languages exacerbates the problems of acquisition.

The increased demand for software has resulted in the rapid growth of suppliers and the wise librarian will exercise caution in the evaluation of software and choice of supplier. The decision of the library to standardize on a particular microcomputer or a limited range of microcomputers should be influenced by the software that is available or likely to be published. Software is a major cost in the use of microcomputers.

A number of institutional bodies have been established to offer advice in this area. These include the National Computing Centre (NCC) Oxford Road, Manchester M1 7ED, which develops computing techniques and provides aids for the more effective use of computers. Members have access to a large database of information and the Centre publishes a number of guides, including a *Directory of hardware* and a *Directory of software*. However, it should be noted that they are still predominantly involved with the larger computers, although they are developing information services for microcomputers. The educational user should also contact his regional centre of the Microelectronics Education Programme (see page 165).

Another important source of information is Computers in Education as a Resource (CEDAR), Imperial College Computer Centre, Exhibition Road, London SW7 2BX. This offers a national service including an enquiry service with databases on books, periodicals, etc and also one on computer-assisted learning packages available in the UK (these are available on microfiche). They also provide a library service, index of experts, and training workshops. There is a regular newsletter *CALNEWS* with information on projects, books and conferences. The Microsystems Centre (11 New Fetter Lane,

London EC4 1PU) provides a similar service for the business world.

Micronet 800 also offers a national service for its members and is available via Prestel. It offers guides to hardware, software, benchtests, buyers guides, details of user clubs, and a news magazine. Telesoftware services are also available.

The publishers of software are numerous. They include: schoolchildren as in Houghton County Primary School (Houghton, Huntingdon, Cambs.) who supply software for the Commodore Pet; specialist suppliers as in Medical Micro System (26 High Street, Bishops Lydeard, Taunton) who supply software such as a doctor's patient file; traditional book suppliers such as Ginn and Co; and computer manufacturers such as Apple Computers (UK) Ltd (Eastman Road, Hemel Hempstead, Herts).

There are a considerable number of subscription services which operate an 'exchange service'. For example, the Central Program Exchange (Department of Computing and Mathematics, Polytechnic of Wolverhampton, Wulfruna Street, Wolverhampton WV1 1LY) offers the subscriber a service which includes the copying of up to ten programs per year free plus extra programs for a small fee. Materials for specific microcomputers are also available, for example PETPACK Master Library (Commodore Information Centre, 360 Euston Road, London NW1 3BL); BBC microcomputers (BBC Microcomputer System, PO Box 7, London W3 6XJ); and Atari Program Exchange (185-195 Ealing Road, Alperton, Wembley, Middlesex).

A serial publication *Small computer program index* ALLM Books, 1981- (21 Beachcroft Road, Bushey, Herts, WD2 2JU) lists programs published in books and periodicals in the UK and USA.

The major printed sources for software are in periodical form. These include general publications such as *Personal computer world* (Computing Publications Ltd, 1978-) which offers guides to software and equipment; and *Which micro and software review* (EMAP). Specialist subject periodicals include *Micro decision* (VNU Business Publn. 1981-) which provides a directory of retailers and software for business users; *Educational computing* which includes a directory of educational computing software. Finally, there are periodicals for particular makes of equipment such as *BBC micro user* (Database Publn. 1983-). The latter type of periodicals are essential once the library has decided on a make of microcomputer. Such periodicals list suppliers for the machine and software, for example for the BBC some 40 suppliers for over 300 programs are noted.

189

Specialist subject sources include the Economics Association who publish an *Annotated guide to CAL materials in economics* quarterly in the journal *Economics*. The Geographic Association Package Evaluation contributes lists and reviews to the journal *Teaching geography*. The Engineering Science (CAL) Program Exchange is based in the Faculty of Engineering, Queen Mary College, Mile End Road, London E1 4NS. The Institution of Electrical Engineers also publish guides in their journal *Electronic systems news*.

There is no general catalogue to microcomputing software. The ILEA Centre for Learning Resources is cataloguing a wide range of software and this could be the basis of a future national catalogue. There is an *International microcomputer software directory* Imprint, 1981 but it is of limited value. The standard source for computing is *The computer users' yearbook* (Computing Publishing Ltd) but this and its sibling publication *International directory of software* are only slowly recognizing the demands of the microcomputer users.

Telesoftware is increasingly an important source for computer programs. This is the transmission of programs from one computer to another by broadcast radio, television or via telephone lines. Independent local radio has experimented in this area and there is a service provided by Belgium national radio. The BBC transmit programs via CEEFAX, and Prestel provide a service called 'Aladdin's Cave' and also transmit this facility on Micronet 800. A Directory of Prestel facilities *The prestel user* (1978-) lists the services available. However, librarians will also have to provide their own index to the service if they are to gain maximum benefit from the complex indexing system. Directel from 1983 will bring out this publication.

Information concerning equipment is available from many of the above services and the benchtest service provided by TEST should also be noted (see page 165).

Steps 4 and 5: Previewing and purchase: The bibliographic organizations and publications listed above can help the librarian to decide which NBM should be considered for further selection. A review may even give information to enable the librarian to purchase the document sight unseen. However, a review of a particular document perhaps may not exist, or may only give insufficient detail for a decision to be made. The librarian will then have to consider previewing the item.

If a library supplier is used it may be possible to obtain the items on approval, and some publishers will supply direct for a short approval period, against either an official requisition or a full cash deposit. Publishers of sound recordings are usually unwilling to send any material on approval because of copyright problems. In larger libraries, such as a public library system, the easiest course might be to buy one copy of everything that seems to be suitable, and then to decide whether further copies are required. Film will normally be hired out for previewing and with a number of suppliers the cost of hire may be offset against the purchase price later paid.

The time involved in previewing should not be underestimated; indeed the cost in staff time may be much more than the purchase cost of the document. It has been argued that the librarian cannot in any case preview NBM for clients who have their own specific needs and that the librarian's view is subjective even when objective guidelines are available. Bearing in mind these points, the librarian still has to make a decision over which items to purchase from the wealth of available materials. Each institution will need to decide on its approach to previewing, but some general points can be made.

A selection panel or committee is usually more accurate than a single assessor. One writer states in this regard that the 'best judgements derive from discussion with a group of mixed expertise; the majority can depend on the specialist in their midst for guidance on factual accuracy (if relevant) but contribute their individual unprejudiced views on the success or effectiveness of presentation'.[1] Wherever possible, more than one person's opinion should be sought, or it should be possible to refer a decision to a selection committee if doubt arises.

The skill of previewing cannot be gained from reading about techniques. The more experience the librarian has had in assessing NBM, the more likely that there will be a valid critical judgement. However, it is possible to consider some general criteria for evaluation. There are similar criteria for the selection of book and non-book materials and the major differences tend to be in the areas of technical organization and packaging. The following points are not a complete list:

1 Relevancy to the library and its clients:
    (a) Relevant to the objectives of the library?
    (b) Relevant to the needs of the clients?
    (c) Can factual material be found in material already in stock?
    (d) Is there already adequate subject coverage in other materials?
    (e) Can it be linked to other material in stock?
    (f) Would it have to be for reference only?
    (g) Is it designed for individual or group use?

191

(g) Suitable format for clients, for example slides rather than filmstrip?

(i) What physical environment is required, for example blackout facilities?

(j) Is suitable equipment available in the library or to clients externally?

2 Subject contents:
   (a) Factual accuracy?
   (b) Currency of information?
   (c) Lack of bias?
   (d) Is it stimulating, produced with sensitivity and understanding of the needs of the proposed users?
   (e) Is the organization of the subject logical?
   (f) Vocabulary: correct for the intended age range?
   (g) Concepts: correct level for the intended audience?

3 Organization of material:
   (a) Contents list and index: are they accurate and do they represent the material?
   (b) Titles and captions: relevant and accurate?
   (c) Narration, dialogue, sound effects: relevant and accurate?
   (d) Balanced approach; for example cinefilm: sequences pertinent and of an appropriate length, balanced use of narration, dialogue and sound effects?
   (e) Has one medium been used where another would have been more appropriate, for example sound tape/slide instead of slide/notes?

4 Technical organization:
   (a) Artistic, stimulating and descriptive?
   (b) Paper: clear, use of white space, correct type, size of paper, links to illustrations?
   (c) Film: sharp image and of good quality? Effective use of colour and correct colour rendering?
   (d) Sound: faithful reproduction, clear and intelligible? If used with visuals good synchronization of sound and image?
   (e) Suitable physical size and format?
   (f) Symbols used readily understood?
   (g) Typography and labelling: legible from correct viewing distance?
   (h) Are there appropriate notes or guides?
   (i) Is accompanying material necessary or merely a gimmick?

5 Packaging:
  (a) Attractive?
  (b) Easy to handle and store?
  (c) Durable and easy to repair?
  (d) Self-explanatory contents list?
6 Cost:
  (a) Value for money?
  (b) Cost to add it to stock in processing time?
  (c) Will material soon be dated and have a limited shelf life?

It should be stressed that librarians must establish personal criteria which reflect the needs of clients. For particular forms, such as sound recordings and film, more precise criteria would have to be supplied.

Once the criteria have been decided upon, it is helpful to formalize them into a policy statement or put them in an assessment form, as can be seen in figure 28. Such forms can ensure a more consistent approach by reviewers, and can also be filed for future reference to prevent the same document being inadvertently previewed twice.

Step 6: reasons for selection or rejection: It is of course not sufficient merely to collect NBM; the client must be encouraged to use such materials. This can be achieved by accessions lists and exhibitions, and participation may also be helped by publicizing the selection criteria and procedures. A few libraries have also published the criteria they use in selecting NBM, while others have published the reviews of their assessment panels. Hertfordshire Library Service produce *Material matters* a journal with three objectives: 'Promotion of materials – to bring items to the attention of users, in accordance with their actual and potential needs; provision of information about materials – to provide such information as will assist the selection of items of the greatest value to the users, in terms of their particular needs – educational, cultural, recreational and informational; promotion of the library service'.

There are obvious problems in this policy of open dissemination of decisions concerning purchase. Criticism from staff and clients is one, and explaining the reasons for rejecting a certain document almost invites someone to ask for it. The heavy commitment in staff time and expense should not be underestimated. However, in considering the importance of selection of materials it would appear vital to inform clients of the reasons for selection and rejection of NBM, either formally or informally.

Non-book Materials Assessment Form

Title	Format
Publisher	
Technical description	
Content summary	

Level: Primary / Secondary / Further / Higher / Adult education / General

	POOR →			→ GOOD	
	1	2	3	4	5
Accurate information					
Unbiased					
Current					
Authority of publisher					
Vocabulary					
Appropriate format for subject					
Interesting					
Logical arrangement					
Suitable pace					
Suitable length					
Colour					
Clarity					
Synchronisation					
Durability					
Value for money					

Extra features: notes, guides, accompanying material

Is storage difficult? Yes / No	Compatible with own machinery? Yes / No
Similar material in stock? Details:	Purchase advice: Yes / No / Discuss
Assessor	Date

Figure 28. Assessment form

The traditional means of publicising new purchases are of course also applicable for NBM. Indeed, their very nature lends itself to exhibitions and displays. Non-clients may well be encouraged to use the library as a result of such activities. Special film weeks have been mounted by some libraries, when films are shown non-stop. Displays of new posters and wall charts can brighten a library's entrance hall as well as drawing attention to new purchases. A number of Public Libraries have organized microcomputer clubs on branch premises and also provided Prestel sets for the public's use.

Step 7: production of material: A librarian who has exhausted all bibliographic avenues and still not found the material to satisfy the client's requirements has one further possibility: to produce the material in house. This has been a common practice for the off-air recording from radio and television. In the UK a licence may be purchased to record all Open University broadcasts, and school broadcasts may be freely copied provided they are only kept for a certain period (three years for radio and television). A number of libraries have been quick to realize the potential of NBM as a learning device. They have used them for in-service training of staff and also for user education. Examples of such programmes have included sound cassettes illustrating reference work, sound tape/slide presentations introducing staff to new computer issue systems, and also illustrating the work of a librarian for career conventions.[2]

The Standing Conference of National and University Libraries (SCONUL) have since 1970 produced and coordinated a number of sound/tape guides to specific subject areas. However, the most ambitious scheme was the Travelling Workshops Experiment in Library User Education, Newcastle-upon-Tyne Polytechnic which was funded by the British Library. Here librarians saw themselves as primarily 'maximizing the use and effectiveness of their collections, rather than acting as custodians'. Learning packages were created including sound cassettes, posters and slides, as well as printed materials. Areas covered included 'Biology', 'Mechanical Engineering', 'Social Welfare' and 'British History'. There is an extensive literature concerning this experiment.[3] Also of interest is Hills, P J et al. *Evaluation of tape-slide guides for library instruction* British Library, 1978 (BLRD 5378 HC).

Non-book materials can also be used for publicity purposes. Wiltshire County Library has produced photographic posters to publicize their NBM service and these are distributed to local schools and institutions. This authority has also produced a number of slide sets related to local needs, for example a set on the canals of Wiltshire. Indeed it is in the local history area that libraries have been the most prolific as producers, with postcards and posters of local views and historical personalities the top sellers.

In summary the process of acquiring NBM involves the librarian in: searching printed sources; contacting institutions and individuals for specialist advice and services; creating criteria for evaluation; deciding which documents to purchase, which to hire and which to preview; and finally establishing a previewing system. If suitable documents cannot be traced librarians may be in a position to produce them for their clients, although it is more likely that they will be linked to their own needs for training of staff and user education.

CATALOGUING, CLASSIFICATION AND INDEXING

The challenge faced by librarians has been succinctly stated by Foskett as one of 'ensuring that individuals who need information can obtain it with the minimum of cost (both in time and money), and without being overwhelmed by large amounts of irrelevant matter.'[4] The process of obtaining this 'relevant' information from the library collection is known as information retrieval. Any document may be sought by a client under a number of headings – form, subject, author, title, publishers, etc. However, the librarian adopts a physical storage system which usually organizes the documents under only one, or perhaps two, of these headings, for example, non-fiction documents by subject. To meet the needs of the clients, therefore, librarians have traditionally dealt with the other possible approaches through a substitute record, the catalogue. This is a familiar sight in most libraries, though its value has been questioned.

Ignoring this problem of use, two questions need to be asked. Do all non-book materials need to be catalogued and classified in the same way and to the same extent? And, is the experience that librarians have gained in cataloguing books applicable to non-book documents or do they have to devise new methods and a new theory? The stress here is on a *general* collection of book and non-book documents. The requirements of libraries with specialized collections serving clients with special interests are beyond the scope of this work. For example, the BBC Film Library has devised its own systems, which are of interest but not generally applicable.

Management decisions

(1) Are substitute records to be made for all the documents in the library? This is a decision that has to be reached before a library begins to catalogue or classify a single document. For example, a primary school may decide that its curriculum and likely use of documents does not require a catalogue. All work in the school may be project-based around set topics with a certain number of documents on each one. Each topic will have a colour code for its documents, for example those on animals having a blue colour on the spine. The teacher will then say 'I want you to look at all the documents with the blue spine code'. Or a public library with an illustrations collection may decide that this material is self-indexing, that is, arranged by subject headings; a client requiring an illustration of the 1973 Sunderland Football Association

197

Cup winning team will look under the major grouping Sport and then under a subject heading Football. This system works more than adequately for very large collections such as the BBC Hulton Picture Library, which has over ten million items arranged basically by A-Z subject headings within five major groupings. Similarly, faced with a slide set, do the librarians catalogue each slide or just the whole item? Their decision will be based on their knowledge of their clients' requirements. An interesting survey of some solutions to this problem has been undertaken by Bradfield.[5]

(2) Accessibility to NBM. Are the documents to be freely available for access by browsers, or are they to be stored on closed access? If a closed-access system is chosen then there is additional pressure to have very detailed catalogue descriptions of each document in order to prevent the client asking for material which may be of little benefit.

In addition, storage by an accession number system relieves the cataloguer of the need to consider helpful classification by browsing. Deciding on an open-access system requires less descriptive information from the catalogue as the client has the opportunity to search through the documents themselves to aid in selection.

(3) The integrated catalogue. Ideally the storage of the library materials should be completely integrated to allow the client to browse amongst the whole stock for a subject rather than have to search through separate form divisions. Standardized packaging may achieve this with sound recordings, slide sets and films, but it is likely that charts, specimens, and models will need to be arranged in parallel. Also, any integrated arrangement of material will always be bound by administrative factors related to buildings, staffing, and security. A solution to these problems is the integrated catalogue which will consist of entries for both NBM and books in the collection.

Some librarians have discovered problems in constructing an integrated catalogue: 'There is a risk of items being lost or overlooked in the plethora of information; the catalogue quickly becomes unwieldy; it is difficult to file the entries successively; constant signalling has to be involved to indicate clearly the media or form being described on any item'.[6] These are technical problems which can be overcome to some extent by the use of material designations, a colour code for all NBM, and clear guidance to the use of the catalogue. At issue is librarians' willingness to overcome these technical problems for the requirements of clients rather than just to construct a catalogue for librarians' own needs. The client benefits from a catalogue that gives a complete record of all the documents in the library collection: there is no problem in looking up a subject like insects and finding everything, whatever its form, recorded in the one catalogue. Or a collection of poems by T S Eliot may be required, and the client remain unaware that the library not only has these in a printed form but also a sound recording of Eliot reading his poems. If the two forms were recorded in separate catalogues the client might easily remain unaware of the last document having no reason to consult the sound recording catalogue. Finally, increasingly practice is for books and non-books to be published together; for example, a book on astronomy may well have a slide set bound into it.

(4) How far can the computer help? The pioneer work of the Learning Materials Recording Study demonstrated clearly that the computer could be used for the organization of audiovisual data on a large scale. The subsequent publication of the *British catalogue of audiovisual materials* illustrated that it was possible to establish 'a single computerized system that gives access to a combined catalogue of the nation's output of documents in all physical forms, whether printed or audiovisual'. The British Library has made these records available through BLAISE (British Library Automated Information Service, 2 Sheraton Street, London W1V 4BH). In the United States the development of OCLC (Ohio College Library Center) and its spread into the United Kingdom has utilized the power of the computer to provide an integrated catalogue of books and non-books of some seven million documents.

The development of microcomputers has brought the concept of a computerized catalogue within the reach of many smaller libraries. These are currently for small databases; for example the Schools Information Retrieval Project has developed a microcomputer-based information retireval system for use in secondary schools that will store up to a maximum of 1000 records per disk.

The needs of client are the important facts in whether or not to computerize a catalogue. This can be seen in the work of the Further Education Unit Regional Curriculum Base at Garnett College, London. Here the client group has been identified as requiring multiple access to a variety of materials. Non-book materials are included because clients require that information, but the management decision was that the computerization would aid the user to categorize the materials by type and level of skills, the form of the materials being unimportant. Thus management decisions are as usual dependent upon the library and its clients. NBM does not impose a particular approach which would drastically alter the cataloguing and classification system already in use, even when it involves a computer.

Cataloguing non-book materials

The first edition of this work found it necessary to argue that a librarian's knowledge of cataloguing books was also relevant for the cataloguing of NBM. There is little doubt now that this particular view has prevailed and that, for example, library schools now contain within their curriculum adequate reference to and practice in the cataloguing and classification of non-book materials. However, it was the publication of the second edition of the Anglo-American Cataloguing Rules that put the imprimatur on the view with its simple statement that 'The rules cover the description and entry of all library materials commonly collected at the present time, and the integrated structure of the text will facilitate the use of the general rules as a basis for cataloguing commonly collected materials of all kinds and library materials yet unknown'.[7] The Librarian's Bible had recognized that librarianship is concerned with information first, and secondly with the form in which the information is encapsulated. However, it may be necessary to repeat the argument with the introduction into libraries of new formats, such as the microcomputer disk and cassette. It is unfortunate that the weakest chapter in AACR2 concerns Machine-Readable Data Files and it does need to be revised for microcomputer materials. Nevertheless, these new information carriers can be catalogued by the librarian and they do not differ in substance from other non-books. The principles that underly AACR2 are a sound guide for the cataloguing of all non-book materials.

Perhaps the clearest exposition of what a client may demand from a catalogue was written by C A Cutter in 1876:

'(1) To enable a person to find a book of which either (a) the author is known, (b) the title is known, (c) the subject is known; (2) To show what the library has (d) by a given author, (e) on a given subject, (f) in a given kind of literature; (3) To assist in the choice of a book (g) as to its edition (bibliographically), (h) as to its character'.[8]

While Cutter was referring to the need to help a client in the choice of 'a book', the passage of one hundred years and the introduction of a number of new information carriers does not invalidate his statement.

The attack made upon the catalogue functions and uses, the arguments concerning the principle of authorship, and the developments of ISBD, of chain indexing, Precis, and computerization are not fundamentally altered by the introduction of non-book materials into the library. The weaknesses and strengths of the library catalogue may be shown up by the introduction of NBM, but the catalogue functions still centre around those expressed by Cutter.

The information given on a catalogue entry for a document may be divided into three areas, which may be seen in the following example from the *British national bibliography*:

Heading   PRESTEL and education: a report of a one year trial/
Description Vincent Thompson. – London:CET,1981. – 29p;30cm
                ISBN 0-8614-055-0 (pbk): Unpriced
Subject description   371.335

The areas are: the descriptive cataloguing of the document (the 'body of the entry'); the establishment of headings for the document, by which the entries are arranged in the catalogue; and a subject description of the document.

The descriptive cataloguing of a document

It must be stressed that this description is applicable not only to the library catalogue but also to the entry of documents in other bibliographic tools. The only difference is that the former must relate to one particular library (or group of libraries) and its clients while the latter normally takes no account of any particular library or its needs. Further, it is not suggested that every part of the physical description is necessary for every library, merely that in order to know what elements to leave out to satisfy a particular library's clients all these elements must be known to start with!

In using AACR2 chapter 1 General Rules for Description as a basis to discuss the physical description of NBM it is important to stress the following points:

The physical description of any item 'should be based in the first instance on the chapter dealing with the class of materials to which that item belongs'. Thus slides should be catalogued according to the rules in chapter 8 Graphic Materials and not solely on chapter 1.

It is likely that only a national bibliographic agency (eg the British Library) will record all the elements described in the areas, ie 'Third level of description'. Other bodies will choose either the first or second level of description.

The description established will not normally be used by itself, but

1.1	Title and statement of responsibility area	
	B. Title proper	The librarian
	C. General material designation	[graphic]
	E. Other title information	: personality plus
	F. Statement of responsibility	; photographs by Susan Shera

1.2	Edition area	
	B. Edition statement	. — 2nd ed

1.3 Material (or type of publication) specific details area
No general use of this area is envisaged for nbm. However, if an item is being described whose contents fall within the scope of cartographic materials and serial publications then see Chapter 3 and Chapter 12.

1.4	Publication, distribution, etc. area	
	B. Place of publication, distribution, etc.	. — Newcastle ; Luton
	D. Name of publisher, distributor, etc.	: Rectory Publications : Bishopscotes
	E. Statement of function of publisher, distributor, etc.	[production company] [distributor]
	F. Date of publication, distribution, etc.	, 1983
	G. Place of manufacture, name of manufacturer, date of manufacture.	

1.5	Physical distribution area	
	B. Extent of item (including specific material designation)	. — 36 slides
	C. Other physical details	: col.
	D. Dimensions	
	E. Accompanying material	+ 1 booklet (18p.; 16 cm)

1.6	Series area	
	B. Title proper of series	. — (Media and the librarian
	G. Numbering within series	; 5)

1.7	Note area	
	B. Notes	. — Also available in filmstrip version. Illustrates the vital role of the librarian in encouraging use of nbm.

1.8	Standard number and terms of availability area	
	B. Standard number (or alternative)	. — 12463
	D. Terms of availability	: £35.00

Figure 29. AACR2: general rules for the description of all library materials, together with a worked example

---

The librarian [graphic] : personality plus/compiled by Jack Lurcher; photographs by Susan Shera. — 2nd ed. — Newcastle: Rectory Publications [production company] ; Luton: Bishopscotes [distributor] , 1983. — 36 slides: col. + 1 booklet (18p.; 16 cm.). — (Media and the librarian; 5). — Also available in filmstrip version. Illustrates the vital role of the librarian in encouraging use of nbm. — 12463: £35.00

Figure 30. Worked example as it could appear on a catalogue card

will usually form part of a complete entry in a catalogue or other bibliographic list. The organizational factors (headings, classification numbers, etc) used in arranging entries in a catalogue do not form any part of the standard description for an item.

The framework of chapter 1 will give the physical description as outlined in figures 29 and 30. The numbering of the framework refers to the specific AACR2 rules. As can be seen from the former this gives: 1. All the elements that are required to describe NBM; 2. Assigns an order to these elements; 3. Prescribes punctuation for the elements.

While suggesting in the example that it is possible to construct from the basic principles similar descriptive entries for both book and non-book materials, it is important to realize that these are problems peculiar to NBM. Using the framework these peculiarities will be discussed, and some of the problems will be pointed out. However, reference should be made to individual cataloguing rules such as, for example, the Aslib film rules.[9]

Source of the description

The chief source of information for printed monographs is the title page. The title page is the prime source of information and few modern books lack a title page. Such information is unusual for NBM, the only traditional representation being to scatter it around the document. Thus on a slide set the information required may be found in a number of different sources none of which carry the 'traditional' weight of the title page. Such sources may be the title slide, information printed on the slide mounts, a set of notes for the slides, information printed on the packaging. AACR2 recognizes this problem by using the concept of 'the chief source of information' in relation to a specific NBM; thus for video recording the film itself (for example, the title frames). However, the individuality of each type of NBM is recognized and guidelines are offered in considering which source of information should be given first preference. The categories for these are:

1 The material itself, including the container where this forms an integral part of the item, for example a cassette or cartridge.

2 The container where this is completely separate from the item, for example a box.

3 Accompanying data, that is guides and other leaflets issued with the item.

4 Other sources, for example, reference works.

The order of preference for each of these categories is given by the specific material chapter. Thus for motion pictures preference is given to textual material before the separate container while for slides preference is given to the container.

A further problem may arise when the item being catalogued consists of more than one form. For example, *An Alaskan adventure*, British Petroleum Educational Service, 1977 is a study kit which contains four filmstrips, a sound cassette, teacher's guide, sheets of stickers, a painting book, six charts, five cut-out sheets of model making, four pamphlets, four copies of pupil's books, and 16 copies of commentary notes. All of these forms have different information on them, and no one is identifiable as being the major constituent of the kit.

The chief source of information for such items is usually the container itself or the cataloguer must create a description that satisfactorily identifies the item.

Finally, in contrast to the above example in which there is an over-abundance of 'chief sources of information' consider one with no apparent sources at all, a model of an oil rig. This has no information on it other than its name 'Sea Quest'. The cataloguer has to use his judgement and create an entry to describe the item, for example Sea Quest: [oil rig]'.

Cataloguing rules cannot always give precise help. Rule 6.0B1 states that the 'chief source of information' for a tape cassette is the cassette and label. However, it is the inlay card that usually gives the most pertinent and easily observable information. Wise cataloguers will exercise their professional skills in choosing the information that gives the clearest description for their clients.

Descriptive cataloguing and the AACR2 framework
In order to discuss the problems arising as part of the descriptive cataloguing of NBM, a focus can be provided by making use of the framework of chapter 1 of AACR2.

1 Title and statement of responsibility area
This contains title statement (1.1), general material designation (1.2), statement of responsibility (1.3).
1.1 Title statement: The title usually poses few questions that are not answered by the rules stated in AACR2. However, there are perhaps three points that need to be mentioned:
   (i) The use of uniform titles: A uniform title is the particular title by which a work that has appeared under varying titles is to be identi-

fied for cataloguing purposes. The choice may be between alternative titles as in these examples from films: *The fearless vampire killers* also known as *Dance of the vampires; Pope Joan* also known as *The devil's imposter; The Barratts of Wimpole Street* also known as *Forbidden alliance*. In these cases, the title would be that on the copy in the library with the original title in the Notes Area.

(ii) Supplied titles: Often NBM may have no title and one must be supplied. Such a situation is very common with illustrations, specimens and models. Thus a Japanese doll has no title page or similar source, unless it comes with a descriptive card, so the cataloguer must supply a title, '[Japanese doll]'. A particular set of slides with no title may be described as '[Beatrix Potter: scenes from her books]'. Essentially, the supplied title must be an appropriate description of the intellectual contents.

(iii) Collective titles: An individual item may contain several works and there may be two or more titles associated with its description. Sound recordings, in particular, often have two or more titles associated with a single item, for example the Open University sound cassette which has *The development of the social sciences* paired with *The social scientist at work*. If there is not a collective title associated with the work then it will be necessary to record each title in the order in which they appear in the chief source of information.

1.2 General material designation: Material designation may be defined as the physical form of the document being catalogued, as a slide or a model. This may be further divided into two elements; a general material designation, for example videorecording, and a specific material designation, for example, videodisc. Material designation is used to give an 'early warning' to the catalogue user. Using the general material designation from the British List a slide illustrating a robin would be written as: 'The robin [graphic]', while a sound cassette would be given as: 'The robin [sound recording]'.

There has been considerable debate concerning the merits of General Material Designation. AACR2 states that it is an 'Optional addition' and there was no agreement concerning the descriptive terms for British and American libraries other than to agree to go their separate ways. Hence the taciturn British chose the term 'graphic' while the expressive Americans chose art original, chart, filmstrip, flash card, picture, slide, technical drawing and transparency!

The LA/NCET code stated that there should be no material designation after the title and that it only appears in the physical description area. The British Library has decided to leave out the General Material Designation. The following examples illustrate the possibilities.

AACR2 British List:

general material designation

> Energetics [graphic] /by R.S. Lowrie – Oxford: Pergamon, 1969. – 6 transparencies: col.

specific material designation

AACR2 North American:

general material designation

> Energetics [transparency] /by R.S. Lowrie. – Oxford: Pergamon, 1969. – 6 transparencies: col.

specific material designation

AACR2 British Library:

> Energetics/by R.S. Lowrie. – Oxford: Pergamon, 1969. – 6 transparencies: col.

specific material designation

There is an obvious appeal in the idea of such an 'early warning system' for the catalogue user who wants to know quickly the form of the document. However, there is a lack of evidence concerning client preference and whether a statement such as 'graphic' is sufficient description for the user. The ability of the client to scan a catalogue card and note the designation quickly has also not been researched. The advent of shortened catalogue entries, for example as in on-line catalogues and indexes to COM catalogue, will mean that the format may not be listed.

There are other methods of 'early warning'. One such is the colour coding of the catalogue cards; in this system all slides would be on blue cards, all sound discs on green cards, etc. However, Weih's objections should be noted: 'Colour coding is not recommended for the following reasons:

1 Photo reproduction of catalogue data is impractical because the use of colour film raises costs.

2 Colour-coding is also impractical for computer produced books, microform, or on-line catalogues.

3 To make colour-coding economically feasible in centralized cataloguing, an internationally accepted standardized colour code would have to be established. At present there is no such standardization. Individual resource centres using such services would have to colour code by hand, a time-consuming task.

4 As new types of media are acquired, the media centre would soon run out of distinctive colours. Shadings of colours could lead to confusion if the quality of the colour were not maintained.

5 Colour coding erodes the all media approach to resource centre materials.[10]

In addition, catalogues reproduced on microfilm would only be able to reproduce such colour differentiation at great expense. However, it may help in an integrated catalogue to have the NBM listed on different coloured cards where the vast majority of stock is of books. The client searching for a NBM item would have a quick visual guide in these circumstances.

Another possibility is a media code in the top right hand corner of the catalogue card, as in this example from Furlong and Platt:

	media code	T
Energetics/by R.S. Lowrie. — Oxford: Pergamon, 1969.—		
6 transparencies: col.		

The usefulness of a media code is open to question, particularly as the client has to remember a further set of letters. Furlong and Platt list sixteen such codes:[11]

F	Film	P	Picture
FL	Film loop	R	Record
FS	Filmstrip	S	Slide
K	Kit	SP	Specimen
MA	Map	TC	Tape: cassette
MO	Model	TR	Tape: reel
MF	Microform	W	Word card
MS	Microscope slide	WA	Wallchart

It is strongly recommended that a media code is not used. Clients do not remember such codes and often require the help of library staff to determine their meaning. To remember codes plus the classification number may be asking too much of the average catalogue user.

The problem of material designation is further complicated by the proliferation of terms to describe the physical forms. It is crucial for library clients that they are helped to identify easily the particular format that they are interested in using. The librarian is faced by a proliferation of terms and often different definition of terms. For example, the term 'chart' can mean a flip chart, wallchart, star map or navigational chart. AACR2 has not completely 'tidied up' this area and indeed a number of terms such as filmstrip, flip chart, photograph, postcard, poster, stereograph, study print and wallchart are not defined in the glossary.

However, AACR2 has established a common vocabulary and perhaps more importantly a forum where librarians can work toward a revised glossary for NBM terminology. For the librarian wishing to identify the books in the library collection, the term 'text' can be used as a general material designation. This is used 'to designate printed material accessible to the naked eye (for example, a book, pamphlet or brochure). However, if it has been decided not to use a GMD there is no specific material designation and it is deemed sufficient to identify a text in the physical description area by a statement of number of pages, etc (though it should be noticed that the ILEA Central Library Resources Services uses the term 'book' as a specific material designation).

To summarize, there needs to be a material designation so that the client can identify the form of the document. Librarians must decide whether or not their clients and the format of the catalogue requires that there should be a general and a specific material designation. Similarly it should be determined whether or not the term 'text' or an equivalent should be featured as a specific material designation.

The next problem is a document which includes more than one format, for example, a sound cassette with a filmstrip, or slightly more complex one with a microcomputer cassette, transparencies, slides and sound cassette. If it has been determined that the library's clients require a general material designation then the term used in the United Kingdom is [multi-media] and [kit] for North America. However, this only applies if no one format is the predominant constituent of the document.

No dominant component

Coffee [multi-media] . – Wakefield Educational Production, 1972.
– 4 pamphlets, 3 samples of coffee, 12 slides, 6 study prints.

Here no one format predominates so the GMD [multi-media] is used.
Each format is arranged in alphabetical order in the physical description.

A predominant component

Churches. – Newton Abbot: Student Recordings, [197-?] –
41 slides: col. + 1 sound cassette.

Slides are the predominant format and it has been decided to record
the accompanying format, the sound cassette, at the end of the physical
description.

It is often difficult to decide which is the predominant component,
and again fine professional judgement is required. The problem of
'accompanying material' will be further discussed (see page 213).

It is often difficult to decide which is the dominant medium, and
again fine professional judgement is required.

1.3 Statement of responsibility: This has been variously defined.
ISBD(G) states that it is 'A statement transcribed from the item being
described, relating to persons or corporate bodies responsible for the
creation of *intellectual* or *artistic* content of a work, or for the *performance* of the content of a work'.[12] LA/NCET uses the term 'primary
intellectual responsibility' and states 'make a statement of primary
intellectual responsibility in respect of a person or body, if any, whose
overall responsibility for the whole of the *intellectual* or *artistic* content
of the work is both (i) clearly attributed as such in the work or other
authoritative source, and (ii) such that the name has a primary significance in the identification of the work'.[13]

AACR2 uses the term 'statement of responsibility' and defines it as
'A statement, transcribed from the item being described, relating to
persons responsible for the intellectual or artistic content of the item,
to corporate bodies from which the content emanates, or to persons or
corporate bodies responsible for the performance of the content of the
item'.[14] For a book, this is usually easily determined and this name will
become the main heading as, it is argued, a client will remember a document by that feature. Thus *Hamlet* was written by Shakespeare and this

is an identifying feature which can readily be established and would be used by catalogue users.

Is this also true for non-book materials? How do users of the catalogue decide who is the creative force behind a document such as a videotape of Laurence Olivier's *Hamlet*? Here there is the problem of performer and his interpretation. Would clients think of the main entry as Shakespeare or Olivier? Do they think of it as Shakespeare's or Olivier's *Hamlet* when they search for it? The question of performer is an added element in the definition of an author. It broadens our interpretation beyond the writer. ISBD(G) has determined a wide range of persons and bodies who may be deemed responsible for a work — writers, composers, graphic artists, choreographers; adaptors of an already existing work; collectors of anthropological and other field recordings; persons responsible for the direction of a performed work; organizations or individuals sponsoring the work of any of the above; performers.

The range of people associated with a non-book material may be seen in the following examples.

Sound recording of the novel *The hobbit*
    author: J R R Tolkien
    performer: Nicol Williamson
    adaptor and producer: Harley Usill
Sound cassette *Improve your golf*
    narrator: Harry Carpenter
    discussion between Dai Rees and Harry Doust
    executive producer: Ivan Berg
Cinefilm *O lucky man*
    producers: Michael Medwin and Lindsay Anderson
    screenplay writer: David Sherwin
    director: Lindsay Anderson
    performers: Malcolm McDowell, Helen Mirren, Authur Lowe
    music and songs: Alan Price.

It is difficult to establish who has the intellectual credit for these works and with whom lies the 'prime intellectual responsibility'. The more cynical may remember Danny Kaye's comment —

Screenplay by Glock,
from a story by Blip,
from a chapter by Ronk,
from a comma by Stokes,
from an idea by Gropes,
based on Joe Miller's jokes.[15]

210

Little wonder that AACR2 Rule 7.1.F1 tries to consider all eventualities by stating that persons or bodies should be listed who are 'considered to be of major importance to the film and the interests of the cataloguing agency'.

A further problem is that the functions of the authors of NBM are not always clear. This can be seen in the credit list for *The American West: myth and legend* EAV, 1976 (Filmstrip/sound cassette), which reads:

supervising editor: Robert Gindick

scripts and picture research, part 1: James H Handelman

scripts and picture research, parts 2 and 3: Verna Tomasson and Robert Gindick

editor in chief: Gladys Carter

music arranged and performed by: Lorre Wyatt

sound engineer: Stephen M Aronson

What is a 'supervising editor'? Is he the same as a compiler or does he receive the scripts and alter them to suit his intellectual or artistic mind? What control does he have over the pictures so carefully researched and the music so creatively arranged and performed? Even if Robert Gindick has the primary intellectual responsibility, is it certain that the next time the term 'supervising editor' is used it will have the same meaning?

The earlier cataloguing rule LA/NCET has perhaps most aptly summed-up the situation as one where 'the creative responsibility for intellectual or artistic content is characteristically shared among several persons and bodies, performing between them a variety of functions, the relative importance of which to the work is difficult to determine and which often permits no analogy with the authorship of books and texts'.[16] Thus it is important to establish first a standard description for a document and then to add headings and/or uniform titles. If an author can be clearly established then enter under author. However, if no author can usefully be given as a heading then a title is used instead.

2 Edition area

There are no problems arising here that previous experience in book materials will not make clear. The use of terms such as '2nd ed' or 'revised version' is familiar.

3 Material (or type of publication) specific details area

No general use of this area is envisaged, but it does point to the problems which arise when one form of material is displayed via another form: for example, a map on an overhead projector transparency or a serial issued in microform. The solution is to draw upon information given in the appropriate part of AACR2, that is for cartographic materials (chapter 3) and serial publications (chapter 12). Thus in the first example chapter 3 would be used to determine the scale designation, etc.

4 Publication, distribution, etc areas

This includes publisher and place of publication, distributor and place of distribution, statement of function of publisher and distributor, date of publication and distribution, and manufacturer. It is not a section that poses any serious problems, and experience gained in cataloguing book imprints is relevant. Decisions between two publishers, various places of publication, and the problems of a lack of date are relatively easily resolved. There are, however, some problems which need to be discussed further.

The company or person responsible for issuing a book is known as the publisher, while on NBM they may be described as publisher, manufacturer, production company or some other identifying tag. Whichever is used, the important fact is that they are responsible for the issue of the intellectual content. If they have not manufactured the item, they are still responsible for having chosen the firm which does so, and will have similarly selected the firm distributing it. It is important to distinguish between the publisher and the manufacturer of the physical item. A firm such as Educational Productions takes other companies' master copies and duplicates for the mass market as well as being publishers in their own right.

Trade names pose a problem, particularly for commercially issued sound recordings. For example, the sound disc *The Animals on the Animals* has the information on its label 'EMI Records (The Gramophone Company Ltd) Regal. Starline'. Starline is the series and Regal is the trademark of The Gramophone Company Ltd. Thus the publisher, following the AACR2 rules, is the trademark 'Regal'.

AACR2 describes a distributor as a company or individual having 'exclusive or shared marketing rights for the item' While it may be helpful to list a sole distributor or even a company with a major distribution right it is doubtful if it is worthwhile listing an item freely available from a number of distributors. Thus Disney items are distributed solely in the UK by the Slide Centre and should be recorded. However,

Longman/Common Ground are freely available and the distributor should not be listed.

The date cannot be found on many documents, particularly on illustrations, posters and photographs. Following AACR 2 Rule 1.4.F7 gives an approximate date, for example [198?]. Often where there is a choice of dates, for example in a multimedia item then give the earliest and latest dates, for example 1979-82. Another problem with dates is when the intellectual content recorded in one form is transcribed to another format without any alteration. For example, Dylan Thomas' *Under Milk Wood* was released as a sound disc in 1954 while the sound cassette version was released in 1969. This would be written as 1954 [ie 1969] with a note explaining the dates.

5 *Physical description area*
This includes the extent of the item (including specific material designation), other physical details, dimension and accompanying material. Reference should also be made to the points discussed under area 1.2, General material designation (page 205).

The aims of this area are to: enable the user to distinguish between the various physical forms of a work (for example, *Michelangelo* by A Bertram is available as a filmstrip or a slide set); assist the user to identify the work; describe the equipment required: for example, a U-matic videocassette will be useless to a client who only has access to a VCR machine; describe the peripherals required for a computer program (for example, joystick); describe all elements present (for example, a slide set with 16 slides plus notes, or a kit including five or six formats).

The description of the physical details should not be a complicated task provided that the cataloguer is aware of terminology such as double frame, overlays, diazo, ultra high ratio, microgroove, and ROM chips, and helps his clients to understand these by providing descriptive notices near the catalogue. More onerous is the timing of recordings, for example sound discs and videocassettes. How much effort needs to be put into precise timing depends upon client needs, but certainly within education such timing is usually very important. AACR2 Rule 8.5.D1 states that all graphic materials except filmstrips, filmslips and stereographs should have their height and width described. However, measuring of graphics, such as posters and wall charts is perhaps not so important except when they are stored by size.

A final problem in this area concerns 'accompanying material', and the comments on page 208 on the cataloguing of documents which contain more than one form should also be noted. In AACR2 this term is used to describe material which is secondary to the predominant component. Rule 1.5E1 gives four ways of recording information about accompanying material.

(a) In a separate entry.

(b) In a multilevel description (see chapter 13).

(c) In a note (see Rule 1.7B11).

(d) At the end of the physical description.

A policy decision must be made by the cataloguing agency in this area. The most appropriate in many libraries would possibly be to record the details at the end of the physical description. Thus The Honey bee/by J.F. Free. – Wakefield: Filmstrip productions for Educational Production, 1966 would have a physical description which would read 1 filmstrip (41 fr.): col. + teacher's notes. If, however, no one component is predominant then Rule 1.10C2 applies and this gives three methods to consider depending on the item being described.

(a) List the extent of each distinct class of material without further physical description. End the element with 'in container', if there is one, and dimensions of the container, thus

10 study cards, 100 student sheets, teachers handbook,

40 spirit masters; 18 X 25 X 19 cm.

This method is particularly useful for study kits where a full physical description is unnecessary for the client.

(b) Give separate physical description for each class of material. Place them in separate lines, thus

Living in space ; – New York: Doubleday Multimedia, 1972.

1 filmstrip (61 fr.): col.

1 sound cassette (12 min.): 3¾ ips, mono.

This approach is particularly important where the client requires a detailed physical description of the format in order to obtain the appropriate equipment.

(c) If an item has a large number of heterogeneous items give a general term in the extent, such as

Newcastle Metro .– Newcastle: Rectory Press, 1983.

74 pieces: ill., facsims., maps.

The Jackdaw portfolios are a typical example of this type of document, and it is to be regretted that AACR2 was unable to give a suitable specific material designation. Some libraries use a term such as portfolio or even kit.

AACR2 does not answer all the questions with regard to physical description; in particular the cataloguer will have to introduce specific material designations without apparent authority from AACR, for example, lessons cards, friezes, computer cassettes or ROM chip. A checklist of these should be marked in the working copies of AACR2.

The cataloguer's main problems are that he may have to play the material to get the full physical details, and he may require a larger time allowance than for cataloguing a book. This is not true for all forms or even all examples within a form, but from personal experience using a proforma system the times seem comparable.

To summarize, the collation of NBM will fit, for the most part, into the existing framework, but the cataloguer has to understand the requisite terminology and technical specifications, and what detail is required for the users of his library's catalogue.

6 Series area

No special problems arise in this area with regard to NBM. It is sometimes difficult to determine whether a phrase on a slide set is a series statement or merely the publishers added information. Thus a slide set with the statement 'Economic history' may be referring to its subject rather than being part of a series on economic history. The cataloguer will have to base a decision on experience and checking the publisher's catalogues. If there is still a doubt, then it should go in the Notes area.

7 Notes area

AACR2 states that the reasons for notes on the catalogue entry is to give 'useful descriptive information that cannot be fitted into other areas of the description'. This area is important for some non-books because it allows the client to establish a clearer picture of the possible value of the document before having to handle it. A film loop is not easily browsed through, and a clear description of its contents on the catalogue card will save some wear and tear through unnecessary previewing.

Because many of these documents are aimed at a particular type or level of client, the nurse in training or the primary school child, it may be important to state this in the notes area so that the user has an idea of the intended audience. This may be difficult for the cataloguer to determine, especially for graphic material such as slides, illustrations and posters. Client level is often found assessed in the publisher's catalogues or the library document assessment forms, if such a system

215

is used in the library (see also the section on acquisition of materials, page 194).

The packaging of the document may also have to be noted, as for instance in the case of a boxed kit which may have to be out of place in the normal shelf-sequence. A document may be kept in closed access for security reasons. Finally, it should be noted if the document is available in another format, perhaps a videorecording available in two formats, or a filmstrip available in single frame and double frame.

8 Standard number and terms of availability area

Some NBM do have International Standard Book Numbers (ISBN) and some libraries may find it useful to have a record of this on their catalogue cards in case of future reordering, as tracing details of this material can be difficult if the publisher's catalogue is not available. It is mainly the documents produced by book publishers such as Longmans that are using ISBN. However, other producers are taking advantage of ISBN, for example the computer materials produced for the Microelectronic Education Programme are appearing with an ISBN. Other publishers do use 'item numbers' which can prove useful when reordering.

The terms of availability area are perhaps more applicable for current bibliographies than for the library catalogue. It is rarely useful to have the price of an item on a library catalogue entry, for inflation will soon outstrip it. However, lacking the equivalent of a *British books in print* to give an up-to-date price, this may offer some guidance if a client has to be charged for losing the document! Details such as whether the item being for hire belong to the bibliography and not the library catalogue.

AACR2 as a framework can be used for all NBM including computer materials. The detailed guidance given in the code for monographs is the result of many years of careful and exacting work by book cataloguers. It is hardly surprising that the chapters on non-book materials are not as detailed and that the non-book cataloguer must rely more on his professional experience. However it is unfortunate that the weakest chapter in Part 1 is chapter 9 Machine-Readable Data Files. This chapter was written before the general availability of computer cassettes and disks and it is not surprising that the chapter limits specific material designations to 'data file, program file and object, program'.[17] Currently a 'Study of Cataloguing Computer Software' (SoCCS) is being carried out with funding from the British Library and the Microelectronics Education Programme. It is hoped that this will lead to a rewriting of chapter 9.

However, there is no reason why the framework of AACR2 should not be used to catalogue computer software, and the skilful cataloguer will adopt the approaches in other chapters, for example chapter 7 Motion Pictures and videorecordings. Thus Rule 7.5B1 allows the cataloguer to add 'a trade name or other technical specification to the term for a videorecording if the use of the item is conditional upon this information'. This would enable the cataloguer to use the phrase 'one computer cassette (BBC Computer Model B)'.

Once the document has been physically described, the next step is to create suitable headings for it.

The headings for a document
The heading is the element by which the entry is filed in the catalogue. Thus a document can be filed by author, title, form or its subject. This last heading will be discussed on pages 218-220.

Author/title
The arguments concerning authorship have been looked at closely in the discussion concerning the statement of responsibility. Once the statement has been established the cataloguer has to decide if one or more of those elements should become headings. In many cases there will be no statement of responsibility and then entry should be under *title*. To some extent the various forms differ in whether or not they have an author heading; sound recordings usually have an author heading; filmstrips, slides, wallcharts and posters sometimes have an author heading; models and motion pictures rarely have one.

The need for entry under author is perhaps open to scrutiny for NBM and will have to be decided from experience of how the clients of the library ask for this material. Many librarians have suggested that the usual approach is by subject and clients rarely search for NBM under a specific author. This view has to be treated with some caution, for it is often that of librarians working in school library resource centres dealing with the requests of teachers and pupils. It may be that other clients are now beginning to treat NBM in a similar way to books; for examples of these see the Materiography series produced by the ILEA Reference Library and Information Service Centre for Learning Resources.

217

Form

This has to be considered as a heading which might be sought for; a client might ask for all the filmstrips in stock on librarianship, for example. In an integrated catalogue this will involve checking each card individually for its material designation. However, this type of enquiry is perhaps so infrequent that it can be dealt wih as it arises by the librarian rather than by a deliberate policy of providing a form entry for each document. Preparation of select form lists is another possibility, if it is a regularly recurring enquiry.

Subject description of a document

Generally speaking, clients use subject headings most often to search the catalogue for NBM. As with books there are two elements to consider: the analysis of the subject content of the document and its subsequent classification; and the establishment of an index which will help clients to retrieve documents about named subjects successfully.

The analysis of the subject content of a document, and the expression of it for the benefit of clients, does not have to differ between books and non-books. A book on home beer brewing, a videotape on methods of brewing beer, a sound cassette giving instructions on how to brew beer, and a specimen of home brewing apparatus – these do not differ in subject, despite the variety of forms. The librarian may choose pre-coordinate systems such as the dictionary catalogue or the classified catalogue, or post-coordinate systems such as uniterm or optical coincidence, but the decision will be a result of an appreciation of the needs of clients and the extent of the collection. All subject indexing systems have strengths and weaknesses and the introduction of NBM may highlight these; it does not cause fundamental changes.

Yet despite this there has been much heated discussion concerning the subject approach, particularly in the writings of Shifrin[18] and Edwards.[19] The Schools' Council funded Beswick[20] to look in particular at the problem within the secondary school. The reader is advised to look at the detail of this discussion in the writings of these authors and in particular Beswick's argument[21] that the classification of NBM was not the true problem. This he considers to be a more fundamental question of the relationship between the searcher for subject information and the information retrieval tools librarians provide. The Learning Materials Recording Study CET, 1981 clearly demonstrated the practicability of merging non-book media with book data for subject purposes and that, for example, there was little difficulty in applying PRECIS to audiovisual materials.

However, for the librarian who has not previously been involved in the subject analysis of NBM it is perhaps as well to point to the main problems.

In analysing a book a librarian can usually establish its subject fairly quickly by looking at the title page and the contents list. From experience, the librarian presumes that the sub-themes of the book do not usually have to be classified as there are likely to be other books in the collection which have these as their main themes. A main subject heading will be given for the book, with perhaps one or two added headings for particularly important sub-themes.

Consider the following example. The librarian is asked to catalogue *The American West: myths and legends* EAV, 1976. (Sound cassette/filmstrip set) and analyses it in this way. There is a teacher's guide which contains the dialogue of the sound recording, but no description of the 278 frames of the filmstrips. The librarian has to look at them though a viewer. The illustrations, which can be quickly glanced at in book form now pose problems as he or she laboriously uses the machine. A conscientious librarian, worried about clients who may not realise from a single classification number the wealth of visual information in the filmstrip, notes that it contains material on cowboys and red Indians and that it is about the falsification of the true history of the American West. It also shows how the media through novelists (such as James Fenimore Cooper) films (through stars such as Gene Autry and John Wayne, and directors such as John Ford), television (through series such as the Lone Ranger) falsified the true picture. The real American West is then portrayed through folksongs, illustrations of the Mexican War, the Californian Gold Rush, Oklahoma Territory, and further illustration by the artist Charles Russell. The idea of Manifest Destiny is used to explain the myth-making, as are Buffalo Bill, the Mormons, the Battle of Little Big Horn, Davy Crockett, Billy the Kid, and pioneer women such as the real Calamity Jane. The librarian knows that all of this information could be used by the clients. But they cannot easily browse through the format, and the librarian knows there is not a great amount of visual information in the library on this subject. The problem is, how far should the document's subject content be analysed?

In other words, how 'exhaustive' should subject indexing be? Is the right policy one of 'summarization', that is a statement of the overall theme of the document, or one of 'depth indexing', statements of all the concepts within the document that might be helpful to clients? If one picture speaks a thousand words, then how many subject entries are required to make certain that all possible subject enquiries are catered for?

Bearing in mind such factors, plus the cost of making an entry and the difficulties of using a bulky catalogue, the answer must be to rely on encouraging clients to phrase subject enquiries in such a way that these difficulties can be overcome. Thus the client searching for an illustration of Buffalo Bill and failing to find a precise subject reference should be encouraged to think of less specific headings such as cowboys and look at the material found under that heading. A client wanting a picture of John Ford may well find a source in printed guides to film material or the librarian may advise him to look in an encyclopaedia. The library collection is a living collection with many possible entries to its material. It is important to remember this in deciding a policy on the exhaustivity of subject indexing. Non-book material may require as a norm more subject entries than books, but this should be kept within limits that take note of cost, the client's ability, and the librarian's own searching skills.

'Specificity' is a problem that should be noted in connection with the analysis of NBM. How far does the system allow precision when specifying the subject of the document? To the newcomer some NBM are perhaps surprisingly more specific in their subject content than books; for example, *Mini-environments, part 4: river bends; Ammonia: the Haber process; Why overtime?; Heavy industry in Great Britain*.

This is not a new problem. Any cataloguer will know of books that are as specific as these and gather dust on his classification shelves until he plucks up courage to deal with them. Yet NBM do seem to have more than their fair share of these very specific subjects.

A further problem is that such specific subjects often require a long classification number. *Why overtime?* could be classified at 658.3222 and *Heavy industry in Great Britain* at 338.0942. These are not particularly extensive numbers but are rather too long to put on a filmstrip container if the classification number is acting as a location device. It may well be necessary to consider giving the full number in the catalogue to act as a guide to the content of the document but only use part of the number, say four digits, to act as a physical location device. In this case, the catalogue card would read 658.3(222) with the digits within parentheses not being given in the actual document.

Conclusion

It is not necessary to introduce new cataloguing, classification and indexing systems solely in order to deal with NBM. It seems pointless to confront clients who have conquered their fears of the classified catalogue, or those, indeed, who may have had long years of practice in using it, with the need to learn a new method for part of the collection. The librarian used to his dictionary catalogue and its peculiarities, and well-versed in explaining it to his clients, should not unnecessarily have to cope with thesauri, punching holes in cards and refiling them when they are left out of place. Future shock is a problem for both librarian and clients and it should not be increased by introducing new retrieval tools unless they are absolutely necessary. If the present system used in the library for the retrieval of books has been successful for the users of the catalogue, then there is no reason why it should not be used for NBM. Extra guidance in finding NBM in the catalogue should suffice.

There has been no attempt in this section to praise or damn any one system of information retrieval. All have their strengths and weaknesses and as has been said, NBM merely highlight these rather than pose any fundamental questions.

MANUAL OF PRACTICE

Cataloguing NBM
This section does not attempt to give all the details concerning the cataloguing necessary for NBM. Instead it highlights the variations from the cataloguing of books, and for a fuller picture the reader is referred to the standard works. As mentioned at the beginning of the section, policy decisions have to be made concerning the links between NBM and books and the provision of an integrated catalogue. Also NBM can generate more entries than for a book, and a decision must be made on the maximum number of entries. However, such a decision should not be inflexible, recognizing that special provision should be made for some documents. A policy on which forms to consider as self-indexing should also be settled at an early stage. Illustrations collections are perhaps the most obvious example; slides may also be treated in this way depending upon the extent of the collection. A decision must also be made concerning simplified cataloguing. The following example illustrates the necessity for the cataloguer to be concerned with the amount of information he needs to supply when describing a document. It is based on AACR 2 Third Level of Description.

Airports [multi-media] /devised and produced with Gerald Lloyd . — London: British Airports Authority: BP Educational Service, 1978.

1 Airport timetable
1 construction sheet.
1 currency exchange card.
1 cut out model (6 sheets): card + instruction sheet.
1 filmstrip (36fr., 4 title fr.): col.; 35mm + commentary notes.
174 miniature flags of the world: col.
1 painting book.
1 slide kit and slide viewer.
1 sound cassette (ca. 30 mins.): 1-7/8 ips, mono.
5 teachers guides.
4 wallcharts: col.; 71 × 101 cm. folded to 36 × 25 cm.
    In box 38 × 29 × 8 cm.
Investigates the world of airports.
For children aged 8-14.
Technical assistance received from Air Education and Recreation Organization.
Construction sheet for a cardboard glider.

Cut out model of a typical airport building and vehicles.
15 copies of filmstrip commentary.
Painting book tells story of two girls travelling to Spain.
Wallcharts concern themes of location, people, aircraft, and travelling.
ISBN 0-901918-91-1; £27.99 (Education: £14.95)

387.7

1. LLOYD, Gerald
2. BP Educational Service
3. BRITISH AIRPORTS AUTHORITY
4. BRITISH PETROLEUM
       see
       BP

First level of description:

Airports/devised and produced with Gerald Lloyd . – British Airports Authority, 1978.

1 airport timetable; 1 construction sheet; 1 currency exchange card;
1 cut out model; 1 filmstrip; flags of the world; 1 painting book;
1 slide kit and slide viewer; 1 sound cassette; 5 teachers guides;
4 wallcharts.

Investigating the world of airports.
Intended for 8-14 year olds.

ISBN 0-901918-91-1

387.7

All that is required?

Airports kit . – British Airports Authority, 1978.

387.7

The cataloguer will have to take considerable care in choosing the level of description appropriate for his clients. The first level of description may be appropriate for the majority of NBM. However, the Physical Description Area for this level (1.5B) is limited to 'extent of the items' and it may be important to add on 'other physical details' (1.5C) and 'Dimensions' (1.5D) as in the speed of a sound disc or the size of a wallchart.

As has previously been mentioned, it may be necessary to shorten a classification number to accommodate it on some packaging, for example, a filmstrip tub.

Unlike the North American scene, where numerous commercial agencies will supply catalogue cards, only one exists in the UK who will supply for all forms of materials.

A decision must also be reached regarding guiding within the library and the catalogue. The printed guides will have to include details concerning the location of NBM, instructions on how NBM are arranged within the catalogue and lists of material designations.

The librarian has to make these policy decisions on the basis of the needs of the library's clients, the forms of documents acquired, the organization of the stock and last but not least the staff available for cataloguing. Once these initial policy decisions have been made the various tools and equipment required can be considered. First an appropriate cataloguing code must be selected. It is strongly recommended that AACR2 is used for the cataloguing of NBM. It will need to be annotated by the practising cataloguer and in particular:

(a) Define any terms that are unclear or required by clients.
(b) Annotate Ch. 21 to make it absolutely clear which rules can be used for all materials and which only for texts, sound recordings, etc.
(c) Decide where extra elements will be required for particular forms if descriptive level 1 or 2 are used.

The *Examples illustrating AACR2* by Eric Hunter and the sample cards in *Non-book materials: the organization of integrated collections* 2nd ed, by Jean Weihs are also essential for the cataloguing room. The LA/NCET code although superseded in part by AACR 2 still remains of value.

For the libraries involved in the cataloguing of computer software it would be appropriate to consider the SoCCS recommendations. While ISBD(G) and ISBD(NBM) are not cataloguing codes, copies of them will always be useful. There should be no reason to adopt another classification scheme, although some subject headings may have to be reconsidered to make allowance for other forms of information.

It may be useful to have copies of some of the printed catalogues from organizations such as the *British catalogue of audiovisual materials* to act as illustration of the use of rules (although note that it also made use of the LA/NCET rules).

Equipment such as tape recorders may also have to be provided within the cataloguing room, as well as timing devices and table rulers.

The organization of the cataloguing process depends upon individual library requirements but some general points can be made. Individual forms should be processed in batches, for example, a number of slide sets together. This will ensure that problems peculiar to a particular form can be treated at the same time, any equipment required being on hand. It is recommended that a document is catalogued first and then subject-analysed. The item will have to be thoroughly searched for descriptive information and this search can be utilized for the subject form. If an assessment form system is used then this can prove useful for subject analysis. Only as a last resort should a document be played or projected as this is time-consuming.

A proforma is very helpful in speeding-up the cataloguing process and these can be designed to meet the individual library's needs. The proforma in figure 31 was designed for practical exercises in cataloguing of NBM by librarianship students, but there is no reason why it should not be used elsewhere. The terminology and pattern is based on AACR 2. The proforma should be completed in the order: description of the document; physical description; series; notes; and item number. This will create a standard item description. Then the main heading and tracings for added entries and references can be given. Finally, the classification and subject indexing can be entered.

Figure 32 illustrates a filled in proforma for a single media document. This would then be handed to a typist or computer punch operator who would produce the catalogue card shown in figure 34. plus any other entries required from the tracings section on the proforma. Figure 33 illustrates the method for a mixed media document. The only major difference is the use of the column 'entry order' on the right hand side of the physical form designator section. This indicates in which order the physical forms should be typed on the catalogue card. Figure 35 shows the resulting catalogue card. Figure 36 shows a proforma for a machine-readable data file.

In summary, the practical cataloguing, classification and indexing of NBM should not cause any major problems. Once policy decisions are made and the cataloguers familiar with NBM and cataloguing tools, a steady output can be expected.

Cataloguing of microcomputer software

The framework of chapter 1 General rules for description should be the guide for the cataloguer of microcomputer software. The information

Cataloguer: initials	Classifier: initials	Location	Acc. No.

Classification	Additional classification

Subject headings + references or Subject index entries

Main heading

Description of the document

Uniform title

Title (or supplied title)

General material designation
Statements of responsibility

Edition

Place

Publisher, Sponsor

Place of distribution

Distributor

Date of publication

Figure 31. Blank proforma for cataloguing and classification of nbm

226

No. of Items	Physical Description	Entry Order
	Sound cassette (min. sec.): ips, mono stereo quad	
	Sound disc (min. sec.): $33\frac{1}{3}$rpm 45rpm, mono stereo quad; in	
	Filmstrip (fr./double fr., title fr.): col. b.&w.; mm.	
	Slide: sd.( ), col. b.&w.	
	Video cassette ( ) (min. sec.): sd. si, col., b.&w., rpm; in	
	Computer cassette ( )	
	Computer floppy/hard disk ( ) in.	
	Poster: col. b.&w. x cm.	
	Wallchart: col. b.&w.; x cm folded to x cm.	

Other specific material designation	Extent	Other Physical details	Dimensions

Series

Notes

Standard number		Terms of availability

Tracings

Figure 31. Continuation

227

Cataloguer: initials	Classifier: initials	Location	Acc. No.
I.C.B.	*R.F.*	*Nevilles Cross Branch*	*85918*

Classification	Additional classification
612.78	

Subject headings + references or Subject index entries

1. SPEECH : physiology   612.78

Main heading   *FRY, D.B.*

Description of the document

Uniform title

Title (or supplied title)   *Science looks at speech*

General material designation   *[sound recording]*
Statements of responsibility   */D.B. Fry ; Interviewer Paul Vaughan*

Edition

Place   *— London*
Publisher, Sponsor   *: Seminar Cassettes*
Place of distribution
Distributor
Date of publication   *, [197- ?]*

Figure 32.   Completed proforma for cataloguing and classification of nbm (sound recording)

No. of Items	Physical Description	Entry Order
1	(Sound cassette) (5 / min. — sec.): 1⅞ ips, (mono) stereo quad	
	Sound disc (min. sec.): 33⅓ rpm 45rpm, mono stereo quad; in	
	Filmstrip (fr./double fr., title fr.): col. b.&w.; mm.	
	Slide: sd.( ), col. b.&w.	
	Video cassette ( ) (min. sec.): sd. si, col., b.&w., rpm; in	
	Computer cassette ( )	
	Computer floppy/hard disk ( ) in.	
	Poster: col. b.&w. x cm.	
	Wallchart: col. b.&w.; x cm folded to x cm.	

Other specific material designation	Extent	Other Physical details	Dimensions	

Series	— (University series)
Notes	Seminar Cassettes : SS10S

Standard number		Terms of availability

Tracings 1. SCIENCE looks at speech
2. VAUGHAN, Paul
3. 612.78

Figure 32. Continuation

229

Cataloguer: initials	Classifier: initials	Location	Acc. No.
ICB	*RF*	Coach Lane Branch	*85917*

Classification	Additional classification

Subject headings + references or Subject index entries

1. COMMON MARKET 382.9142

2. EUROPEAN ECONOMIC COMMUNITY 382.9142

3. E.E.C. (EUROPEAN ECONOMIC COMMUNITY)
382.9142

Main heading   *HAYWARD, O.G.*

Description of the document

Uniform title

Title (or supplied title)   *The Common Market*

General material designation   *[multimedia]*
Statements of responsibility   */ by O.G. Hayward*

Edition   *— London*

Place

Publisher, Sponsor   *: C.I. Audio Visual*

Place of distribution

Distributor

Date of publication   *, c. 1971*

Figure 33. Completed proforma for cataloguing and classification of nbm (multi-media)

No. of Items	Physical Description	Entry Order
1	~~Sound cassette~~ *40* min. — sec.): $1\frac{7}{8}$ ips, (mono) stereo quad	*1*
	Sound disc (min. sec.): $33\frac{1}{3}$ rpm 45rpm, mono stereo quad; in	
	Filmstrip (fr./double fr., title fr.): col. b.&w.; mm.	
16	~~Slide~~: sd.( ), (col.) b.&w.	*2*
	Video cassette ( ) (min. sec.): sd. si, col., b.&w., rpm; in	
	Computer cassette ( )	
	Computer floppy/hard disk ( ) in.	
	Poster: col. b.&w. x cm.	
	Wallchart: col. b.&w.; x cm folded to x cm.	

Other specific material designation	Extent	Other Physical details	Dimensions

Series — *(International Studies ; IS 1).*

Notes — *Historical background to the E.E.C.; organisation and prospects. Teachers' notes*

Standard number		Terms of availability	

Tracings *1. The COMMON MARKET*
2. INTERNATIONAL STUDIES
3. 382.9142

Figure 33. Continuation

231

```
612.78

FRY, D. B.

Science looks at speech [sound recording] / D. B. Fry;
interviewer Paul Vaughan. — London: Seminar Cassettes,
[197–?] .

1 sound cassette (51 min.): $1\frac{7}{8}$ ips, mono.— (University series).

Seminar Cassettes: SS105
```

Figure 34. Completed catalogue card for 'Science looks at speech'

```
382.9142

HAYWARD, O. G.

The Common Market [multi-media] /by O.G. Hayward .—
London: C.I. Audio Visual, 1971.

    1 sound cassette (40 min.: $1\frac{7}{8}$ ips, mono.
    16 slides: col. — (University series).
        Historical background to the EEC, organisation and
        prospects. Teachers notes.
```

Figure 35. Completed catalogue card for 'The Common Market'

given in chapter 9 Machine-readable data files is not particularly helpful and should be in the main ignored: do not use this chapter as
the cataloguing standard. Until an official AACR 2 guide is published
follow the advice given in the Study of Cataloguing Computer Software.
(There is an American guide Dodd, S *Cataloguing machine-readable
data files: an interpretative manual* American Library Association,
1982.) A typical catalogue entry could read:

232

REEVE, A.J.

Business games [machine readable data file] / author A.J. Reeve. —
Cambridge: Acornsoft, 1982.

1 computer cassette (BBC computer model B): single sided.
+ booklet (9p; 24 cm)

Contents: 'Stokmark' a game which simulates conditions of
the stock market —
'Telemark' simulates financial control of a firm.

Acornsoft: item no. SBE 03

658.407

The cataloguer will require access to computing equipment. Management
will need to offer support for training and should encourage links with
other libraries cataloguing computer software.

Cataloguer: initials	Classifier: initials	Location	Acc. No.
ICB	*RF*	*Widespen Branch*	*4987*

Classification	Additional classification
658.407	

Subject headings + references or Subject index entries

Main heading   *REEVE, A.J.*

Description of the document

Uniform title

Title (or supplied title)   *Business games*

General material designation   *[machine readable data file]*
Statements of responsibility   */author A.J. Reeve.*

Edition

Place   *— Cambridge*

Publisher, Sponsor   *: Acornsoft*

Place of distribution

Distributor

Date of publication   *, 1982.*

Figure 36. Completed proforma for cataloguing and classification of nbm (machine-readable data file)

No. of Items	Physical Description	Entry Order
	Sound cassette (min. sec.): ips, mono stereo quad	
	Sound disc (min. sec.): $33\frac{1}{3}$rpm 45rpm, mono stereo quad; in	
	Filmstrip (fr./double fr., title fr.): col. b.&w.; mm.	
	Slide: sd.( ), col. b.&w.	
	Video cassette ( ) (min. sec.): sd. si, col., b.&w., rpm; in	
1	Computer cassette *(BBC computer model B)* *: single sided*	
	Computer floppy/hard disk ( ) in.	
	Poster: col. b.&w. x cm.	
	Wallchart: col. b.&w.; x cm folded to x cm.	

	Other specific material designation	Extent	Other Physical details	Dimensions
+	*booklet*	*[9p.*		*; 24 cm.)*

Series

Notes *Contents : 'Stokmark' a game which simulates conditions of the stock market – 'Telemark' simulates financial control of a firm. Acornsoft: item no. SBE 03*

Standard number		Terms of availability

Tracings

Figure 36. Continuation

235

STORAGE AND RETRIEVAL

For both user and librarian, the topic of storage raises some of the greatest complexities concerning non-book materials. Books have been placed on shelves for hundreds of years, and this system presents reasonable accessibility combined with fairly economic storage. When non-book materials first appeared on the scene, they appeared so radical in format that librarians felt that only new systems could be adopted. Tied in with this was a concern that these materials were more overtly desirable than books and presented considerable problems of security. Certainly some NBM are expensive, but they cannot honestly be considered excessively so in comparison with the current cost of books.

As a result of these concerns for security and alternative methods of storage, non-books commonly had their library life confined behind lock and key in closed-access sections. Videotapes, and now disks and cassettes for computers, tend to be even more protected than the other media, for in many institutions the user is not allowed even to handle them. There are reports of teams of robots being used now in Japan to draw the videocassette from stock and insert it into the player for the user. More commonly, the tape was selected from the catalogue by the user, but the library staff placed it on the recorder and relayed it by cable to special viewing positions where the client could view it. Perhaps because the library staff feared and were anxious about the equipment they felt the client was subject to similar feelings and would cause untold damage and destruction.

Out of the gradual diminution of closed-access restrictions came the next stage of media collection storage. Stacks or cabinets of non-book materials grew alongside bookshelves, but each collection was mono-media. Thus there appeared the filmstrip corner, the audiotape collection, the slide cabinets. The client faced with this arrangement had to come to the collection with a prior decision that a filmstrip was needed. If the catalogue was organized so that books and non-book materials were integrated, it was possible that a casual search for a subject would reveal the presence of a variety of formats on it. In the absence of such information, however, the client was faced with deliberately searching for the subject within the medium that had been pre-selected.

Recognition of these drawbacks has encouraged library organizations towards the final logical step of inter-shelving the different media. However, with certain items, this policy presents considerable storage problems. With the appearance of the computer as a major source of materials, it has to be asked again whether this is the best policy, even for computer programs. Most microcomputer systems will develop networking systems amongst a group that can in theory number well over a hundred. One of the advantages of this system is that one disk system can be used to serve out programs to all the microcomputers in the network, although the users will be limited to those programs on the disks in use at that time. A central distribution is therefore possible although in the end probably inconvenient. A system like this is not economic for a network of under twelve computers.

Alternatively, the programs may be held on a large mainframe computer, the user working at an independent terminal and drawing from the central equipment what he needs. That central mainframe could be a viewdata system like Prestel or that of a company, and the programs could be downloaded to a terminal in a domestic setting through the telephone system. Whether this is a practical proposition is dependent on the complexity of the program being examined, the economics of the operation and what the user wishes to do with the program. In making any decisions on this, it is necessary to take account of the relative importance of the documentation that accompanies the program. While this may be retrieved at the beginning of the program itself, experience shows that it is more effective if it is permanently available to the user on paper. It is, too, an important aid to browsing. With the technology at its current stage, it seems likely that local availability is probably more valuable and convenient for the user than a central distribution system for the majority of materials. Some programs from mainframes will be useful, but more research is necessary to determine which is the most appropriate for different uses. Certainly, many computer items can be intershelved with other materials. In the section that follows the various media will be discussed, progressing from independent storage to the position of inter-shelving all formats including books.

Firstly, some consideration of the criteria for selecting a storage system is necessary. Such criteria need to reflect both the needs of the clients and the managerial problems of the librarian. Underlying them must be the demand for maximum use combined with optimum security, safety and availability. Any decisions that are made will necessarily be compromises, for the totally secure system will totally preclude free availability, but in reaching such decisions the librarian should at least have considered the reasons and have some understanding of the consequences.

1 Labelling

A useful guide, USPEC 12, concerned with labelling NBM has been produced by the Council for Educational Technology. While consideration will be given to labelling in more detail later, it is useful at this stage to be aware of the main issues. Labels should:

(a) carry information which ties various parts of a production together
(b) have space for local additional information
(c) explain any equipment standards required for use
(d) carry a brief description of content and treatment, particularly with regard to materials that are difficult to browse
(e) explain any prior knowledge that the user should have or indicate a level of treatment and its objectives where relevant
(f) be legible to the level of literacy likely for the potential user
(g) be so affixed that they do not come off easily.

2 Browsing

While some non-book materials are difficult to browse through easily, every effort should be made to increase the possibility. This may mean additional information on labels, transparent packaging, small representations or adjacent equipment for simple and quick scanning. Disks and magnetic tape are the most complex items for browsing amongst, but both can be dipped into just like a book, provided the external labelling gives adequate guidance.

3 Keeping the parts together

Most formats separate readily into a number of parts. These may be merely the material and its box, but the individual pieces may be more numerous than this. Cross-labelling does help to bring the pieces together, but it is also important that external labels provide all the necessary information about how many and what items are inside.

4 Security

Storage should meet problems of security without imposing prohibitive conditions on use. There are some potentially unpreventable losses because the items concerned are so small, such as microforms and individual slides. However, many of the standard library security systems act effectively with non-book materials (care must be taken to avoid magnetic systems being used with magnetic tape, or X-ray systems with film). Some security systems also act effectively with equipment as well. In most libraries, equipment is most satisfactorily secured by screwing it firmly to benches and shelves. Finally, a decision has to be made to carefully balance the cost of security against the cost of replacement. Naturally, unique and irreplaceable material is looked after more carefully, only copies being made available for general use.

5 Packaging
The organization of the packaging should be so arranged that it facilitates storage. Progressively, libraries are moving towards inter-shelving, so it is increasingly a major criterion of choice. In addition, the packaging should be durable, reflecting the degree and manner of use that is to be made of the material. Some packages are so durable, in fact, that access to the contents can be excessively troublesome, while others open so readily that the librarian is fortunate to find the contents still present even after resting on the shelf. Finally, the packaging should protect the contents from damage, but in so doing should not damage the user. The principal enemies of NBM are dust, excessive temperature variation, and humidity, all of which should be allowed for by a good packaging system.

Difficulties over storage come, not from the type of the material, but from the different formats in which they are arranged. It is therefore necessary to deal with most of the NBM formats separately.

Portfolios of paper materials and photographic prints
The early system adopted was to file the materials in the wallets in which they were produced in drawers or in racks. Although the wallets had flaps, an accidental drop could shed the contents. It was rare to find the external labels indicating a clear listing of the contents or for them to be cross-labelled to their own packaging. More recent packaging systems have begun to use binders, ring, lever-arch or even albums to secure the materials. The contents are more secure and in some cases better protected. The packages can be shelved easily. More concern must be expressed over the labelling so that each item can be cross-referenced to its container, and the container itself carry the relevant information on its contents.

Filmstrips
These are usually supplied in small canisters with separate explanatory notes. In many places they are reorganized as slides, but this section
239

refers to those libraries where a decision has been made to keep them as filmstrips.

Early storage problems were solved by storing filmstrips in special narrow drawers. Inside the drawer a form was placed with holes cut out into which the canisters could be fixed. Either in that or an adjacent drawer the notes were stored. The latter, incidentally, vary considerably in size and shape. One firm produced its filmstrips in extra long tube containers which not only held the pictures but also a rolled-up version of the notes.

In order to make filmstrips more accessible, shelving systems were adopted. One method was to place a tray on the shelf on which the canisters and their notes were arranged. Another was to produce special shelves, about two inches deep and slightly angled, on which the canisters could be placed. Rearranging the order was simple as they rolled easily up and down the shelf, the notes stacked in pamphlet boxes below.

A more recent development has been the production of a binder with a flap for the notes and a cut-out hole in a pad of sponge rubber for the canister. Variations on this by the formation of complete cardboard boxes with a cardboard former for the hole are also available. The extra protection this provides hardly increases the protection afforded to the filmstrip, as it is already adequately preserved inside its canister.

A further system is an extension of the transparent plastic wallet for slides which is suspended in a filing or similar cabinet on a metal rod. For filmstrips, the wallet acts like a bag to contain the canister, notes and any other material that the user may require.

If inter-shelving is a major factor, then the binder or boxes that stand upright on the shelves is the most suitable system to adopt. Unlike most of the other systems described, the notes are packaged in the same container as the filmstrip, and there is also adequate space for an audiotape if that is also needed. The disadvantage of the system is that the packaging introduces an extra cost.

Adequate labelling can only come from careful cross-referencing. The filmstrip itself (probably scratched on or stuck to the black leader), the canister and the notes need to carry the relevant titling and numbering to ensure that they are kept together, and this information needs to be transferred to any external container. Well-prepared notes should provide the user with a browsing facility, but it is not difficult to extract the filmstrip and hold it up to the light or over a light box to obtain an impression of the quality of the visual content.

240

Slides

All slides should be mounted before storage. Mounts can be divided into three main types; cardboard, plastic without glass, and plastic with glass. Many commercial processors supply the slides in card mounts, but these have the disadvantage of bending. Once this has happened, they must be replaced. Damage occurs particularly when the slides are pressed into viewers, or as a result of misdirected lever action which tears the edges. Plastic mounts do not have these disadvantages. But whichever mounting method is used, the film itself is exposed without protection and may be damaged, fingered or become covered in dust. To avoid this, plastic mounts with glass may be used. They tend to be thicker than other plastic types and very much more expensive. If a trace of moisture is either present on mounting or is introduced through humidity changes, there is a distortion to the light as it passes through, giving an appearance like a rainbow. This is called a Newton ring, the pattern moving with the heat from the projector light. Some glass mounts are advertised as anti-Newton and eliminate this distortion. They are naturally even more expensive.

In making decisions about the type of mount to choose, it is essential to take account of the way in which the slides are to be used. Commonly, master sets are mounted in anti-Newton glass types, reference sets in ordinary glass mounts and distribution copies in plastic mounts. In all cases, however, the slides must be labelled. Each should have a spot in the bottom left hand corner, and frequently this carries the number which indicates its position in the set. Other labels should give the set title if there is one, and maybe the production company. In library collections, it is wiser to avoid using a code number only, although this too may be added to the other labels.

The common domestic storage method is a box with individual slots for each slide. To be retrieved for use, they must be extracted one by one and inserted into the projector or its magazine. For identification, an indexing system is needed to decide which slide is which. New slides which need to be inserted into the sequence mean a complete reshuffle, a time-consuming activity. Such a system of storage is difficult to inter-shelve with other media, and this normally leads to a separate slide area.

A development of this system which aids intershelving is to house the slides in projector magazines. Care needs to be taken as some do not seal satisfactorily and the slides fall out. The system can be expensive; more especially if the magazine is not completely filled.

241

In both these systems, browsing is only possible by putting the slides on a projector or lifting them individually to the light. A more popular and simple system has been developed in which the slides are stored in a transparent plastic wallet, each in a separate slot. The number of slides per wallet varies with the size of each slot. Too tight a fitting slot can introduce possible damage, the slide rubbing against the sharp transparent edge. Too loose a slot means that the slides can readily fall out if the wallet is tipped up, but this can be prevented to some extent by a covering flap, either over each slot or the entire wallet. This system allows the user to hold the wallets to the light for simple browsing. These wallets may be hung in drawers of special cupboards or filing cabinets, but for inter-shelving the same system may be used as the pages of a book-like file or in simple boxes. Care needs to be taken to ensure that the slides do not slip out of their slots. For checking purposes, the information on the file or box should include the number of slides, and it may be an asset to cut away any spare unused slots.

Microforms
While microfilm material itself is illegible without magnification, this must be compensated for by the presence of eye-readable information on roll microfilm. This may be attached to the spool, the cassette or the cartridge, on aperture cards to the card, on microfiche on the top band and any other covering in which this may be stored. The extent of the information should be sufficiently comprehensive to identify the important sections rapidly.

Roll microfilm is readily stored on shelves, as the various methods of holding the material can be easily placed in boxes. To give further body to the material, it may be helpful to place the reel, cassette or cartridge in a book-file or another box.

Aperture cards are primarily used for holding technical information, and so intershelving is not usually required. Such cards are commonly placed in drawers, or in machine sorting systems.

Microfiche of all types are normally held in paper folders, and as these are approximately 6in × 4in in dimensions, can be simply stored in a small drawer. In large numbers, microfiche can be stored in book-like files, or in ring binders in plastic slots. For inter-shelving purposes, the latter can be adapted to form a sheet in between two card boards with a backing as in a book. Provided the plastic is fairly tight, the fiche protected in its paper folder, there should be no danger of it falling out.

Cinefilms

As browsing amongst films is difficult, information concerning the material should be comprehensive. With some films, there may be a short precis to give users an opportunity to obtain some understanding of the content before projection. A few projectors also have footage counters which give users an opportunity to wind the film fast to a selected point. If such equipment is available, information linking important sections to certain footage measurements can be included. Because the format of film varies, the external labels should give a clear indication of this. This is particularly important with 8mm films.

Loop films are issued in boxes which lend themselves to shelving. As they are usually comparatively small, it may be necessary to insert them into box files to give them more substance. Reels of film are supplied in boxes, often unfortunately with easily detached lids. Some means of securing or reboxing is necessary if the shelving of the boxes on end is to be the method of storage. The wider film standards, 16mm and 35mm, are commonly held in circular metal cans. Putting the former in strong boxes is a frequent practice to aid shelving. Where just rows of films are shelved, a two-bar shelf can be used into which these cans will rest. However, it should be noted that the weight of films of these standards is considerable. In many libraries 35mm films are stacked in piles rather than on end, and the shelving used here must be particularly strong.

Films may be seriously damaged by dust, excessive heat and humidity. Apart from maintaining constant suitable environmental conditions, protection from dust is essential and can only be sustained by keeping the reels securely boxed when not in use. It should not be necessary to expose the film material on its reel for initial information on its content.

Tape-slides

Because of the different standards of pulsing, it is very important for the user to know which system has been employed. It is possible to switch off the relays responsible for tape-pause, and equipment may be left in this way. If tape pauses are part of the programme, it should be mentioned on the labelling.

The information on the tape should be cross-referenced to the slide set it accompanies, and the slide-set to the tape. Mention should be made on both parts of the production of the number of slides, and the length of the programme indicated on the tape and any enclosing packaging. While the parts of tape-slide programmes can be stored separately, this encourages confusion and difficulty. If the slides are stored in a magazine, the tape may be glued to the outside of the container, or forced inside it. This system does lend itself to shelving, but in a rather ugly way. Hanging slide sets in transparent wallets in cabinets can be a useful system, and a small pocket fixed to the back of the wallet can be used for the tape.

For inter-shelving, the use of a book-file or box is a simple and convenient method. The slides would be stored in wallet-pages, the tape in a special card or sponge rubber former. Any variation in the form of the visual element could be stored in a similar manner.

Sound tapes

Magnetic tapes are obviously difficult to browse through; there is nothing to see. Comprehensive information is therefore necessary, giving a precis of the content, the length of the whole tape, and its parts if they are clearly differentiated. Such lengths should represent time, not footage. If there are odometers which are reasonably uniform in their readings available on the equipment in the library, position readings of major sections of the tapes can be helpfully included. In practice, sampling or browsing through the contents of a tape can be obtained by using the fast forward or rewind controls on a player to predetermined points, and then playing that part of the tape. To make use of this facility, however, some suitable equipment should be available close to the various storage areas.

Technical information should also be included, particularly in reference to speeds and track layout employed with open reel tapes. Cassettes, being standardized, require only limited labelling, such as stereo or mono (in fact these are always compatible, so it is unnecessary to mention it), the tape coating if it is chromium dioxide or if it is a metal tape, and the Dolby system if it has been used in the recording.

Tapes are usually boxed, open reel commonly in cardboard containers (the lids of which readily fall off), cassettes in hinged plastic holders. These cases are important to prevent dust getting into the reels. As boxes, tape and information can easily be separated, cross-referencing is necessary. The space is clearly provided on the outside of the cassette, and no attempt should be made to write on the tape as this rubs against the heads. However the outside of the leader part of the tape on an open reel can be used safely. Alternatively a sticky label can be attached to the reel to carry information.

The decisions for cassettes of computer programs are similar to those for audio recordings. However, it is important to ensure that the fact that it is a cassette for a computer is clearly indicated, and also the make, model and operating system or series of the machine is marked on the external label. Care should be taken to cross-reference to any documentation. Commercial publishers are tending to publish these as a cardboard or plastic folder, the cassette in a holder on one side, the paperwork on the other, the whole being similar to a small book in appearance and therefore shelvable in this way.

While separate stores for tapes can be arranged on shelves, they are given more substance by placing them in book-files or large boxes. The method also gives more space for background information. If this method is adopted, the tape should be in a box inside the external container to provide extra protection from damage and dust. Because of possible damage, the shelving on which tapes are placed should be as far as possible from any magnetic source.

Magnetic disks
Like all magnetic stores, these disks cannot be browsed easily, and depend on accompanying documentation for effective use. As they are relatively fragile and readily damaged by dust and grease, it is essential that they are stored in their paper sleeves, and preferably within another container. Two arrangements are common. One is to place the disks as a collection inside a small box with a lid, each containing about ten of them. With several programs on each disk this means that each box could contain eighty to a hundred different programs. Although they may be related, this does not encourage ease of access, and unwanted disks get fingered during searches for the one that is required. There will also be difficulties in linking relevant paperwork to each program. The other common technique is to place each disk with a limited number of programs stored on it in a cardboard or plastic folder, the disk being inside a flap on the left, the paperwork describing its use on the right. This is the system adopted by commercial publishers, the end product being very similar to a slim book which can therefore be stored accordingly. The major disadvantage is that much space on the disks will be unused, but the cost of this is not high.

Each disk bears a label, but only the lightest pressure must be used to write on it or else the disk surface within its cardboard jacket will be marked and damaged. Felt-tip pens are recommended for this purpose. The principal information, in addition to program names, authors and

245

producers, is that which identifies the computer with which the disk can be used. This means listing the make, model and disk operating system or format, as there is no other way of identifying this information from the external appearance of the disk. All small disks for computers look identical.

As magnetic disks wear out with use and are relatively easily damaged or corrupted, it is common practice to prepare a copy to be kept safe in reserve. There is no qualitative difference between the original and any copies made from it, as all are storing digital information. Thus it does not matter whether the original or the copy is issued for general use. Some publishers sell a copy with the original in the package that is sent out, some release copyright for this purpose and recommend that a duplicate is prepared. To prevent accidental erasure, it is advisable to cover the write protection notch with the appropriate adhesive tab. While it is easy to remove and therefore purposefully amend the disk, its presence helps to avoid genuine accidents.

Disks are damaged by excessive heat, high humidity and direct sunlight, so they should be stored in a reasonable environment. Pressure leads to bending and distortion of the surface and this has to be avoided. Also, because the information is stored on them magnetically, they have to be kept away from the strong magnetic fields like those produced by television sets or even the transformers in the computers. However, despite their delicacy, they usually have a considerable lifespan before certain parts become worn out.

Videotapes

The requirements for videotapes are very similar to those of sound tapes, both in terms of information needs and storage systems. The technical information should include the model or system of equipment on which the programme was recorded. While this is obviously necessary with open reel tape, it may also be necessary with cassettes, because the same format may be used with completely incompatible equipment. Currently, for example, the VC or LVC cassettes are used with both the 1500 series Philips system and the incompatible 1700 series.

Nearly all videotapes are supplied in easily shelved boxes, which usually stay shut, and are reasonably substantial. In cassette boxes, there are usually reel bracing inserts, either loose or as part of the container. Separation into tape, information and box is similar to that with the soundtape, but under no circumstances should information be written on the tape itself.

246

Overhead projector transparencies

Only specialized libraries dealing with education and training are likely to have these materials to store. Because they are normally only used by instructors, it is usual to store them as a separate collection and not attempt to intershelve.

If transparencies are not framed, they are most suitably kept in folders, wallets, or pseudo-record sleeves, separated from each other for ease of use and protection by paper. Framed transparencies may be stored in box files, ring binders or in folders in large filing cabinets.

Information about individual transparencies may be written on the upper or most easily scanned edge of frames, summaries being given on the outside of folders. When wallets are used, information can be written on labels on the outside. Some coding mechanism should be developed to bring the various transparencies back together after use.

Discs

The accepted packaging for discs is a double sleeve, the inner a protective paper cover (better than plastic because this material induces static), the outer a strong laminated card which generally carries a comprehensive summary of relevant information. The individual bands are usually identified, and there is an increasing trend to include the length in time of each. Labels may be fixed to the outer surface of the sleeve for library numbering, and this should be repeated on the label on the centre of the disc. It is also possible to write on the spine of the outer sleeve if the storage method makes this important.

The storage of discs presents paradoxical tendencies. For convenience in browsing and selection, clients prefer a bin system in which the front of the sleeve faces outwards and the collection can be flipped through. But in order to preserve the quality of discs, they should be stored vertically and fairly rigidly, the most convenient way being on a shelf with the spine outwards. Both systems may be found in shops, the latter usually only accessible to the assistants, the empty sleeves in bins, browsed through by customers. If records are stored vertically, the shelves should have dividers, nine to twelve inches apart. Discs are heavy, so the shelving needs to be strong.

There are no trends towards intershelving discs, and any move in this direction is likely to be even more damaging to the disc than the use of bins. If the library wishes to intershelve material available on discs, it is wiser to purchase or re-record (with permission) on cassette tapes and store these.

Laserdiscs

The videodiscs are sold in cardboard sleeves like records while compact discs for audio are marketed in boxes, which are adequate protection from most sources of damage. So early is the experience of producing these discs that it is not certain how they will be labelled nor is it yet clear what information users will require to assist them. Certainly, there is a need to identify the difference between active and long play videodiscs but whether codes for different areas of the discs need to be identified is not yet clear. Similarly the compact disc works on time from the beginning and it may be helpful to users to list the intervals between movements on the disc, or they may be happy with the fast advance between tracks.

Another feature of the marketing of these discs is that they are claimed to be almost indestructible. Certainly normal handling and accidental scratching has no effect on the quality of play, and there are as yet no indications of heat or moisture damage to them. They do bend, but the pressure has to be high to make this happen. Because of the way in which the recording is made, there is no threat from magnetic fields or other physical phenomena.

Shelving of compact discs is certainly possible as the box will stand on end and is not dissimilar in size from a book. Videodiscs are 30cm in diameter, however, and this means that normal shelving will not be possible. A bin system, similar to that for long play discs, may be the most appropriate.

External labelling

To end this section on storage, it is helpful to return to external labelling. Frequently the information on materials produced from commercial sources is inadequate and needs to be supplemented by library staff.

External labelling is important for two reasons. It provides the user with browsing information, and indicates such constraints on operation that may immediately dismiss it from consideration. Secondly, if the information is sufficiently comprehensive, it saves the user from opening and exploring the package if it proves irrelevant, and thereby prevents potential damage to the contents.

As a minimum, the information on the spine should give the title, author and/or presenter, publisher's insignia and any series or item title and number. Sufficient space should be left for local library labels. On the front and/or rear of the container, further information concerning the level and content of the package is useful, together with the various formats included, particularly where these may lead to incompatibility problems.

The comprehensiveness of this information needs to be increased in the case of extensive multimedia packages, including references to the relevant users and the most suitable manner of use. The packaging and storage of these mixtures have not been described. There is no reason why such collections should not be boxed and stored on end on shelves, just like rather fat books.

COPYRIGHT

With the development of inexpensive copying equipment, it is very simple for users to make copies of published materials. Librarians are already aware of the difficulties surrounding the copying of paper materials and the ease with which infringements of the copyright act can occur. Restrictions are almost impossible to apply when there is public access to photocopying equipment in places where there is no practical means of control.

Non-book materials also are fairly simple to copy and control is impossible. Photographs do present a few technical complexities to the amateur, particularly if they are slides, filmstrips or microforms. A camera set-up can be arranged to make copies of slides and filmstrips, and diazo copies of microfiche can also be produced with accessible equipment although the quality is unlikely to be high. Once in the possession of a user, it is impossible to prevent copying if material is allowed out of the library.

Roll microfilm is more complex, and at present it is very unlikely that the amateur could make copies without utilizing expensive equipment. The same is especially true of cinefilm. To make a usable copy of this, it is necessary to make a negative first from which a copy-print is then produced. Unless there has been deliberate arrangement to set up a laboratory in which this work can be done, it would normally be necessary to involve a commercial laboratory, where any deception is likely to be noticed. Of course, it is possible to film a presentation of a cinefilm, but apart from the obvious lighting problems, there is also some difficulty in synchronizing the filming camera with the projector. Even filming television which scans at a different speed is unsatisfactory as the black frame lines are frequently seen in the picture.

Audio and videorecordings are, however, particularly simple to copy. An audiotape recorder connected to a record player, a radio or another tape recorder, is simple to organize, and almost perfect copies can then be made. Indeed, modern domestic music centres are deliberately wired so that audiocassette copies of radio and discs can be made to a very high standard through electronic connections. There is no doubt that the simplicity of this is disturbing to record manufacturers.

Video cassettes are widely copied, and indeed sold, and notorious 'pirated' editions have been made available. Usually the quality of these recordings is very poor, but many people seem satisfied by them. This is particularly worrying for commercial companies that officially market the tapes, production companies and even broadcasting organizations. Many attempts have been made to identify technical preventive mechanisms, but no satisfactory system has yet emerged.

It is possible to introduce unique signals on the original which can be identified on a copy and traced. However, this means that the rights owner has to find the illegal copies and this is generally not easy to do. Similar identification tags can be inserted in computer programs, and there are other machine code systems that have been developed to prevent copying. For some people, these present a 'challenge' to be overcome and there are commonly none that cannot be circumvented. All that it does is prevent the casual and non-technical user from making a copy, and this in itself may be an advantage. In the early days of computer program development, the free exchange of listings of programs was commonplace and indeed encouraged. This makes it more difficult now to assert the rights of writers and developers. The users who contravene the copyright act most widely are educators who give copies to students, small club and disco operators, and people in their own homes making personal copies. In practice, activities like this cannot be prevented.

Copyright regulations are of course a nuisance. It would be very much simpler to allow people to make as many copies as they like, and to ignore the legislation when it is so easy to abuse. However, it is important to remember that many livelihoods are dependent upon the products. Musicians and artists of all kinds earn their living by selling their creativity, and the more sales the more they earn. One best-seller can subsidize the vastly larger number that earn little. Most serious producers of NBM reinvest profits in supporting the development of further materials. Infringement of copyright therefore short-circuits this cycle in a way which is ultimately deleterious. Even though it is awkward to organize, protection of the rights of providers is important in ensuring the continued production of new materials, and such protection can be improved not by altering their rights but only by altering the act to ensure simpler and more effective control.

The present UK Copyright Act was passed in 1956, and it is supported by the Performers' Protection Acts of 1958 and 1963.[22] Between them, these acts legalize the complexity of owners' rights in materials. Simply, rights exist not only for the content, but also for the performances and for the format of presentation. Thus in the case of a disc of a piece of music, rights are owned by the composer, by the musicians and by the recording company. To acquire permission to copy, all these rights have to be cleared. The procedure involves identifying the copyright holders and applying for permission. Although a fee may be charged, it is unusual for rights not to be granted. Certain materials, however, cinefilms and broadcast television in particular, can rarely be copied. The safest rule to apply is that copying, either in the same or a different format, is illegal without first obtaining permission. The notion of fair copying for private study does not usually apply to non-book materials, the exception to this being paper copies of some parts of microforms of printed originals.

Some basic conclusions as a guide to UK practice can be drawn and are listed below, but for further details of the few exceptions, users are referred to the original acts or to interpretative texts.[23]

1 Without suitable licences or permission, making multiple copies of any material whether for free distribution or for sale is illegal.

2 Copyright lapses as follows:

(a) photographs — fifty years after being taken

(b) drawings and artistic work — fifty years after the artist died and fifty years since first publication.

(c) literary, dramatic or musical works — fifty years after the author's death and fifty years since the work was first published, broadcast, publicly performed or issued on record.

However, it is important to note that there remains copyright in the form of the presentation, so that copying a record of a Beethoven symphony is illegal if the disc was made less than fifty years ago.

3 It is illegal to make single slides or overhead projector transparencies of printed materials for educational purposes.

4 Licences may be obtained to transfer discs to tapes, to record in audio and visual form schools and educational broadcasts in educational institutions, to videorecord Open University programmes. These are blanket licences though with important constraints.

5 Public performance of any copyright musical or dramatic work is illegal without prior permission. The rights in musical works include the rights in the recording of the disc.

In 1977 the Whitford Committee[24] on copyright reported and a green paper *Reform of the law relating to copyright, designs and performers' protection. A Consultative Document* (Cmnd 8302) was published in July 1981. However, in spite of considerable agitation, no action has yet been taken by the government. In brief, the Whitford

Committee concluded that a system of licensing should be introduced to allow free copying, the exception being in the case of general broadcast material, and that some form of excess charging on copying equipment should be levied. The fees from the licences and such excess charges should be distributed by appropriate groups to rights holders, but the means by which this was to be done was not detailed. The conclusions are very sensible from the users' viewpoint, but their administration and the elimination of anomalies raises a good deal of concern. However, the excess charge system is favoured in West Germany, and in Sweden licensing methods have been adopted. Certainly a tidier form of enforcing the rights of copyright holders is much overdue with the increasing facility for copying that modern equipment provides. Such a system should ensure that users can have reasonable access to the materials they require without fundamentally depriving the holders of rights of a fair reward for their labours.

The position on copyright in the USA has changed since the publication of Public Law 94-553 *Copyright revision act 1976*. Copying for a library collection is generally *not* permissible. However, under this new law, portions of sound recordings, films and filmstrips can be copied for student use *only* in an educational context. Public and instructional television programmes may be recorded for educational use, but the tapes must be wiped clean after seven days. If the user comes to a private agreement with the broadcasting company, copies may be retained for a longer period. Some libraries may also be allowed to record news programmes from commercial stations. As the limitations within the law are not yet entirely clear, users are recommended to refer to an interpretative publication.[25]

Part 5

MANAGEMENT

INTRODUCTION

If users and materials are to interact successfully within the library, good management techniques are essential. Without them, the user is left to flounder in a mass of disordered material without either advice or guidance. The basic techniques for managing a library are of course appropriate for both book and non-book collections. In this chapter, the discussion is limited to those extra problems introduced by the presence of NBM, and deals with the four topics of: the physical environment, staffing requirements, financial implications and problems of control.

A very thorough guide to the organization and management of NBM in a college setting has been provided by the Council for Educational Technology in their packs 'Learning resources in colleges'.[1] Although aimed at the educational market the questionnaires provided are of value to any library manager considering the place of NBM in the library and its community.

Many of the problems of management are a result of the inadequacies of clients' conceptions and their difficulties in making use of the service provided. To some extent NBM add to these problems, for many of the formats require the availability and use of specialized equipment. Here is a new dimension to the much discussed topic of 'user education'. The technologies involved in 'information technology' will lead to a re-examination of the library as a provider of information. Libraries are developing in some areas community video workshops. In America they have been involved in telecasting their own and other productions. The Library Association has stated that librarians must be involved in the public debate with regards to optical fibre lines and cable television networks. Public Libraries have cooperated with local community groups in providing viewdata facilities and in loaning out microcomputers. It is not the purpose of the comments in this chapter to consider the problems involved in managing activities like these. Nevertheless, it is worth noting that libraries could have a central role in 'managing' these developments for the local community and ensuring that all members have the right of access to this source of power. For to a remarkable extent information is a source of power in Western society; it is of vital importance for the industrial, commercial and cultural success of the United Kingdom.

A great deal of research is now taking place into the ways and means of educating the library user. NBM are widely employed by library staff to introduce facilities to clients, ranging from the simple chart or map to complex programmes involving tape-slide and television recordings. In educational institutions, seminars and lectures for students on the techniques of searching are frequently supported by overhead projector transparencies, slides, tapes and teaching packages. 'Librarians now see their primary role as maximizing the use and effectiveness of their collections, rather than acting as custodians.'[2] There has been tremendous interest in research into information skills and the aim of this has been summarized as 'getting the user to use the library with maximum effect'.

The development of the idea of an information skills curriculum has emphasized the sequences of stages inherent in any finding-out activity. These have been summarized as:

1 What do I need to do? (formulation and analysis of need)
2 Where could I go? (identification and appraisal of likely sources)
3 How do I get the information? (tracing and locating individual resources)
4 Which resources shall I use? (examining, selecting and rejecting individual resources)
5 How shall I use the resources? (interrogating resources)
6 What should I make a record of? (recording and storing information)
7 Have I got the information I need? (interpretation, analysis, synthesis, evaluation)
8 How should I present it? (presentation, communication, shape)
9 What have I achieved? (evaluation).[3]

Here the library and its resources have been placed in an overall pattern of the use of information. The roles of the school teacher and librarian are of great importance in developing such early knowledge.[4] As so many schools use NBM as a natural part of their teaching, and children are using much of the appropriate equipment at home, the process is not new or difficult. However, for the next few years until methods of organization and storage are firmly established, the process of searching and browsing for NBM may require guidance. The development of simple information retrieval computer software such as 'Factfile: primary school database programs' will assist this process.[5]

The Travelling Workshops Experiment in library user education was a major testing ground for the study of user education. Its most important aim was 'to demonstrate to teaching staff in higher education how various aspects of information handling may be taught and incorporated in to the students curriculum'.[6] It also tested the value of teaching packages, centrally produced, concluding that they may be more effective than individual programmes which have been unable to draw upon a wide range of experience. These packages comprised student handbooks, practical work sound tapes, slides and posters. The conclusion of the report emphasizes that 'it is the context of user education that most influences its relevance. Content and method are of secondary importance; this is borne out by the often striking differences in the success of the (same) TWE materials and approaches, when used in two different situations'.[7] It is the use made of NBM and the style of the presentation which is important.

The problem for NBM use rests far more on the inadequacies of the older clients than on the young. Not only are they less willing to trust and use the materials (as for example in the antipathy to microforms vis-à-vis books) but they are also more fearful and reluctant to handle the equipment. As far as the library staff are concerned, considerable effort will have to be required to overcome this distaste by means of example and recommendation. The difficulties with equipment can be allayed by the development of simple procedure charts or pamphlets which must be carefully placed with the individual items. A number of libraries, particularly in the educational world, have already developed successful ones.

When NBM are issued to new clients, librarians may also feel it is necessary to enquire whether they have the technical ability and facilities to use and look after them. A common-sense approach to this should be adopted, initial questions perhaps being raised around knowledge of the recording standards, speed, pulsing, etc of the materials. Clients may even benefit from simple advice or discussion on techniques of use and obtaining the greatest value from the materials.

User education raises much wider problems than those discussed here. Effective exploitation of all information resources is an area that requires much further research to develop appropriate strategies and techniques. However, NBM add only a few additional issues to those encountered with all materials and these have been mentioned above. Carefully planned procedures and structured learning packages using NBM can also assist in their resolution. While many of these may be provided from a central source, perhaps as core material, additional items are likely to be necessary from local sources to supply answers to the special needs of the clients of a particular institution.

The physical environment
Incorporating NBM into the library invariably raises questions about its physical conditions and layout. Many of these are more the result of staff trepidation than real problems, and in this section the intention is to consider the actual effects of these materials. In general, apart from the points discussed below, NBM do not require special features or consideration. Conditions that are suitbable for books are usually satisfactory for NBM.

Coping with hazards
The major hazards to NBM are extremes of temperature and humidity, dust and magnetic fields. If staff and clients can work comfortably in the environment, then the temperature and humidity levels are likely to be satisfactory for materials and equipment. Note should be taken of the likely damage if these conditions vary excessively (see pages 61-66), and a check should be made regularly if there is any doubt. Staff should also take care that conditions do not alter much when the library is closed.

Problems with magnetic fields are unusual. Electric motors and transformers may be present in the library to provide supplies for particular equipment like air conditioners or cleaners, and they should be kept away from NBM using magnetic tape. Some security devices also include magnetic devices and these should be checked for their effects.

The worst hazard is undoubtedly dust, not only because it coats film and lenses, but also because it tends to be ground into the materials as they are used, causing poor reproduction or even scratches. While a totally dust-free atmosphere is impractical, every effort should be made to ensure cleanliness. When not in use, all NBM and equipment should be kept covered, and a regular system for cleaning the machinery is advisable. Plastic materials need to be wiped with anti-static cloths at fairly frequent intervals, particularly if plastic protection sleeves are used around them.

Electricity supply
Most equipment requires a mains supply of electricity for economic operation. While some can make use of battery power sources, these are very expensive. It may be worthwhile investing in rechargeable batteries. There is no guide to numbers of power sockets, the simplest rule being that there are never enough.

For safety reasons all sockets should be flush with the surface to which they are fixed and have individual switches. They should also be internally guarded, access to the live and neutral parts being prevented until the plug removes a guard through insertion of the earth bar. As a further safety measure, they should be easy to reach to insert or remove plugs without having to pull on the wires or having to bend them acutely as they emerge from the plug, both of which can be dangerous.

There are a number of possible systems for locating the sockets. Unless there is a definite policy to make use of fixed furniture, when electrical conduits to the sockets on the tables are simply arranged, the problem of flexibility is the most difficult to surmount. Certainly wires trailing around the floors are to be avoided at all costs as they are very dangerous – for both the equipment and the users. Some libraries have chosen floor sockets, sometimes covered by flaps of carpet. While these are usually safe, some types of shoe heels can cause problems. Wires are still present at ground level with all the potential dangers implicit in this. In libraries where there are pillars, sockets can be provided on them and on the walls, benches being moved close to them when equipment needs supplies. Another system is to hang sockets from the ceiling, a safe method (unless users walk into them) but aesthetically not very pleasing.

Although each library will make its own decisions, it is necessary to bear in mind both the safety and the convenience factors. In the latter category, it is sensible to site the sockets at table top height, about 0.75m from the ground, to avoid the need for the user to stoop. Anything which prevents easy access is an encouragement to misuse and possible danger.

Lighting

Many NBM deteriorate under direct exposure to sunlight, so this should be avoided, particularly with photographic materials. However, the major problem is the difficulty of seeing pictures on a screen when the surrounding light is bright. To reduce this, many rear projection screens are easily protected by having hoods around them. In some circumstances, it may be considered necessary to keep the equipment in special areas of reduced light, but generally this is not essential. Provided some care and consideration is given to the direction and level of lighting, the problem is not difficult to surmount.

Where equipment uses number display systems similar to that used in pocket calculators, there may be visibility difficulties in bright light.

This is particularly apparent where fluorescent tubes are used, and some means of shading such displays may be necessary. Some modern tape recorders use these types of number in the odometer and difficulties may arise with them.

Fluorescent tube lighting may be the cause of interference with electronic equipment, particularly obvious on television monitors/ receivers. In prime condition, the lights usually produce no problem, but defective tubes, especially at the end of their life, generate transmitted waves which can cause crackles on sound reception and white lines on television screens.

Now that television sets or monitors are used for continual reading and study, it is necessary to consider the brightness of light on them. Stray reflections should be avoided where possible, and the user should be able to sit about a metre away from a 14in screen and view and work in comfort. The ambient light needs to be at a similar brightness to that of the screen so as to reduce any potential eyestrain.

Viewing/listening positions
When NBM first appeared in libraries, there was some anxiety about possible disturbing effects on the book users. The problems of distribution of mains power and security also seemed insurmountable unless the viewing/listening areas were enclosed in some way. As a result, there was a rapid development of carrels, small enclosures of either three sides only or complete, in which the equipment was housed. In some libraries, NBM, or rather those considered to be audiovisual, are kept and used in only one special room. This makes cross-referencing between information in different types of document even more difficult. In others, carrels are blocked together in one part or spread in small patches for particular subject areas. It is apparent that a client wishing to use paper materials will go to the open tables, and to explore NBM a carrel.

The resulting seclusion meant that the activities of NBM-using clients did not distract other users, and that any noise from the equipment was restricted to a small area. However, they were seen to be doing something special, and NBM became imbued with a special quality which made their use different from that of other documents. More recent trends of thinking, and indeed the argument of this book, incline towards the attitude that NBM and all other documents are equally valuable information carriers. Any secreting of NBM users into special areas runs against this thinking.

261

Further support for the development of isolated carrels came from the complexity of some equipment. Tape-slide presentation, for instance, requires a sound tape recorder, a connecting box, an automatic slide projector and a screen. In the early days all these were separate items, which were most conveniently kept joined together in specially made furniture cabinets. The Surrey carrel, developed at the University of Surrey, was a successful development of this type. A number of other institutions produced their own, particularly medical schools. In some libraries, a decision was made that television programmes would be distributed on demand from a central bank of videotape recorders and not put on by the client personally. To view them, carrels were essential, fixed structures wired to the video distribution centre. In American colleges, the 1960s saw a considerable development of these systems to various levels of sophistication. Known as dial-access-retrieval, the client dialled a telephone code for the particular programme required from the selection being transmitted at the time. However, this never proved attractive to British institutions, partly because of its considerable expense, but more importantly because of its inflexibility.

Nevertheless, if the full complexity of dial-access-retrieval was discarded, librarians still felt it necessary to isolate NBM use to carrels. A number of commercial models are available, many demountable and therefore easily moved to different areas. For convenience, most of them also interlock, usually in fours, and where they are fixed, a central core carries all the wiring which is distributed four ways. Some of the most successful have been made to the special designs of Dundee College of Education. A further development in the carrels produced for Plymouth Polytechnic is a sliding top which acts as a shield against interference from overhead lighting, and also locks up the carrel completely when pulled further out.

Yet the necessity for carrels at all must be questioned. With improving technology and client skills, the early anxieties over mechanical noise and user incompetence have been reduced. If the philosophy of similar value between books and NBM is to be evident in practice, surely it is better that they should be seen to be used in any part of the library.

Distractions for other library users can prove much less than many expect. Generally, viewing screens are comparatively small in the library as they are used by individuals or pairs at most. The special group viewing rooms are excluded from this discussion. A reader who is distracted by people moving around the library is likely to be also distracted by a bright picture in another part of the room, but most other people are not. Noise is now rarely a problem. Whether in carrels or not, sound is listened to by users through headphones, and so others are unaware of it. Mechanical movement is still very noisy in cine film projectors because of the activity of the claw in drawing the film through the channel, and this will not be eliminated, unless an entirely new system is developed. There may also be a problem with microcomputers and their peripherals. A number of microcomputers provide a sound system, for example the BBC micro. This can be irritating to users. Similarly the provision of printers can cause a noise problem. However, mechanical noise from other equipment is limited to the sound of cooling fans which is unobtrusive when compared with most air-conditioning and microcomputers. Apart from the problem of cinefilm projectors, distraction as an argument in favour of carrels is increasingly weak. However, it may be necessary to identify particular areas for siting the connecting equipment to mainframe computer systems like Prestel or major databases overseas. The telephone connection charges can be high if it is not used with discrimination, and controlled user sections for this may be advisable.

Complex equipment is also not such a difficulty as it was. As has been stated, users are becoming progressively more aware and confident with it through their own experience in school and home. Machines which used to be separate and bulky are now manufactured as one compact model. A number of different tape-slide replay models are now available which sit easily on a table and require a minimal level of operator skill to use. The modern videocassette equipment is also relatively foolproof and can be entrusted to the client with considerable confidence.

Security will always be a problem, and librarians are right to be anxious about the attractive nature of much NBM equipment for the potential thief. It is worth noting that some of the library security systems developed to prevent the loss of books can be used to similar good effect with NBM equipment. While carrels afford a measure of protection against loss, usually by screwing or chaining the equipment down, similar measures can be taken with equipment placed more openly in the library. Naturally, unscrewing has to be possible to allow for servicing and repair, and the determined thief will find a way of doing this surreptitiously. Nevertheless, the screw is a deterrent against the casual loss.

Whether the library decides on a separate room for NBM, carrels, or the open table, display and use will depend on a balance of weighting between the points mentioned above. All three choices offer an acceptable practice for which there are particular advantages for different libraries. A final point is worth noting, however; the equipment for NBM does occupy space, and therefore if the client is to make notes or refer to other materials at the same position, adequate table-top area has to be provided.

Browsing

If users are to be encouraged to browse through the library's NBM, it should not be necessary for them to take the materials to the main viewing/listening positions. The provision of light boxes for transparent materials and simple sound cassette players for listining to tapes can be fixed alongside stacks easily and inexpensively. With cinefilms, computer software, and videotapes, browsing is difficult, and must be confined to the printed information supplies with the containers.

Technical area

A library dealing with NBM will normally require access to or have a technical area. This will have three main functions:

1 Repair of equipment: A store of spare parts, including lamps, will be necessary for instant replacement. Depending on the skills of the staff, it may be possible to undertake repairs also. A sufficiency of measuring devices for identifying faults, soldering irons, mechanical jigs, etc may be present.

2 Repair of materials: The sophistication of this will depend on the level and type of stock present in the library, and a calculation of the relative costs of instant in-house repairs against more time-consuming external agencies. Simple laminating equipment and binding will normally cover damage to paper materials. Damaged still pictures are most economically discarded, but cinefilm can be spliced. To identify areas of damage in a cinefilm, sophisticated and expensive apparatus is available to automatically check a reel, but unless there is a large stock this may be more cheaply undertaken by hand. Sound tape can also be spliced, but videotape should be re-recorded. Damaged plastic materials are best discarded, and action to be taken on models, specimens etc will depend on their value and their nature. Decisions on the level of repair to be undertaken will dictate the quantity and type of equipment provided.

3 Production: The standard of provision of equipment and space for this will also depend on policy decisions. If duplicate copies are to be issued to clients, then provision is necessary for the appropriate machinery. Original materials may also be made: this may require simply transferring one format to another, for example microfilming periodicals or transferring disc recordings to sound cassettes; another method may be making off-air recordings from broadcasts, in which case good aerials connecting to the equipment will normally be essential. The library may also have decided on the active creation of new materials to fill apparent gaps in its stock, and the level of provision will depend on the forms in which such NBM are to be made. Any decisions on this will need to be considered in relation to the costs of in-house production compared to using an external agency.

Staffing requirements

Do NBM cause special staffing problems? Some would argue that they only demand extra skills from the professional librarians, while others point to the need for extra differently qualified personnel. This resulted in a major consideration of staffing structures in the work of Gerald Collier for the Council of Educational Technology.[8] This was an attempt to analyse and clarify 'the managerial and professional level tasks involved in providing a teaching and learning support service or unit in a wide variety of educational institutions'. It recognized that information provision was embracing the work of librarians, media specialists and computer staff. Integration is the aim here but the rigid demarcations drawn up by these groups have prevented in some institutions this aim being reached. In this section the issues about staffing are discussed, but it must be emphasized that this is only in terms of the impact of NBM. Some of the points will have a more general application, although the development of the concept is based on the results of introducing these materials. If a library is adding to its stock, it may be necessary to increase the staff to deal with it; that is a normal calculation for the management which is not of importance here. NBM may be additional stock in this sense and require that response, but that is a decision based on the quantity of materials, not their nature. Here the discussion is concerned with the impact of stock of a different type and the effect that that has on the skills of the staff employed.

The audiovisual librarian?

When libraries first admitted audiovisual materials like slides and video-recordings, the initial response was to employ a special librarian to look after them. Few of the professional staff had any experience with such materials. Basic training mostly emphasized books, and the bibliographic tools commonly available and used were slanted in their direction. A similar response had been made towards records and music scores when these were introduced into the general library, and in this case, as the field had a subject coherence, this was very logical. But the AV librarian was in a different situation. The subjects were disparate, only the materials forming the link.

AV librarians were also allocated only a limited proportion of the full range of NBM. For example, it was unusual to find them responsible for portfolios or even microforms. The latter were usually carriers of government publications, back runs of newspapers and periodicals, and assigned to the relevant subject specialists. To the AV librarian was given the responsibility of all the 'awkward' materials, from slides to wall charts and models.

Such an approach is the antithesis of normal academic library practice. The trend over the years has been to greater subject specialization, fundamentally for two reasons: firstly, such a system meant that one member of staff at least became deeply familiar with one particular field and hence was able to operate a sensible and carefully thought out acquisition policy; secondly, such specialization produced more effective advice to clients because of a deeper knowledge of the field and a fuller appreciation of the likely interests. A specialist AV librarian could only offer a good knowledge of the different formats and the relevant equipment, but understanding of the content was naturally superficial.

The philosophy underlying this book is that NBM and books are equally valuable as information carriers within the capabilities of their formats. Conversely, the existence of the specialist AV librarian emphasized the opposite, highlighting the difference between the two types of materials rather than the similarity of the information they carried. At the beginning of this evolution in the library's responsibilities, the management solution to inadequate staffing may well have been considered the only logical one. However, now it is surely clear that all subject specialists should be responsible for the NBM in their area, and it is towards the necessary in-service training of such staff and the appropriate basic training of new entrants that the profession must look.

In the modern library, clients will expect to find the NBM in the same area as the other materials on the subject, and to seek advice on all the relevant stock from the same person, not one for books and someone else for the others. To this end, all staff should understand 'the application of librarianship to the new media which should be covered in the initial education of every librarian, whatever his eventual specialization'.[9]

The skills required

To be able to exploit NBM, it is necessary for the librarian to have certain extra skills. Here, only a series of general points are made to demonstrate the range of needs.

1 Technical skill: It is *not* necessary for the professional staff to be technical experts, and it is important to avoid 'the everpresent danger ... that the machines can be transmuted from simply a means of unlocking informational riches to an end in themselves, with ... interest becoming centred upon how to work the magic boxes and their care in sickness and health'.[9] For some people there is a compulsive delight in exploring the mysteries of electrical equipment and gadgetry, but this fascination is not a requirement for a librarian. It is important that the machines are seen as a means to an end, not the end itself.

All the same, it is necessary for the staff to be able to use the equipment with confidence, and be able to assist clients to do so as well. A basic knowledge of how the equipment works, following what is described in this book, is all that is normally needed by way of preparation to achieve the appropriate information revealing operation. If the equipment does not work, a qualified technician is needed, not a librarian. However, it is probable that most professional staff will also be required to undertake basic maintenance as outlined in chapter three. The growth of the domestic market for NBM equipment, for example videorecorders, has meant that manufacturers have had to make the equipment more idiot proof; they have supplied better instruction manuals. Another important factor is that the younger generation of librarians have themselves grown up with the technology and have often attended equipment training courses at library schools.

Some librarians who work with NBM would also argue that there is much to be gained from the development of an empathy with these materials, similar to that many people have with books. The truth behind this is difficult to ascertain − it is almost impossible to measure − but it probably evolves from enjoyment of the way the information is transmitted and an appreciation of the techniques of production. While this is not a technical skill, its possession leads to a more constructive approach to the care of the materials and sensible advice on

267

their exploitation. While a knowledge of computer programming skills may be of assistance to the librarian involved with computer software they are not a necessary prerequisite. The provision of software with adequate documentation is crucial in assisting the user, rather than the ability to explain how the software was written.

2 Bibliographic skill: While the bibliographical tools are less well organized than for books, there are still a considerable number that can be used. The approach is not quite so straightforward as the use of *British books in print*, but their exploitation is not difficult, and should be a skill acquired by all librarians. Where there are Prestel facilities the librarian will need to provide a manual index to the commonest subjects sought by his clients. The long-winded tree indexing is expensive to use and frustrates the user who wants a quick answer.

3 Advising clients: The exploitation of stock will always involve advising clients, helping them to locate appropriate items and to make use of them. The certain technical variations in the organization and storage of NBM, and sometimes even limitations on their use, will mean that guidance may often be more necessary than is the case with books.

Advice on selection and use will be related to an analysis of the client's needs and situation. Because some NBM require equipment, advice will be needed to ensure that the client has the appropriate items and understands the problems of compatibility. However, more important is advice on the appropriateness of selections for the particular circumstances, the only relevant question to answer is whether the materials are designed for individual or group use.

Educational circumstances are, however, different. While some NBM have been created for independent study by students, many will be found in educational libraries for class use by teachers. Compared with books, NBM can be used in teaching in a wide variety of ways, and the librarian who is exploiting his stock fully should be giving relevant advice. This demands a considerable understanding of teaching methods which are not normally part of the background of the librarian. Although some would suggest that such knowledge is unnecessary because the professional teacher should know what he has to do with his particular classes, considerable uncertainty arises when he is faced with a varied stock offering a number of different opportunities. Advice, supported by a realistic understanding, is then very useful, particularly if further information on successful use by other people can also be given.

The importance of such skills is gradually being recognized. Some librarians are now seeking additional teaching qualifications, although

268

the full teacher-training course is probably excessively detailed. Unfortunately other relevant courses are difficult to find. A British Library report 'recommends that librarians in academic institutions attend the introductory courses on teaching now being organized for new academic staff' and suggests that 'a suitable course to follow might be the City and Guilds of London Institute's Teacher Certificate'.[10] *The Review Committee on Education for Information Use: Final Report* summarizes the present situation in user education and makes recommendations and indicates areas where further research or expansion of activities is necessary or desirable. One result of this was a learning pack designed to improve the librarian's teaching skills and providing guidance and rationale for the creation and use of NBM such as OHP's and tape-slide programmes. Other courses which would be beneficial to librarians would be those leading to diplomas in curriculum development and educational technology. A list of training programmes is given in the *Audiovisual and microcomputer handbook.*[11]

The argument here tends to the need for librarians in educational institutions to have considerable knowledge of teaching and also the methods of student learning. Not all the activities of professional staff require such understanding. For example, cataloguing and basic bibliographic control can be undertaken without it, and this may lead to the development of different types of staff — those that advise clients requiring this type of educational skill, and those dealing with the mechanics of organization and control.

Such knowledge of learning may also have other benefits. Firstly, assistance to students in finding appropriate study pathways can be given from a background of deeper understanding, and an exploitation of a wider variety of approaches to the subject might well be made possible, using the full range of NBM. Secondly, many NBM are published with very little information on how they are to be used for effective teaching/learning. To improve this, the librarian may feel it is helpful to provide basic guidance sheets including headings such as the learning objectives, the equipment and other materials required, briefing on how to set up and organize the setting, and even perhaps a debriefing which lists possible ways of following up the work to develop its potential further. In order to prepare such sheets as these, more knowledge than comes from present training in librarianship is necessary.

The concepts outlined here are still controversial, but they are mentioned because they evolve from the presence of NBM in the library of an educational institution. The level of efficient exploitation is one decided upon, to a considerable extent, by the general management policy. Because NBM offer such a variety of approaches to learning it is difficult to conceive of useful advice being given without such a background of knowledge.

4 Advising colleagues: While NBM are still unaccepted by a number of professional staff, librarians committed to their use may employ their skills in demonstrating and explaining their value. This requires an ability to advise and assist without causing irritation, and can be very useful and encouraging in an embryonic organization.

5 Being aware of developments: No librarian in the present technological age can feel that all methods of storing and exploiting information have now been fully developed. New techniques will continue to emerge, new means and materials evolve. It is therefore important that the modern librarian has an open mind, and will watch for new approaches and evaluate their benefits for his institution. The profession has had an unfortunate reputation for stasis, an unwillingness to recognize trends and manipulate them to its advantage. However, although the first generation of NBM have caused a rethinking and a somewhat reluctant acceptance of them, it is clear that the next generation are being received more willingly. The eagerness of librarians to pilot viewdata systems and the formation by the Library Association of an 'Information Technology Group' are indications that the profession has perhaps learnt the lesson of earlier debates concerning NBM.

Soon the librarian will be faced with different storage systems for computers like ROM packs and holograms as possible stock items, ready to be loaned out for use on domestic machines. There will be new distribution systems, maybe even cable links between the library and the households in the immediate community. Are libraries prepared for these, and are there additional skills needed by the professional staff? Until they actually appear, this is impossible to answer clearly. What is clear, is that their arrival should not be a time for anxieties.

Technical assistance

A library with equipment for NBM will need professional technical assistance to undertake regular servicing and cope with the inevitable serious repairs. Whether full-time posts are created or not will depend on the amount and types of equipment involved. The technicians should be fully qualified whether by experience or through academic courses. It is probably wiser to look for electronic rather than mechanical expertise, as the latter can be readily acquired by a person with the former skills. Most serious mechanical breakdowns have to be returned to the factory or accredited servicing agencies because they require special tooling which is uneconomic for the library to acquire for the few occasions it is likely to be needed.

Other technical experts, such as photographers, will depend on the policy adopted towards duplications of NBM for clients and in-house production. A team of skilled technicians can be costly, and the library will need to decide whether it can employ them, or whether hiring from an outside agency may not be more appropriate.

Summary
As was made clear at the beginning of this section, the discussion has been limited to the additional staffing needs caused by the incorporation of NBM. There can be no conclusion as to the numbers or level of staff required.

The viewpoint here, as in the whole of this book, has centred on the general library. However, some librarians are already employed in subject resource centres, the stock limited to one small topic area. Just as they will be using subject indexing systems appropriate to their collections, so they will also be responding to the particular needs of their special situation by using further technical skills to those mentioned above. Some will even be undertaking simple production work. Their relationship to their clients will be different, and in academic resource centres they will be noting the work of Pat Noble on resource-based learning.

The comments in this section have concentrated on the general basic needs of the librarian, not those introduced by special circumstances. Given a good training in the skills outlined above, the professional librarian should be able readily to adapt and modify his or her approach to meet the needs of specialist clients in these more limited surroundings.

Financial implications
When the constraints preventing the development of the effective use of NBM within the library were discussed (see page 43) the problem of the book fund was mentioned. This has always been the centre of librarians' budgeting requirements and it has appeared in the past sacrosanct. Continuing the theme of this book that it is the information carriers and their exploitation that should be considered sacrosanct, it must be realized now that there is little justification for separate

271

estimates for books and non-book materials in libraries. This becomes clear particularly with the development of on-line bibliographical services where the same information is provided as in the printed services. Indeed one decision may be to dispense with the expensive capital costs of providing a shelf copy of say *Chemical abstracts* compared to a user-financed service to the on-line provision. If the library is to react to its clients' needs, it must not be hampered by separate funds, and it will need to consider the view as expressed by Hallworth 'that the book fund becomes a materials fund, which allows experts of various kinds within the system to apply a corporate approach for the good of the total service; separate funds for each different form of stock is an anachronism'.[12]

The financial implications of housing NBM within the library should not be considered a result of an extra, rather tiresome, even gimmicky, addition to services, but rather as a recognition of what the library should be doing – supplying a *complete* information service.

While extra staff may be needed, these are not necessary to cope specifically with the NBM but rather to deal with the increased volume of stock. In many cases additional NBM can be dealt with satisfactorily by the present staff, although the cost of retraining them may be involved. It may be necessary to establish a technical department to service equipment, or it may prove less expensive to rely on outside contracts.

Perhaps the major financial implication is the cost of equipment. The initial purchase price should be keenly studied; discounts are available and bulk purchasing can also result in significant savings.

Maintenance of equipment has been discussed in chapter three, and some people have suggested that ten per cent of the initial cost should be allowed annually for this. It is also important to budget for the complete replacement of a piece of equipment after five years. There may also be increased insurance costs, especially where clients have free access to electrical equipment, and also extra premiums for theft. The running cost of equipment is small although extra estimates will have to be made for spare projector bulbs and other replaceable items. If it is decided to use carrels or special storage systems for the equipment, this will be extra to the initial purchase price. There is also the use of services which depend upon telephone links, for example telesoftware or Viewdata. This will involve telephone costs, costs for accessing the service and often a charge for using particular pages. The library may decide to earmark a certain sum of money for this service and withdraw the provision when this money is spent rather than give an open-ended commitment.

Finally, there is the ever-present problem of equipment development and the obsolescence of old models. In presenting the final requirements, the librarian must make allowances for this for 'it reflects the need to be aware of and responsive to advances in technology, equipment, and materials. The multimedia library manager needs to ask, for example, what advances have been made in microforms? These advances in technology become budget concerns because they mean that technology has solved a problem or met a need, or created new fiscal requirements that must be reflected in the budget'.[13]

The librarian may also be faced with a novel situation, the decision whether to purchase or hire. This is true especially for cinefilm and videorecordings, which may be hired through a number of commercial libraries. Therefore an amount must be earmarked for hiring material. If material is previewed before purchase it may also be necessary to hire, although this can often be subsequently deducted from the cost.

The majority of NBM are no more expensive than books and therefore any increase in the materials fund should not be excessive. However, one area of extra cost may be that of repackaging and processing. The servicing of NBM may mean extra staff particularly if standardized packaging is not used. In particular, filmstrips, sound discs and film can be expensive in staff time. If a policy of integrated shelving is adopted then repackaging in book-like containers will have to be considered. Many publishers are now providing their materials in suitable packages. The microcomputer publishers, such as Acornsoft, seem to be following a similar pattern. There is a bonus in that labelling and pocketing of such rebound documents is more analogous to that of books and new library stationery need not be bought. Indeed, a library supplier will often label and pocket free of charge using the library's own stationery. The full range of library processing, class lettering, issue cards, accession number, ownership stamp, will be more easily fixed to a standardized packaging than the original published format. The cost of repackaging should also be compared to the extra cost in separate shelving if a non-standard approach is adopted. Consider, for example, the additional expense of purchasing sound cassette stands, plastic wallets and filing cabinets for slides.

The cost of security must also be taken into account. Certain formats, such as sound cassettes, and equipment are susceptible to theft and need to be protected. However, this should fit into the security system already in use in the library. For a library without such a system it may be necessary to consider installing one as a result of the decision to purchase NBM.

The selection of stock may be more expensive in staff time because of the nature of some formats and the cost of equipment for previewing. Similarly the cataloguing process may be slower and there may indeed be a major cost factor to consider if the book cataloguing is by MARC tape as the majority of NBM are not included in these services. Thus a larger staff may be required to cope with a smaller quantity of material. Developments from the British Library through the BLAISE Service which now includes AVMARC and the proposals for a UK Library Database System offer the possibility of one database for all documents. Certainly some UK libraries have managed to computerize the cataloguing of books and NBM in one system, as in the Humberside Public Libraries, and the ILEA Central Library Resources Service.

A final element in the financial implications is the difficult one of charging for the service. A number of public libraries are charging clients for borrowing sound discs, cassettes and pictures. This is a tempting approach to get a new service started. Prestel, for example, can be provided by a coin slot service. The political philosophy involved here is outside the scope of this book, but the central tenet must surely be to provide the same service for all materials. Thus the logical step would be to charge for books. Indeed it can be argued that the success of charging for NBM has recently caused some pressure from financial committees to impose such charges. Indeed, the financial implications of NBM may be very much wider than just those of the cost of material, equipment, processing and staffing!

Physical control

The question of the centralization of service must be discussed. There seems little doubt that centralized processing is the most efficient. Particularly within educational institutions it has been argued that NBM should be located in the areas where learning takes place, perhaps as a result of their traditional use as teaching aids. However, this takes no account of the use of NBM by other departments, their value in individual study situations and the need for access outside teaching times. If the materials are in the library access can be controlled for the benefit of all. Within the public library it may be necessary to process centrally but the individual branches can then be left safely to establish their own stock. Expense has caused one or two branches of some public

274

libraries to be established as 'the sound cassette library' or 'the picture library'. This can result in resentment from some clients who cannot visit these branches. Where possible there should be equity of service.

The physical processing of the documents should be done centrally or by an outside supplier. As with all materials processing there will be four objectives: to identify the library's ownership; to process for issue; to locate where the document will be stored; and to protect from damage and theft. Individual formats can result in time-consuming procedures; for example, marking the ownership of a filmstrip could involve scratching an identifying mark on the film leader, labelling the filmstrip tub and its lid, stamping the notes, and finally labelling the container for the notes and filmstrip. Decisions also have to be made on the balance between time-consuming processing and security. A set of 36 slides could have an accession number on each of them or just on the container, a choice between absolute security or the minimum necessary. The librarian involved in the processing procedure must have knowledge of the storage facilities and the possible damage and deterioration the NBM will face from continued use. Computer floppy disks should not have their security tags removed. Linked to this is the lack of browsability of some of the forms and the need to provide full information labels on the actual item. While the physical processing method is a highly logical exercise and includes the use of work flows, the librarian still needs to use his initiative and imagination to cope with the variety of NBM.

Shelving may be in specialized cabinets, or integrated with the book stock. In either case shelving staff should be trained to be careful and accurate in placement of NBM: for example, videorecordings should be securely fastened in their containers; film cans should be carefully handled to prevent damage and staff should not carry an excessive weight; sound discs should be stored vertically without pressure on them; illustrations will need to be accurately replaced in sequence.

There must be a policy decision as to whether material shall be on loan or for reference only. This is a decision that cannot usually be made for all NBM or even one particular form. Rather it depends on the needs of the clients. There may be pressure to restrict access to specific groups, for example only lecturers or the representatives of a particular organization. This should be resisted as a general policy, for all clients should have access to all services. The degree of access will depend on individual circumstances. Some material may be for reference only. Microcomputer software is often only available within

275

the library because of the use of expensive equipment. A film collection with a large demand for its stock may restrict loan to a short period, perhaps 48 hours, or the 16mm films may be limited to individuals representing groups and no provision made for one person viewing. However, bearing these points in mind, 'circulation is a primary task of the multimedia library. Its goal is to maximize the availability of all materials to the patron and to actually implement (sic) the use of such materials'.[14]

The method of loan issuing adopted must be able to handle all materials, whether a book, a filmstrip or a model of a dinosaur. There are numerous systems available and these should be assessed on how simply and accurately all material can be issued. However, problems may arise in deciding how far to check NBM prior to issue. If there are 16 slides in a set and only 15 are returned, the client may claim that it was missing on issue. There is a similar problem with damage to sound discs and film. The best method is to check on return and make an accurate record, then to use damage labels for sound discs (on which scratches may be marked). For slide sets a supply of 2in X 2in cards with 'slide number – missing' printed on them to place in vacant pockets. Videocassettes and microcomputer software are time-consuming to check and the librarian must often rely on a complaint from a subsequent client. A decision on when documents should be withdrawn from stock should be left to the judgement of the librarian. The slide set could be withdrawn from circulation until a replacement slide has been obtained, but individual slides are sometimes difficult to acquire. Portfolios and kits are a difficult problem with their profusion of items. The easiest solution is to provide a contents list with a note asking users to inform the library of any missing items when they return the kit.

Security is a problem in most libraries and the introduction of NBM and in particular the equipment, has made the library a temptation for thieves. Equipment such as sound cassette recorders are easily resold. Both equipment and documents can be protected by sensors. All systems should be checked with the manufacturers for their use with magnetic tape as these may be affected by the electrical field incorporated in some devices. Loss may also be prevented by siting equipment close to the issue point or any other easily observable area.

The librarian concerned with managing his library to the highest standards often relies on outside evidence to help finalize his decisions and to offer as evidence to his controlling bodies. The British librarian

276

must rely upon the more general statements concerning library provision, for example the recommendations contained in *College libraries: guidelines for professional service and resource provision* 3rd ed. Library Association, 1982. There is no British equivalent to the two standards of the American Library Association, Public Library Association, Audiovisual Committee: *Guidelines for audiovisual materials and services for large public libraries* and *Recommendations for audiovisual materials and services for small and medium sized public libraries* Chicago, ALA, 1975.

The British school librarian is better served by *Library resource provision in schools* new ed, Library Association, 1977, which includes recommendations for school library resource centres and the School Library Service. They should also note the *Guidelines for the planning and organization of school library media centres* IFLA, 1979.

Conclusion

The addition of non-book material to the library stock does not cause major problems for management. In this chapter, the areas where significant problems may arise have been looked at, and the logical conclusion should be that a rational analysis of the problems leads to only minor modifications of existing arrangements. Perhaps the most important, and unmentioned, role of management is to encourage in the library staff a commitment to the concept of NBM as valuable information carriers and thence an eagerness to purchase and exploit them. Traditional book-orientated librarians will treat NBM sceptically, perhaps to the extent of creating unsurmountable problems, but staff with a wider outlook and efficient training will work hard to overcome any difficulties that may arise. Providing clients with the opportunity to use a variety of materials will encourage more interest from them, and probably also increase their number. In this way, the library may find itself playing a central role in the development of the life of the community it serves.

Part 6

REFERENCES AND BIBLIOGRAPHY

REFERENCES: PART 1 – BACKGROUND

1   Burke, E *A philosophical enquiry into the origin of our ideas of the sublime and beautiful* 1st ed, 1757, p1.

2   Cabeceiras, J *The multimedia library: materials, selection and use* 2nd ed, New York: Academic Press, 1982.

3   Fleischer, E and Goodman, H *Cataloguing audiovisual materials: a manual based on the Anglo-American Cataloguing Rules II* New York: Neal-Schuman, 1980.

4   McNally, P T *Non-book materials* 2nd ed, South Melbourne: MacMillan, 1981.

5   Tite, C *A guide to media resources in psychopathology* London: LLRS Publications, 1982.

6   Winslow, K *Video: information technology of the 80's* in: Association of Research Librarians *Minutes of ninety-sixth meeting . . .* Washington, DC: ARL, 1980, pp9-12.

7   Henderson, J and Humphreys, F *Audiovisual and microcomputer handbook* 3rd ed, Kogan Page, 1982.

8   Gilbert, L A *Non-book materials: their bibliographic control: a proposed computer system for the cataloguing of audio-visual materials in the United Kingdom* National Council for Educational Technology, 1971 (NCET working paper no 6).

9   British Standard Specification 5408: *Glossary of documentation terms* 1976.

10   Very few listings are available, but they are either highly technical or only of American terminology. A further problem is that the physical form of a given document may be described in more than one way. The following offer a recent history of the development of the terminology:

Anglo American Cataloguing Rules 2nd ed, American Library Association: Canadian Library Association, Library Association, 1978. (Note glossary and terms in Rule 1.1C1 General Material designation and in the specialist chapters.)

Library Association, Media Cataloguing Rules Committee *Non-book materials cataloguing rules* LA/NCET, 1973, p9. (Lists the forms, and some definitions given in the text.)

Gilbert, L *Non-book materials: their bibliographic control* NCET, 1971, pp12-15. (Defines some of the terms in LA/NCET.)

Groves, P S *Non-print media in academic libraries* ALA, 1975, pp 48-50. (A useful structured listing.)

IFLA ISBD (NBM) *International standard bibliographic description for non-book materials* 1977, pp54-58.

Personal computer world London: Sportscene Publishers (PCW) Ltd. Each month an invaluable quick reference guide to microcomputer jargon is published called 'Newcomers start here'.

Weihs, J R *Non-book materials: the organization of integrated collections* 2nd ed, Ottawa: Canadian Library Association, 1979. (Extremely useful source, highly recommended. Glossary pp109-110.)

Also note: British Standard Specification, op cit.

11 The phonogramm-Archiv of the Akademie der Wissenschaften was set up on April 27th 1899. Three major aims: (a) to survey the languages and dialects of Europe, and then the rest of the world; (b) performances of music, particularly of primitive races; (c) voices of famous people.

12 Campbell, A K D *Non-book materials and non-bibliographic services in public libraries: a study of their development and of the controversies which have surrounded them from 1850 to 1964.* FLA thesis, 1965, University Microfilms, p116.

13 Ibid, p131.

14 Lever, A 'The cinematograph and chronophone as educators in public libraries' *The librarian* 3(5) December 1912, pp195-200.

15 Pinion, C 'Video home lending service in public libraries' *Audiovisual librarian* 9(1) Winter 1983, pp18-23.

16 Baxter, P *Libraries and computer materials* London: British Library, 1982 (BLRD 5690).

17 Gibson, G 'Sound recordings' in: Groves, op cit, p82.

18 Doubleday, W E (W E D) 'Current view' *Library Association record* 15th February 1917, pp41-42.

19 Campbell, op cit, p134.

20 Ibid, p130. Quoting L McColvin.

21 Smith, F S 'Music and gramophones in public libraries' *The library assistant* (316) March 1925, p64.

22 Campbell, op cit, p171. Quoting E A Savage.

23 Ibid, p130. Quoting W B Sayers.

24 Ibid, p165.

25 National Committee for Visual Aids in Education *Planning a visual education department* NCVAE, 1948, p1.

26 As reported in:

Fothergill, R *Resource Centres in colleges of education* National Council for Educational Technology (NCET working paper no 10).

Beswick, N *School resource centres* Evans/Methuen, 1972 (Schools Council working paper 43).

27 The full history of the development of NBM in British libraries has still to be written. Many of the facts given in this section are drawn from Campbell, op cit, and Kelly, T A *History of public libraries in Great Britain 1845-1965* Library Association, 1973.

28 *The whisperers* United Artists, 1966 (cinefilm).

29 Fothergill, R and Hurley, S *Child abuse: a teaching pack* Open University Educational Enterprises, 1978 (multimedia).

30 Cross, C 'The making of the British: five invasions (600BC-1066AD)' *The observer* C I Audio Visual, 1972.

REFERENCES: PART 2 – THE USER

1 Unesco 'Text of the resolution adopted unanimously by the fifteenth session of the General Conference of Unesco at its forty-second plenary meeting on Wednesday, 20th November 1968, at Unesco House, Paris' in: International Film and Television Council *International conference on the cataloguing of audiovisual materials* London, 1973, IFTC, 1975, p30.

2 Pedler, R 'The China project' in: *Ford Teaching Project* Unit 4, Teacher Case Studies, University of East Anglia.

3 GB Dept of Education and Science, Committee of Enquiry *A language for life* HMSO, 1975, p318 (Sir Alan Bullock, Chairman).

4 Ibid, pxxxi.

5 Schools Council Project files and index. Regular updating service which listed all the projects the Schools Council were involved with.

6 Noble, P *Resource-based learning in post compulsory education* Kogan Page, 1980, p15.

7 Harrison, H 'Media resources in the Open University Library' *Audiovisual librarian* 1 (1) Summer 1973, pp9-10.

8 Twining, J *Open learning for technicians* Thorne, 1982.

9 Ennals, R 'Historical simulation' (*Practical computing* July 1979) in: Sledge, D *Microcomputers in education* CET, 1979.

10 Higher Education Learning Programmes Information Service *Catalogue* 7th ed, 1982-83, BUFC, 1982.

11 Ravilious, C P 'Call and response: an experiment in audio-visual participation' *Audiovisual librarian* 1(6) 1974/5, pp238-244.

12 Kodak survey *Screen digest* June 1976.

13 'Midlands VHS decision threatens Sony's network dominance' *Audiovisual* (134) February 1983, p19.

Reevell, P 'How mums got the first video disc' *Audiovisual* (122) February, 1983, pp34-40.

14 Fairfax, O et al. *Audiovisual materials: development of a national cataloguing and information service* Council for Educational Technology (CET working paper no 12), p24.

15 Tripp, P 'Audio cassettes for local government' *Assistant librarian* January 1977, pp6-7.

16 Allason, J 'Micros smack the million mark' *The observer* 27th March 1983, p20.

17 *Social trends* no 13, HMSO, 1983.

18 'Decisions 1: distribution – siting an oil terminal' Shell-Mex and

BP and Bath University School of Education, (nd). Exercise on decision-making in industry based on real problems. Useful for 6th form, further education, higher education and industrial organizations. Material included for 16-20 students.

19 *Collier's encyclopedia*, Crowell-Collier, 1970. Volume 9 has an insert between pp138-139 of 4 colour transparencies of 'The internal-combustion automobile engine'.

20 *Social trends* op cit.

21 Pinion, C 'Video home lending services in public libraries' *Audiovisual librarian* 9(1) Winter 1983, p18.

22 For example, Dun Laoghaire Public Library, Eire have installed Apple II microcomputers in the Young People's section of each service point in the branch.

23 Campbell, H C 'Media for man in the street' in: International Film and Television Council *International conference on the cataloguing of audio-visual materials* London, 1973, IFTC, 1975, p83.

24 Swank, R 'Sight and sound in the world of books' *Library journal* September 15th 1953.

25 Ely, D P 'The contemporary college library: change by evolution or revolution' *Educational technology* 11 (May) 1971, pp17-19.

26 Library Advisory Council (England) *Report of the new media in libraries working party* LAC, 1976 (LCE (76) 6), p6. Quoting chief librarian of Toronto Public Libraries.

27 Enright, B J *New media and the library in education* London: Bingley; Hamden (Conn); Linnet, 1972, p36. Quoting R C Swank.

28 American Library Association Public Library Association. Audio-visual Committee *Guidelines for audio-visual materials and services for large public libraries* ALA, 1975, p12.

29 Hancock, A 'Cataloguing and information handling for integrated audiovisual media utilisation at the national level' in: International Film and Television Council *International conference on the cataloguing of audio-visual materials* London, 1973, IFTC, 1975, pp106-107.

30 British Universities Film Council, BUFC Information Service *Publicity leaflet*.

31 Unesco, op cit.

32 Munro, D J 'Bromley audio survey' *Library Association record* 77(4) April 1975, p86.

33 Baggs, C and Thompson, A H 'Video in libraries' *Audiovisual librarian* 8(1) Winter 1982, p26.

34 Coleman, P and Yorke, D 'A public library experiments with market research' *Library Association record* 77(5) May 1975, pp107-109.

35 Pinion, C op cit.

36 *GB Public Libraries and Museums Act 1964* Eliz II ch 75, p6.

37 Ibid, p7.

38 Library Advisory Council (England), op cit, p6. Quotes the chief librarian of Toronto Public Libraries.

39 Bagg, C and Thompson, C A, op cit.

40 Papert, S *Mindstorms: children, computers and powerful ideas* Harvester Press, 1980, p4.

41 Library Advisory Council (England), op cit.

42 Dewey, M *Dewey decimal classification and relative index* 18th ed, Forest Press, 1971, p3.

43 Toffler, A *Future shock* Pan, 1971, p19.

44 *Videotex, viewdata and teletext* Northwood Hills: Online Publications, 1980.

45 Brownlow, K *The parade's gone by* Abacus, 1973, p149.

46 GB *The British Library* (White paper) Cmnd 4572. Note also the trenchant comment on the role of the British Library by the editor of the *Audiovisual librarian* in *AVL* 9(2) Spring 1983, pp62-63.

47 Coward, R E 'Bibliographic requirements relating to non-book materials, their relationship to the British Library, and developments thereafter' in: Andrew, J *Developments in the organization of non-book materials* Library Association, 1977, p20.

48 Trebble, A 'BBC Sound Archives: a general account, including a description of classification and cataloguing practice' *Audiovisual librarian* 2(2) Summer 1975, p68. Kavanagh, J 'The BBC's written archive centre' *Audiovisual librarian* 9(2) Spring 1983, pp83-85.

49 Moss, D 'Pictures: Radio Times Hulton Picture Library' in: Aslib Audiovisual Group *Audio-visual workshop May 7th-8th 1970* Aslib, 1971, p13.

50 This body has published Wall, J *Directory of British photographic collections* Royal Photographic Society, 1977.

51 National Film Archive *Catalogue: pt 1 Silent news films 1895-1933* 2nd ed, British Film Institute, 1965, p(4). From the introduction by the curator, Ernest Lindgren.

52 Murrey, J F *Orkney Sound Archive Project* (Occasional Working Paper 10) SCET. CET has also funded a pilot project to test the feasibility of making local radio material available through the public library, specifically for educational purposes.

53 Bond, M 'The development of a parliamentary sound archive at Westminster'. *Journal of the Society of Archivists* 6(6) October 1980, p335.

54 Hope, A 'Off the record forever?' *Times educational supplement* March 14th 1975. Argues that most sound and vision material is destroyed, and looks at some of the problems of preservation. Quotes Paul Madden, television officer of the National Film Archive.

55 Brownlow, op cit.

56 Ballantyne, J 'Audiovisual archives: recent developments' *Audiovisual librarian* 7(3) Summer, 1981, pp15-16.

57 Harrar, H J 'Photographs, pictures and prints' in: Groves, op cit, p173.

REFERENCES: PART 3 – THE MATERIALS

1 User Specifications (USPECs). Council for Educational Technology.

USPEC 2   *Synchronized tape-visual systems (using compact cassettes)* 2nd ed, 1976.
USPEC 3   *Overhead projectors* 2nd ed, 1976.
USPEC 4   *Cassette audio tape-recorders and playback units (monophonic)* 2nd ed, 1979.
USPEC 5   *Marker boards and pens* 1978.
USPEC 6   *Combined filmstrips/slide projectors* 1975.
USPEC 7   *Projection screen* 1980.
USPEC 8a   *Plugs and connectors (audio and audiovisual)* 2nd ed, 1981.
USPEC 8b   *Matching (audio and audiovisual)* 2nd ed, 1981.
USPEC 9   *Code of operating practice for overhead projectors* 1978.
USPEC 10   *A guide to the selection and use of episcopes* 1981.
USPEC 11   *Pens and inks for use with overhead projector transparencies* 2nd ed, 1976.
USPEC 12   *Storage containers for teaching and learning material* 1981.
USPEC 13   *VHF radio receivers* 2nd ed, 1981.
USPEC 14   *Microform readers* 1975.
USPEC 15   *A guide to the selection of video cassette/cartridge recorders and playback units* 1977.
USPEC 16   *Synchronized tape-visual operating practice* 1974.
USPEC 17   *Headphones and headsets* 2nd ed.
USPEC 18   *Audio card readers.*
USPEC 19   *Symbols for use on audio visual equipment* 1974.
USPEC 20   *Frames for overhead projector transparencies* 1976.
USPEC 21   *A guide to the preparation of operating and maintenance documents for audiovisual equipment* 1981.
USPEC 22   *Slide and filmstrip viewers for individual use* 1977.
USPEC 23   *Magazine slide projectors for 50 X 50mm slides* 1979.
USPEC 25   *A guide to the selection of electronic calculators* 1978.
USPEC 28   *VHF radio cassette recorders* 1983.
USPEC 29   *A guide to the selection of reprographic systems.*
USPEC 30   *A guide to the selection of sound amplifying systems.*
USPEC 31   *Stands and trolleys for audio-visual equipment.*
USPEC 32   *A guide to the selection of microcomputers* 1980.
USPEC 32a *A guide to the selection of printers for microcomputers* 1982.

USPEC 32b *Wordprocessing systems in education: a guide to the applications and selection of suitable equipment* 1982.

USPEC 32c *A guide to the use of microcomputers for real-time applications in control/monitoring systems.*

USPEC 32d *A guide to the application and use of videotex in education.*

USPEC 33 *Electronic clock-timer units.*

USPEC *Focus on safety* 1979.

2 Relevant British Standards for microforms and equipment.

4187: Microfiche

    1973 Part 1: 60 frame format

    1973 Part 2: 98 frame format

    1978 Part 3: 208, 270, 325 and 420 frame formats

4191: 1976 Specification for microform readers

5444: 1977 Preparation of copy for microcopying

5632: 1978 Microfilm jackets, A6 size

5644: 1978 Computer output microfiche (COM), A6 size

6054: 1981 Glossary of terms for micrographics

Other useful standards on microfilming are:

1153: 1975 Storage of microfilm

1371: 1973 35mm and 16mm microfilms, spools and reels

5513: 1977 35mm microcopying of newspaper cuttings on A6 microfiche

5525: 1977 35mm microcopying of maps and plans

4210: 1977 35mm microcopying of technical drawings

3 International electro-technical Commission Publication 574-10, part 10 Audiocassette systems, 1977.

REFERENCES: PART 4 — THE USER AND THE MATERIALS

1 Jones, J 'The appraisal of audiovisual software' *British Universities Film Council newsletter* (30) February 1977, p12.

2 Edwards, J *Materials as aids for teaching and librarianship of the newer media* Council for Educational Technology, 1977.

3 Clark, D *The travelling workshop experiment in library user education* London: British Library, 1981 (BLRD 5602). Gives numerous references.

4 Foskett, A C *The subject approach to information* 4th ed, London: Bingley; USA: Linnet, 1977, p1.

5 Bradfield, V J *Slide collections: a user requirement survey* British Library, 1976 (BL report no 5309).

6 Harrison, H 'Media resources in the Open University Library' *Audiovisual librarian* 1(1) Summer 1973, pp13-14.

See also the correspondence arising from Newins, J 'Diversification and multimedia control: the Leeds Polytechnic Beckett Park Site Library' *Audiovisual librarian* 7(4) Autumn 1981, p9 and 8(2) Spring 1982, p83.

7 *Anglo-American cataloguing rules* 2nd ed, 1978, p1.

8 Cutter, C A *Rules for a dictionary catalogue* 4th ed, rewritten, Government Printing Office, 1904. First Edition was 1876.

9 Aslib Film Production Libraries Group, Cataloguing Committee, *Film cataloguing rules* Aslib, 1963.

10 Weihs, J R *Non-book materials: the organization of integrated collections* 2nd ed, Canadian Library Association, 1979, p8.

11 Furlong N and Platt P *Cataloguing rules for books and other media in primary and secondary schools* 5th ed, School Library Association, 1976, p8.

12 *International Standard Bibliographic Description: General* IFLA, 1977, p5.

13 Library Association Media Cataloguing Rules Committee *Non-book materials cataloguing rules* National Council for Educational Technology with the Library Association, 1973, p21.

14 *Anglo-American cataloguing rules* op cit, p571.

15 Price, S 'Up the Umzimvubu' *The observer* 21 March 1976, p33.

16 LA/NCET, p16.

17 Templeton, R and Witten, A *Study of cataloguing computer software: applying AACR 2 to microcomputer programs* British Library/ MEP, 1983 (BLRD Report on Project no SI/N/370) unpublished, and

Dodd, S *Cataloguing machine-readable datafiles: an interpretative manual* American Library Association, 1982.

18 Shifrin, M A 'A distinction more apparent than real' *Times educational supplement* April 4th 1975, pp48, 49, 50.

Shifrin, M A 'OCCI: the reservations' Soundtape in: *Support materials for courses in educational technology. Module 3 Management of resources* NCET, 1973.

19 Edwards, R P A 'A surprisingly controversial subject' *Times educational supplement* November 8th 1974, pp27-28.

Edwards, R P A *Resources in schools* Evans, 1973, ch 5 'Retrieval systems'.

20 Beswick, N *School resource centres* Evans/Methuen, 1972 (Schools Council working paper 43).

21 Beswick, N *Resource-based learning* Heinemann Educational, 1977, ch 7.

22 The legal state on copyright is complicated but the following references provide the basis on which most actions are taken in the UK.

Berne convention for the protection of literary and artistic works of September 9 1886, last revised Paris 1971 Cmnd 5002.

Copyright Act 1956 Eliz II ch 74.

Dramatic and Musical Performers' Protection Act, 1958. Subsequently modified by the:

Performers' Protection Act 1963 and the

Performers' Protection Act 1972.

The Copyright (Libraries) Regulations 1957 (Statutory Instrument 1957 no 868). British Copyright Council *Photocopying and the law: a guide for librarians and teachers and other suppliers and users of photocopies of copyright works* BCC, 1970.

Two useful statements on broadcasts may be found in:

NCET Working Group on Rights *Copyright and education* NCET, 1972 (working paper no 8).

Appendix E: Statement by the British Broadcasting Corporation, pp72-73.

Appendix F: Statement by the Independent Television Companies Association Ltd, pp74-78.

23 Three excellent works are:

NCET Working Group on Rights *Copyright and education: a Guide to the use of copyright material in educational institutions* NCET, 1972 (working paper no 8).

Crabb, G *Copyright clearance: a practical guide* CET, 1977 (guideline 2). A very simple algorithm to use.

McFarlane, G *A practical introduction to copyright* McGraw-Hill, 1982.

24 GB Board of Trade *Copyright and designs law: report of the committee to consider the law on copyright and designs* HMSO, 1977 (Cmnd 6732) (Mr Justice Whitford, Chairman).

25 *Librarians' copyright kit: what you must know* 2nd ed, Chicago, ALA, 1982.

REFERENCES: PART 5 – MANAGEMENT

1 Donovan, K G *Learning resources in colleges: their organisation and management* Council for Educational Technology, 1981.

2 Clark, D *The travelling workshops experiment* British Library, 1981, p1.

3 Marland, M *Information skills in the secondary curriculum* Methuen Educational, 1981, p50.

4 There is an extensive literature of this field. See:

'Educating information users in schools' *Research review* no 4 1983. British Library Research and Development, 1983.

Brake, T *The need to know: teaching the importance of information* British Library, 1980.

Irving, A *Starting to teach study skills* Edward Arnold, 1982.

Malloy, I *User education in schools: an annotated bibliography* Infuse Publications, 1982 (microfiche).

5 *Factfile: primary school database programs* Cambridge University Press, 1982 (Computer cassette for BBC B, RML 480Z, and Sinclair Spectrum.)

6 Clark, D op cit, p2.

7 Clark, D op cit, p175.

8 Collier, G *Teaching and learning support services: 1. Higher education 2. Further education 3. Secondary comprehensive, middle and primary schools* Council for Educational Technology, 1981.

9 Butchart, I C, Shaw, W B and Watson, W M 'Course guide 1: the application of the librarianship of the new media which should be covered in the initial education of every librarian, whatever his eventual specialization' in: *Media awareness for librarians: course guidelines* Council for Educational Technology, 1977, pp11-18.

10 Review Committee on Education for Information Use *Final report* British Library, 1977 (Research and Development Reports 5325 HC), p11. Summarises a report by M Stevenson for the Committee (BLRD 5320), 1976.

11 Henderson, J and Humphreys, F *Audiovisual and microcomputer handbook* 3rd ed, Kogan Page, 1982, pp108-111.

12 Hallworth, F 'Publicity and promotion' in: Lock, R N *Manual of library economy* London: Bingley; USA: Linnet, 1977, p375.

13 Hicks, W B and Tillin, A M *Managing multi-media libraries* Bowker 1977, p116.

14 Hicks, op cit, p183.

BIBLIOGRAPHY

The books listed below are an update of the works presented in the first edition.

Baxter, P *Libraries and computer materials* London: British Library, 1982 (BLRD 5690).

Beswick, B *Producing lists of learning materials* London: Council for Educational Technology, 1979.

Butchart, I C *AACR 2 and the cataloguing of audiovisual materials* in: Roe, G *Seminar on AACR 2* London: Library Association, 1980.

Cabeceiras, J *The multi-media library: materials, selection and use* 2nd ed, New York: Academic Press, 1982.

Clark, D *The Travelling Workshops Experiment in library user education* London: British Library, 1981 (BLRD 5602).

Clinton, A *Printed ephemera: collections, organisation and access* London: Bingley, 1981.

Collier, G *Teaching and learning support services: 1. Higher Education 2. Further Education 3. Secondary comprehensive, middle and primary schools* London: Council for Educational Technology, 1981.

Crabb, G *Copyright clearance: a practical guide* London: Council for Educational Technology, 1977.

Croghan, A *A bibliographic system for non-book media* 2nd ed, London: Coburgh, 1979.

Davies, R A *School library media program: instructional force for excellence* 2nd ed, New York: Bowker, 1979.

Donovan, K G *Learning resources in colleges: their organisation and management* London: Council for Educational Technology, 1981.

Duke, J *Interactive video: implications for education and training* (CET Working paper 22), London: Council for Educational Technology, 1983.

Dunston Community Workshop/Social Arts Trust *Dunston Community Television: a guide for community group wanting to participate in the cable tv revolution* Dunston Community Workshop, 1982.

Edridge, S *Non-book materials in libraries: guidelines for library practice* Wellington: New Zealand Library Association, 1980.

Evans, C *The mighty micro* London: Gollancz, 1979.

Evans, H *Picture librarianship* London: Bingley, 1980.

Ferris, D J *Learning materials recording study* London: British Library, Council for Educational Technology, 1981.

Fleischer, E and Goodman, H *Cataloguing audiovisual materials: a manual based on the Anglo-American Cataloguing Rules II* New York: Neal-Schuman, 1980.

Folcarelli, R J *The microform connection: a basic guide for libraries* New York: Bowker, 1982.

Forester, T (ed) *The microelectronics revolution* Oxford: Basil Blackwell, 1980.

Gordon, C *Resource organisation in primary schools* London: Council for Educational Technology, 1979.

Greene, S *A survey of audio-visual provision and usage in an academic library* London: Polytechnic of the South Bank, 1979.

Greene, S *A selective bibliography of audiovisual materials on computer technology and its applications* Head Computers Ltd, 1983.

Greenhalgh, M *Audio cassettes: guide to selection and management* Oxford: School Library Association, 1982.

Hagler, R *Non-book materials: Chapter 7 through 11* in: Clack, D H *The making of a code: the issues underlying AACR 2* Chicago: American Library Association, 1980.

Harrison, H *Picture librarianship* London: Library Association, 1981.

Hawkridge, D *New information technology in education* London Croom Helm, 1983.

Hills, P J *Evaluation of tape-slide guides for library instruction* London: British Library, 1979 (BLRD 5378HC).

Hills, P J (ed) *The future of the printed word* London: Frances Pinter, 1980.

Horder, A *Video discs: their application to information storage and retrieval* 2nd ed, Hertford: National Reprographic Centre for Documentation, 1981.

Hunter, E *AACR 2: an introduction to the second edition of Anglo American Cataloguing rules* London: Bingley; Hamden: Linnet Books, 1979.

Ireland, R *Producing guides to local resources* London: Council for Educational Technology, 1979.

Irvine, B J *Slide libraries: a guide for academic institutions, museums and special collections* 2nd ed, Littleton, Colorado: Libraries Unlimited. 1979.

Irvine Smith, R and Campbell, B *Information technology revolution* York: Longman, 1981.

Large, P *The micro revolution* Glasgow: Fontana, 1980.

Library Association, School libraries Group *The microelectronics revolution and its implications for the school library* Mansfield: SLG. 1982.

Library Association *Information technology and the school library/ resource centre: guidelines for the school librarian* Loughborough: Library Association/MEP, 1983.

Maddison, J *Information technology and education: an annotated guide to printed, audiovisual and multimedia resources* London: Open University, 1983.

Marland, M *Information skills in the secondary curriculum* London: Methuen Educational, 1981 (Schools Council Curriculum Bulletin 9).

Martin, J *The wired society* New Jersey: Prentice Hall, 1978.

Merrill, I and Drob, H *Criteria for planning the College and University learning resources center* London: AECT, 1977.

Noble, P *Resource-based learning in post compulsory education* London: Kogan Page; New York: Nichols, 1980.

Oliver, E *Researcher's guide to British film and television collections* London: BUFC, 1981.

Owen, K *Videotex in education: a new technology briefing* London: Council for Educational Technology, 1982.

Page, C F and Kitching, J *Technical aids to teaching in higher education* 2nd ed, Brighton: Society for Research into Higher Education, 1976.

Papert, S *Mindstorms: children, computers and powerful ideas* Brighton: Harvester Press, 1980.

Rorvig, M E *Microcomputers and libraries: a guide to technology, products and applications* White Plains, NY: Knowledge Industry, 1981.

Royan, B and McElroy, R A *Minis and micros: smaller computers for smaller libraries* Library Association College of Further and Higher Education Group, 1981.

SHEMROC *Video recording in schools: a guide to currently available videorecording and playback machines* Sheffield: Shemroc, 1981.

Smith, A *Goodbye Gutenberg* Oxford: Oxford University Press, 1980.

Stonier, T *The wealth of information* London: Thames Methuen, 1983.

Sullivan, C *Local community information on Prestel: one of the Birmingham local information file* Aslib, 1981.

Tagg, W and Templeton, R *Computer materials: a survey of producers, distributors, publishers and catalogues* British Library, 1982 (BLRD Report on Project no. S1/G/524) unpublished.

Sigel, E *Videodiscs: the technology, applications and future* White Plains, NY: Knowledge Industry, 1980.

Templeton, R and Witten, A *Study of cataloguing computer software: applying AACR 2 to microcomputer programs* British Library/ MEP, 1983 (BLRD Report on Project no. S1/N/370) unpublished.

Thompson, V *Prestel and education: a report of a one-year trial* London: Council for Educational Technology, 1981.

Thornbury, P *Resource organisation in secondary schools: report of an investigation* London: Council for Educational Technology, 1979.

Weihs, J R *Nonbook materials: the organisation of integrated collections* 2nd ed, Ottawa: Canadian Library Association, 1979.

Zorkoczy, P *Information technology, an introduction* London: Pitman, 1982.

INDEX

Cinefilms (continued)
    printed sources for 183-184
    projectors 102-105
        manual of practice 148-150
    publishers 159-160
    repair 69-71, 264
    shelving 264
    statement of responsibility 211
    storage 243
Cinemode 72, 73 (fig 6) 72
City and Guilds of London Institute's
    Teacher Certificate 269
Classification: constraints 45
Cleveland Public Library, Ohio 9
Clients
    advice to 268-270
    cataloguing for 215
    definition 22
    survey of demands 41-43
    user education 256-258
Closed access system 198
Clough, F F 185
*College libraries: guidelines for
    professional service and
    resource provision* 277
College with a difference 171
Collets 186
Colliers encyclopedia 32
Colour coding 206-207
Comic mode 72, 73 (fig 6) 72
Commonwealth Institute 37
Compact disc
    physical aspects 88
*Complete media monitor: guide to
    learning resources* 174
Computer
    cataloguing 199-200
    future applications 44
    output on microfiche 73
Computer programme (BBC) 31
Concord Films Council Ltd 183
Condensors 94
Constraints on development 41-46
Consumers Association 179
Contemporary Films Ltd 172, 183
Copyright 250-253
    guidelines 252
    radio 195, 252
    television 195, 252
    United States 253
Copyright Act UK (1911) 47
Copyright Act UK (1956) 251
Copyright Revision Act of 1976 253

Council for Educational Technology
    for the United Kingdom
    see CET
Croghan, A 174
Cutter, C A 200
Cuming, G J 185

DES Working Party 44
Date of publication 213
Denver Public Library, Colorado 8
Depth indexing 219
Descriptive cataloguing 201-216
Design Centre Selection, 1981-82
    181
Design Council 181
Dewey, M 45
Dial-access-retrieval 262
*Directory of British photographic
    collections* 180
Discourses 186
Discs
    care and maintenance 87-88
    physical aspects 87-88
    see also Magnetic discs, Sound
        discs, Sound recordings, Video
        recordings
Distribution area (cataloguing) 212-
    213
Distribution: siting of an oil terminal
    32
Distributors 161-162
    cataloguing 212-213
Documents
    clients' requirements 36-40
    definition 4
Dodd, S 232
Dolby system 114, 244
Dominant medium 209, 214
Doubleday, W E 11
Dundee College of Education 171,
    262
Dunn and Wilson 172
Durham, J 164

EPIE
    see Educational Products Infor-
        mation Exchange Institute
'Early warning system' 206
East Sussex County Library 30
Economics Association 190
Edition area 211
Education
    and cinefilm 11

299

306